I0029039

THE KEY TO THE SELF

Understanding Yourself Through Depth Psychological Astrology

Marianne Meister

CHIRON PUBLICATIONS • ASHEVILLE, NORTH CAROLINA

www.ChironPublications.com

Interior and cover design by Danijela Mijailovic
Printed primarily in the United States of America.

ISBN 978-1-68503-048-3 paperback
ISBN 978-1-68503-049-0 hardcover
ISBN 978-1-68503-050-6 electronic
ISBN 978-1-68503-051-3 limited edition paperback

Library of Congress Cataloging-in-Publication Data

Names: Meister, Marianne, 1952- author.
Title: The key to the self : understanding yourself through depth psychological
    astrology / Marianne Meister.
Description: Asheville, North Carolina : Chiron Publications, [2022] | Includes
    bibliographical references. | Summary: "Our fate is NOT written in the stars, as
    the popular form of interpreting horoscopes would like us to believe. Instead,
    a serious approach to astrology describes an individual's special dispositions
    and developmental possibilities that can be lived out in entirely different ways.
    The experienced Jungian analyst and astrologer Marianne Meister connects
    this reputable astrological approach with the theories of C.G. Jung's Analytical
    Psychology. In her Depth Psychological Astrology, she works out the various
    basic patterns of the personality and makes it possible for readers to discover their
    own inclinations, needs, and potential. This book shows that the experiential
    knowledge from astrology and depth psychology can be used like a roadmap as
    important help in orientation on the path of life"-- Provided by publisher.
Identifiers: LCCN 2022031282 (print) | LCCN 2022031283 (ebook) | ISBN
    9781685030483 (paperback) | ISBN 9781685030490 (hardcover) | ISBN
    9781685030506 (ebook) | ISBN 9781685030513 (3 limited edition paperback)
Subjects: LCSH: Self psychology. | Jungian psychology.
Classification: LCC BF173 .M3595 2022 (print) | LCC BF173 (ebook) | DDC
    150.19/5--dc23/eng/20220729
LC record available at https://lccn.loc.gov/2022031282
LC ebook record available at https://lccn.loc.gov/2022031283

Contents

Introduction: The Meaning of Depth Psychological Astrology   1

1. Images of the Gods Within Us: Planets as Archetypes   7
Consciousness and the Unconscious   7
C. G. Jung's Concept of the Archetype   9
The Ten Planets in Astrology   13
Synopsis: Images of the Gods Within Us   35

2. A Typology of Depth Psychological Astrology   41
The Four Elements in Astrology: Fire, Earth, Air, and Water in
the Twelve Signs of the Zodiac   41
The Four Functions of the Self According to C. G. Jung: Thinking,
Feeling, Sensation, and Intuition   85
Synopsis: The Four Basic Characters (Fire/Intuition, Earth/Sensation,
Air/Thinking, and Water/Feeling)   106

3. Inside and Out: Two Psychological Orientations   111
Extraversion and Introversion According to C. G. Jung   112
The Circle with Its Semi-Circles, Quadrants, and Houses in
Astrology   113
Synopsis: Extraversion and Introversion in Jungian Psychology
and Astrology   123

**4. Interacting Dispositions and the Influences of the
Surrounding World: Aspect Structure and Complex Structure**   143

Aspect Structure in the Horoscope   144
C. G. Jung's Complex Theory   155
Synopsis: Our Inner Imprints   160

5. **Depth Psychological Astrology and Self-Knowledge:**
Eight Horoscope Examples   163

Self-Reference and Self-Interest: Focus on the Ascendant and
Position of the Self   166
Rootedness in the Family and the Self: Focus on the Lower
Heaven   189
Relationship with the Surrounding World and Interest in
Other People: Focus on the Descendent and Position
of the Familiar Other Person   210
Relationship with the World and Roles in Public Life:
Focus on the Midheaven   223

Conclusion   229

Notes   233

Bibliography   245

Picture credits   249

Introduction: The Meaning of Depth Psychological Astrology

Astrology is an ancient empirical teaching that extends back to the Babylonians. It follows a venerable concept of correlations with the assumption that the essential forces at work in the macrocosm correspond with those in the microcosm—and this means within human beings. For Thomas Ring, founder and outstanding representative of modern astrology, these are the "forces of life"[1] based on an autonomous life principle that cannot be described in physico-chemical or microbiological terms.

Fritz Riemann, another well-known astrologer who was also a prominent psychoanalyst, said "that a spiritual principle has an immanent effect in the world of appearances—whatever we may call it—and is recognizable on both the large and the small scale."[2] This shows that he agreed with natural philosophy, which was very powerful at least up to the time of Goethe.

According to Thomas Ring, the life-creating forces are embodied in the cosmos. Astrology allows us to "read" or discover the rules at play in these forces or, in more technical terms, the way these forces function in the movements of celestial bodies—especially in those of the planets in the sky. The constellation of the planets in an individual's birth chart precisely describes how these life-creating forces are expressed in this person, not as irreversible decrees or predetermined events, but in particular dispositions and tendencies. Of course, the birth chart must be viewed and interpreted within the context of the influences of heritage and the surrounding world. And the horoscope says nothing about what people make of their abilities and talents. As Ring mentions, there is always a "self-determining factor"[3] at work in how astrological forces are embodied and enacted, which is not determined by the horoscope, because it expresses the freedom inherent to human beings.

If astrology and the Jungian concepts of the "archetype" and "archetypal image" or "archetypal symbols" are brought into a relationship with each other, we see that the planets—whose names relate directly to mythology—can be understood as archetypal images and/or symbols. There is an interesting quote from Jung that supports this perspective: "Astrology consists of symbolic configurations, as does the collective unconscious with which psychology is concerned: The planets are the 'gods,' symbols of the powers of the unconscious."[4]

In astrology, the signs of the zodiac (such as Aries, Aquarius, Pisces, etc.), the houses (which are the twelve archetypal areas of life or fields of interest that are central for human beings; see the subchapter on "The Circle with Its Semi-Circles, Quadrants, and Houses in Astrology" in Chapter 3), and the aspects of the planets (which means the type of communication or relationship between the planets; see Chapter 4) are important. The signs of the zodiac, houses, and planetary aspects are also archetypal because they depict universal patterns at work in all human history and experience. However, the birth chart shows how these universal patterns are arranged and take form in an individual. As Jung said: "It seems as if the horoscope corresponds to a definite moment in the colloquy of the gods, that is to say the psychic archetypes."[5]

So astrology assumes that there is an unique, but archetypally based, background that structures the personality and wants to be expressed in the process of life. To what extent and how human beings develop what is inherent to their horoscope depends to a certain degree on their personal freedom and is largely their own responsibility, though not completely.

Astrology can be very helpful for people on the path to self-discovery, which is simultaneously the path that will lead them to their place in the greater whole. Goethe speaks of the horoscope or cosmogram as the "law . . . such must thou be" in his *Orphic Sayings*. This poem aptly expresses the basic idea of astrology:

> According as the sun and planets saw,
> From their bright thrones, the moment of thy birth,
> Such is thy Destiny: and by that Law
> Thou must go on—and on—upon the earth.
> Such must thou be; Thyself thou canst not fly;
> So still do Sibyls speak, have prophets spoken;
> The living stamp, received from Nature's die,
> No time can change, no art has ever broken.[6]

Astrology, as the "older sister of psychology,"[7] deserves to step out of the shadows, because it is invaluable for self-knowledge. The more familiar we are with our strengths and weaknesses, our potentials and passions, the greater our freedom to constructively shape our life. Then we can experience contentment and happiness instead of feeling blocked and bound by frustrations and resentments. The less we know about ourselves, the stronger is our tendency to unconsciously maneuver ourselves into the same dead ends—either in how we treat ourselves or in our interactions with others. Like a map for our travels, the birth chart can provide invaluable orientation on our path through life. It is not uncommon for unconscious creative abilities to slumber within us, which can be recognized in the birth chart. When they are awakened from their deep sleep, they can help us to achieve a greater state of inner balance.

On the other hand, reality also sets limits on people which may be difficult to understand and accept. The possible problems that an individual might face in dealing with reality, as well as ways to address them, can be recognized in the birth chart (Saturn constellation). For example, the physical body is a reality. It is increasingly being subjected to cosmetic operations and other invasive procedures of all types as a matter of course—because people cannot accept it as it is. A further difficulty in dealing with limits is shown in the manifold manifestations of addictive behavior (shown in the birth chart by the Neptune constellation). This can be expressed as shopping addiction, abuse of drugs or medication, excessive consumption of alcohol, anorexia, or compulsive overeating (obesity). Boundaries can elicit overreactions or avoidance. Clearly recognizing and identifying such tendencies in the birth chart can be the first step toward an improvement.

Since we often have such difficulty in correctly drawing the necessary boundaries, we wind up with all types of problems. These frequently affect our relationships and interactions with other people. Because we are not only individuals but also social beings, relationships play an essential role in our life. For newborns, the mothering and caring environment is absolutely necessary for survival (above all, this can be recognized in the birth chart by the placement of the Moon as a structural indication of the maternal element). However, supportive relationships are significant not only for the small child but also for people of all ages. Even very successful professionals are not exempt from this problem since they are often unhappy in their private life—or at least may have struggled with the same relationship difficulties for years.

Within the scope of a depth psychological approach, the birth chart has proven to be very useful and helpful in discovering constructive paths out of relationship dead ends and into new territory. For example, couples who no longer can talk to each other and are trapped in a state of mutual misunderstanding—because they project their wishes, ideals, or dread onto each other and therefore prevent a genuine encounter— might find their way to an improved mutual understanding. As a result, they can develop a greater tolerance toward each other.

It can be equally helpful and liberating to take the horoscope into account when there are problems in raising a child. For example, a mother's difficulties in communicating with her offspring may be related to the child having an entirely different disposition. Comparing the horoscopes—above all, the similarities and differences in the lunar constellations of the mother and child—is generally very helpful in parental counselling.

The great advantage of combining astrology with C. G. Jung's theoretic approach is that the two models mutually enrich and supplement each other. Jung directly connects astrology with his theory of archetypes: "The starry vault of heaven is in truth the open book of cosmic projection, in which are reflected the mythologems, i.e. the archetypes. In this vision, astrology and alchemy, the two classical functionaries of the psychology of the collective unconscious, join hands."[8] The birth chart, which is the map of our intrinsic dispositions,

4

reveals its greater depth to the eye trained in depth psychology and psychodynamics.

Conversely, it is highly beneficial for the psychoanalytic process to occasionally include the birth chart. The latter initially provides a structural overview of the patient's or client's dispositions, and secondly provides insights into specific topics affecting the individual like the "mother." For example, a motherly figure in a dream can be related to the Moon's position in the horoscope. This results in an additional perspective on this dream image, which can then be better understood and classified.

In his various writings, Jung deals intensively with astrology and discusses topics such as the quality of time, as well as synchronicity.[9] In his essay "On Synchronicity," Jung explores the possibility that astrology can be explained causally, in contrast to the widespread conception of it as acausally operative—and therefore based on the principle of synchronicity. But he ultimately sees astrology as an intuitive technique that is "based on the acausal connecting principle or synchronicity."[10] In a letter from 5/26/1954 he wrote:

> Obvious astrology has much to offer psychology . . . So far as I can judge, it would seem to me advantageous for astrology to take the existence of psychology into account, above all the psychology of the personality and of the unconscious. I am almost sure that something could be learnt from the symbolic method of interpretation; for that has to do with the interpretation of the archetypes (the gods) and their mutual relations . . . The psychology of the unconscious is particularly concerned with archetypal symbols.[11]

Beyond the general usefulness of the birth chart, Jung also recognized the importance of the *transits* in particular.[12] Transits are the planets that currently activate a certain part of the horoscope in the individual's life through the various aspects: i.e. formation of angles with the planets, the axes (Ascendant–Descendent [AC–DC] and Midheaven–Imum Coeli [MC–IC]), and the houses in the birth chart (see Chapter 3's subsection on "The Circle with Its Semi-Circles, Quadrants, and Houses in Astrology" for more about the AC, DC, MC, IC, and the houses).

These aspects of the moving planets (transits) in relationship to the above-mentioned incisive factors in the birth chart may create conjunctions, oppositions, squares, trines, or sextiles (see Chapter 4's subchapter on "Aspect Structure in the Horoscope"). For example, if we have a Saturn transit across a certain planet, the latter is put to the test—since Saturn embodies the principle of reality, a reality check occurs. What the individual experiences when going through such transits often feels fateful.

The transits are especially significant in a difficult psychological diagnosis because they provide a new perspective, which allows an expanded understanding of the personality in question and the difficulties that have brought them to the psychotherapeutic practice. As Jung put it, "I must say that I very often found that the astrological data elucidated certain points which I otherwise would have been unable to understand."[13]

The specific effect of the transits exerted by certain planets and aspects (see Chapter 4 on the aspect possibilities, i.e. relationships between the planets) in the birth chart can be better explained with an acausal than a causal perspective. Jung called this acausal principle "synchronicity,"[14] which is a way to understand how the cosmos can be meaningfully coordinated, each moment reflecting a unique configuration of life-forces. This provides the basis for the astrological view that different moments in time express distinct qualitative characteristics that are constellated at the moment of birth, which the birth chart portrays.

1
Images of the Gods Within Us: Planets as Archetypes

Consciousness and the Unconscious

The human psyche as understood in depth psychology is based on the distinction between conscious and unconscious levels of experiencing and acting. This duality of our perceiving, feeling, thinking, and acting has now been recognized by many experts and interested members of the general public. This perspective evokes the question as to why and for what purpose it can be meaningful or even necessary to give due consideration to the unconscious in our life. That it is meaningful and necessary to do so, was a view opposed by many within influential scientific circles a hundred years ago.

Even today, many psychological faculties hardly recognize the unconscious or consider its language of symbols as relevant enough to be systematically researched. One of the pioneers of depth psychology, Sigmund Freud, felt this rejection very intensely because his advocacy for taking the unconscious seriously—and his development of psychoanalysis as a way to approach it—resulted in a career setback at the university in Vienna and many public condemnations. However, Freud and his younger colleague Carl Gustav Jung, based on their knowledge and experience of it, remained steadfast in their acknowledgment of the power of the unconscious—since they were both virtually forced to deal with it in their own way.

The older of the two pioneers, Sigmund Freud (1856–1939), was motivated to engage in self-analysis in 1897 because he repeatedly came up against the limits of his conscious will in dealing with his own depression and fears. Freud, who had reached midlife, recognized that unconscious forces within him were stronger than his conscious will. This led him to make the following statement: "My recovery can only come about through work in the unconscious; I cannot manage with conscious efforts alone."[15] His experience with himself and others showed him that the conscious self is not the master in its own house, but a plaything of the unconscious. Mistakes such as slips of the tongue, forgetfulness, and so forth are indications of how the unconscious can subvert the conscious will.

Carl Gustav Jung (1875–1961), the famous Swiss psychiatrist, had a very similar experience. The C. G. Jung Institute Zurich was founded in 1948 on the basis of his theories. Together with other Jung institutes and societies, especially in German-language regions of Europe and in the USA, the Zurich Institute continues to teach and further develop these theories. When Jung fell into a serious depression and remained stuck in it after his separation from Freud, he was forced to recognize that he could not make any further progress by rational means or with the traditional approaches of his psychiatric profession. It became clear to Jung that this crisis was an expression of a one-sided attitude toward life that overestimated the conscious will and rationality. He saw that the life crisis he was facing could only be worked through when the one-sidedness of the conscious attitude was corrected and brought into balance.

This means that it is necessary to include the unconscious when we want to be in a state of psychological and physical balance—instead of ignoring and suppressing it. If we do not actively relate to our unconscious psychological life, sooner or later it will come to us without being asked and we will experience its power negatively. We are at the mercy of whatever remains unconscious and often feel powerless—suffering at the hands of unseen forces that undermine our conscious plans and intentions.

So the term of *compensation*, expressing the way the unconscious counters and addresses one-sidedness in the conscious attitude, is very central in the theory and practice of Jungian depth psychology. It is revealed by daily experiences in psychotherapeutic and psychoanalytic practice, where dreams, images, sand pictures, and other symbolic material—conveying valuable communications from the unconscious—are the focus of the client's or patient's attention and that of the psychotherapist or Jungian analyst who works with depth psychology. The symbol, which by definition encompasses both unconscious and conscious life, is the actual medium of development in the human psyche.[16]

What is important for astrology is Jung's understanding of the unconscious, which differs from Freud's, because it takes into consideration the *collective unconscious* in addition to the *personal unconscious* that Freud had intensively investigated. This deeper level of the psyche was already becoming apparent to Jung when he was still a senior physician at Zurich's Burghölzli Psychiatric University Hospital trying to understand the fantasies of schizophrenia patients. He recognized that these fantasies cannot belong to the personal unconscious since it only contains experiences accrued during an individual's life, but have been forgotten and/or suppressed at some point. On the other hand, the accumulated history and experience of the entirety of human ancestry can be found within the collective unconscious. The latter is common to all human beings and structures the psyche of every individual, every experience, every creative expression.[17] These various levels of the unconscious can be easily recognized in dreams and active imagination, in images and drawings, as well as in sand pictures and other symbolic designs.

C. G. Jung's Concept of the Archetype

It is to Jung's credit that he researched the role of the collective unconscious and the archetypes, as well as giving psychology and psychotherapy the corresponding concepts as instruments for a deeper understanding of the human psyche. So we now know that an archetype is active behind every complex.

Generally speaking, an archetype is a *structural disposition* that makes it possible for individuals to have certain experiences that are typical of their species. *Structural* means that this disposition is not fixed to a specific content but is a container, a form that can be expressed by and draw together many symbols, images, and emotions around a certain core of meaning.

This kind of structural disposition is evident when we examine the inborn ability of small children to learn every kind of language: Throughout the entire world and in every type of language community, children learn the language that they hear quite naturally. This is based on the structural possibility of learning languages. Seen in terms of content, children can learn any language.[18] The archetypal capacity and potential for language gets filled in uniquely by whatever actual language is learned.

Analogously, the archetypes are seen in Jungian theory as an *a priori* system of the psyche, always already at work in our predispositions and preparedness for certain experiences. In this process, there are as many archetypes as possible experiences. This is obviously not just about the innate possibility of learning a language.

Jung differentiates between two aspects of the archetype: He calls the purely structural archetype, the "archetype per se,"[19] which is still entirely abstract, i.e. the individual's potential for having multi-faceted experiences. When the concrete experience is added, which is usually paired with emotion, he speaks of the "archetype that has become an image."[20]

Such "archetypal images" manifest as certain dream figures that act autonomously, for example. As a rule, archetypal dream figures exert a great fascination on those who dream, because they express universal psychological principles, collective forces—virtually "gods" that are bigger and more powerful than the individual. So children experience a *divine mother* or mother archetype behind every human mother, and this is what gives her such great power over her children.

With regard to human children, who in comparison to other mammals (the species to which human beings ultimately belong), are born one year too early and are correspondingly dependent beings—are innately prepared to be parented. This is fortunate since they would die without adequate mothering. However, not every child can accept and utilize the mothering equally well, which can definitely be observed when comparing siblings. This is also very clearly recognizable in the different horoscopes, which can show structurally sparse or fully present motherly qualities— depending on whether the Moon (mother and child symbolism) is aspected by Saturn (the boundary-setting principle) or Jupiter (the principle of abundance and optimism), i.e. in relation to Saturn or Jupiter (cf. the subsection on "The Ten Planets in Astrology" in Chapter 1, as well as "Aspect Structure in the Horoscope" in Chapter 4).

About the diversity of dispositions that infants bring with them in all their similarity regarding the archetypes, which are important for their development, Jung wrote:

> There *is* an a priori factor in all human activities, namely the inborn, preconscious and unconscious individual structure of the psyche. The preconscious psyche—for example, that of a new-born infant—is not an empty vessel into which, under favorable conditions, practically anything can be poured. On the contrary, it is a tremendously complicated, sharply defined individual entity which appears indeterminate to us only because we cannot see it directly. But the moment the first visible manifestations of psychic life begin to appear, one would have to be blind not to recognize their individual character, that is the unique personality behind them.[21]

On the one hand, *how* a mother archetype appears depends on the child's structural disposition—and therefore additionally on the mother's archetypal disposition, which can be seen in her birth chart as well. On the other hand, it also depends on the child's experience with his or her personal mother or foster mother. If the personal mother generally succeeds in adequately relating to her growing child with his or her changing needs in the course of development, it is highly likely that a more positive mother archetype will be constellated. Through the mostly positive experiences with the personal mother or another person who performs the mother function, the child usually develops a rather positive basic attitude of trust in the immediate environment and later in the larger world—a sense of being safe and supported. This is how we recognize a more positive mother complex. If the mother does not succeed and cannot offer the child the attention that they need, in keeping with their corresponding age, or only inadequately does so for some reason—the child usually starts to develop a more negative mother complex. The topic of complexes will be discussed in greater detail below.

Depending on whether the mother archetype is constellated in a more life-supporting or life-inhibiting way, the child's subjective experience of his or her personal mother will be more positive or more negative, and vice versa.[22] The fit of the personalities plays a significant role in this regard: Depending on her own disposition, a mother can better comprehend her child or not understand them well. When the child and the mother fit together well, it is relatively easy for the mother to be a "sufficiently good mother"[23] for the child. But if the chemistry is not right, the child may always get the wrong thing because the mother can hardly find access to the child and their needs due to her entirely different personality—even if she tries very hard.[24]

The experiences that the mother and the child (as well as the father and the child or the father and the mother) have with each other express certain patterns, which in turn further influence the relationship—and therefore also the child's individuation. The concrete relationship between children or adolescents and their parents (as well as that of the parents with each other)—including verbal and nonverbal, conscious and unconscious communication—is therefore ultimately based for its quality on the archetypes involved, and on the archetypal images that have become constellated in the relational interactions. Consequently, Jung's archetypes (which are incidentally similar to Stierlin's modes of relationship[25]) have a structuring character on concrete, interactive behavior.

The archetypes of *anima* and *animus* that embody the feminine and the masculine respectively, and become expressed in specific cultural images are very strongly based on the mother and father archetype in the initial stage. This is shown in dreams and concrete experiences when the appearance of the anima or animus strongly reflects the parental or even sibling images at the beginning of the individuation process by bearing certain similar qualities or traits. In concrete encounters with others, people who are similar to the parent or sibling often exert a power of attraction. When we are affected by this, we fall in love. But this is not always to our advantage if we do not become aware of these mechanisms. However, the anima and animus can increasingly distance themselves from the parent archetypes or complexes.

When this is the case, a strong fascination is exerted by the anima and animus in dream figures who may be drastically different than the parental images. This can extend to completely unknown persons, princesses or princes, queens and kings, or even priestesses and priests, witches and sorcerers, etc. These figures each leave a deep impression on the dreamer and are often remembered for a very long time. Like any archetype, anima and animus can show themselves as very positive or even distinctly negative. They can trigger enthusiasm and love or be experienced as frightening and threatening. They can lead us to ourselves or into the abyss.

Anima and animus appear not only in human form in dreams, but also in an animal forms that may have mythological, fairytale-like, or demonic traits. On the one hand, these may be realistic creatures such as dogs, cats, or snakes; on the other hand, they may also be mythological beings such as dragons or even mixed creatures. Dreamers are typically pursued by a giant animal, which usually triggers intense feelings of fear—or they experience it as helpful when they are carried by a winged dragon over an abyss or a sea.

In their force, archetypal images exceed the person's strength and require a careful reflection. If the archetype gains the upper hand, the individuality of the person is lost and they become a type. Their humanness is blown up, and the affected person is pompous, inflated, and identifies with the archetype—whether this is God or the Devil, or any numinous figure. This occurrence can be observed most clearly and impressively in psychosis, where the person has lost contact with reality and no longer notices what has happened.[26]

Astrology provides a wonderful instrument for dealing with the most common archetypes.

The Ten Planets in Astrology

Sorcerers and witches as archetypes at work in individual and collective experience prove to be special manifestations of the father and mother archetype. In the birth chart, they correspond to the Sun and Moon. In the individual psyche, such overpowering, fascinating, and sometimes frightening archetypal figures can occur in dreams. Culturally they frequently appear as witches and sorcerers in the world's fairy tales and myths.

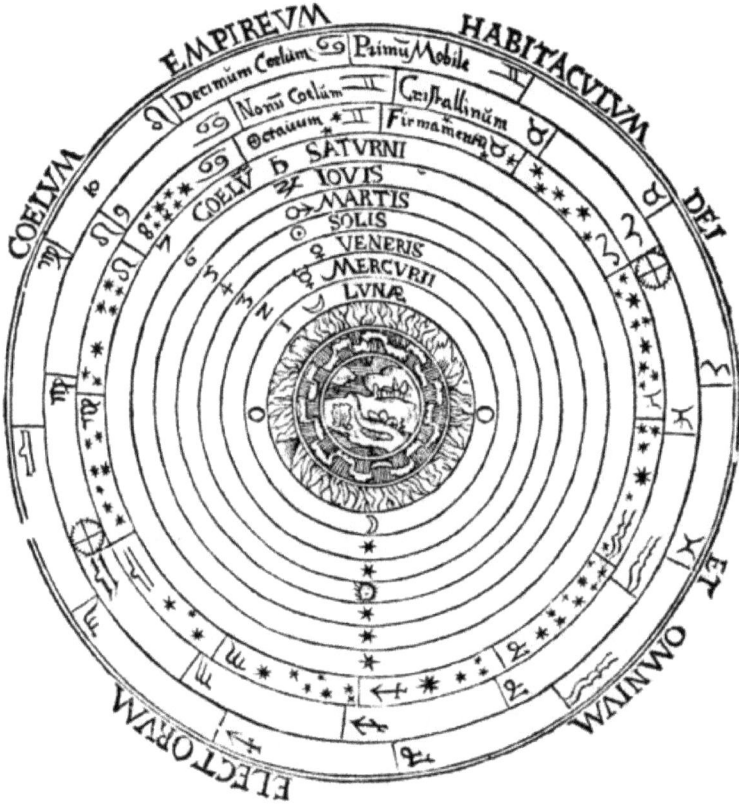

Ill.1.: Map of the Universum Cosmographia by Peter Apian (1539)

As stated in the introduction, the planets are "symbols of the powers of the unconscious"[27] that transcend the human dimension, which is why they are portrayed and experienced as *gods*. The same applies to the archetypes, as shown previously. The following section presents each of the *ten planets,* symbols for the main archetypal powers that play a role in our lives and have various effects on us through their different interactions with each other. Their "conversations" with each other or planetary aspects are the subject of Chapter 3.

My descriptions of the ten planets will focus on their most important meanings for astrological practice. The seven *personal planets* – the Sun, the Moon, Mercury, Mars, Venus, Jupiter, and Saturn— that are relevant for personality development and therefore also for the structure of complexes—take up more space than the three *transpersonal* or *collective planets* of Uranus, Neptune, and Pluto, which transcend the individual personality.

The planetary principles correspond not only to emotional and mental phenomena, but also to physical dispositions. This includes both strengths and weaknesses, which are listed in keywords at the end of each description. However, the physical impact of the three *trans-Saturnal planets* of Uranus, Neptune, and Pluto is not sufficiently known for, because they have an impersonal and collective nature. As a result, corresponding physical dispositions will be omitted from their descriptions.

☉ The Sun

In astrology, the Sun is the main driving force in the individual, moving them toward the development of the entire personality. All of the other planets should assist in this goal or place themselves in its service. Readers who are already familiar with Jungian theory will see this definition of the Sun as the "main driving force of life" with a certain governing function as a symbol for the self, which is the central archetype in a human being's development. It controls individuation and with it the process of becoming both unique and whole. The astrological concept of the Sun as a controlling entity is based on the analogy of the central position that the Sun assumes within the solar system: For millions of years, it has been circled by the other planets with orbits of various distances from it.

Jungian experience shows that the will to develop (as symbolized by the Sun principle) may be relativized, weakened, or even thwarted in the individual's life by many types of opposing forces—symbolized by Saturn (see below), Neptune, Pluto, or Uranus (see below). So the desire to develop as extensively as possible with all of our talents does not automatically lead to its concrete realization (more about this in Chapters 3 and 5).

Just like the actual sun, whose warmth and light allow life to develop on our planet, the archetypal Sun in the horoscope symbolizes the expression and affirmation of life. It is regarded as the principle in which vitality and the will to develop are inherent. In contrast to the Moon principle, which is associated with the unconscious, the Sun represents the ability to become self-aware and behave accordingly. Consciousness and personal responsibility are linked with each other to a high degree, because the more we are conscious of ourselves, the better we can think and act with personal responsibility.

The *logos* (rational principle) and the intellect therefore belong within the Sun's horizon of meaning. The Sun is associated with the male principle and therefore also with the father, which is projected quite unconsciously onto the father by the small child. The Sun principle is obviously experienced with varying intensity and differentiation through the personal father, depending on how well the father's personality fits the disposition of the Sun's father principle (father image) within the child, and how present the actual father is. Consequently, the father complements the mother, who is associated with archetypal maternal qualities. Seen in astrological terms, she is associated with the Moon.

In human experience, the father (the Sun) and mother (the Moon) have primal significance. On the one hand, this is due to the overpowering unconscious archetypal deities that are behind the personal parents; on the other hand, this is because of the child's complete and existential dependence on them from the very start—and the associated formative relationship experiences with the parents.

Without a biological father, there is no child. His sperm must unite with the mother's egg so that the latter becomes fertilized. In turn, the male seed depends on the female egg, which takes it in. Only in this way can both develop into a third being, which consists of elements from both of them, but becomes something new and distinct.

In the growing child, the father's individual image is built upon an archetypal basis, and through the concrete experience of the father. In most cases, this paternal inner image is substantially nourished by the biological father; but sometimes the latter is missing and replaced by other men. In addition to their own father, children generally become acquainted with other people who express other facets of the sun-like or male principle—like a brother, cousin, boyfriend, uncle, or neighbor, just to mention some of the most obvious possibilities. Also included in this category are older trusted men such as a grandfather or great uncle. Older men—age is connected with Saturn (see the section on Saturn)—obviously represent the sun-like traits differently through their experience, than young men or boys. They usually show more calmness and have an larger view of situations, which in the best case even includes a certain wisdom due to their long life experience.

During school years, authority figures such as teachers and sometimes also the male pastor, pediatrician, or general practitioner, and later the male boss or professor embody the sun-like nature. There are also masculine figures who are far removed from everyday experience, but play an important role in the collective like male artists and stars such as singers, actors, and athletes, or even the successful male CEO of a major corporation or head of state. Under undemocratic circumstances this could even include a male despot or dictator—or perhaps a king, emperor, or pope.

The Sun as a main archetypal symbol, corresponding to the archetype of the self, can also be projected onto a male saint or god. Religious feelings and deep faith in a god or saintly figure are based on this potential in human beings to project their longing for wholeness and their concept of it onto god-like figures. There are many luminous figures available as possible objects for our idealizations and projections of wholeness: Jesus, Buddha, Mohammed, or Krishna are male examples here. The different manifestations of the sun-like traits that come to dominate at any particular time are co-determined by the aspects to the Sun, i.e. by the relationship that the planets have with it, as well as by cultural imprints.

In a woman's horoscope, the Sun represents many of the same qualities as in a man's chart. For example, it also symbolizes the self as the main archetype that guides her development into an individual. However, in addition to self-realization, the Sun—together with Mars and in its overall constellation with the other planetary principles—is very central in the woman's psyche for how she experiences men in everyday life and ultimately chooses her partner. This is because the Sun and Mars shape the qualities of the animus, whose characteristic attributes are largely based on the unconscious archetypal form behind the father image, as well as on the unconscious and conscious experience of the actual father. This archetypal quality, which ultimately has an effect on how every actual relationship with a man is experienced, very frequently leads to an excessive and usually mostly unconscious wish to find a hero, prince, or king in the actual partner. But if the animus is very shadowed, a tyrant, or merciless jailer or persecutor in human form—or even a destroying demon—may be projected onto the male counterpart.

As reality shows in a variety of ways, the true acceptance of a partner in his human limitations is only possible when the woman can deal with the corresponding dis-illusionments experienced when facing her male counterpart's limits—not making him responsible for the failing her own projections of male idealizations. This is easier said than done, because it requires self-reflection and a lifelong striving for self-knowledge. This striving ultimately reveals that she carries these male qualities within herself and has them at her disposal to shape her life. In any case, dealing with the animus is a principal challenge for every woman. Fighting for and setting boundaries for herself, distinguishing her own mental qualities and defending herself with courage, as well as the ability to commit herself to a cause (on both the physical and mental levels) and taking a stand for her own viewpoint—all these abilities depend on the development of the animus in the woman's psyche.

Problematic facets of the Sun qualities in the human psyche can be expressed in an exaggerated aspiration to be the center of attention, a craving for recognition, and vanity, as well as striving for power and dominance at the expense of other people's freedom. Many people with a narcissistic disorder show these attributes in an especially pronounced way.

As always, when astrological powers are at work, whether the sunlight warms and promotes life or manifests too much or too little heat—whether it burns life as a scorching, blazing fire or cannot give enough light and warmth—depends on a variety of factors. Above all, this applies to the overall constellation in which the Sun is embedded, genetic disposition, and the influences of the surrounding world. And as mentioned earlier, this ultimately includes a factor of freedom that is difficult to define and transcends all influences and conditioning.

The Sun in the body: heart and circulation.

☾ The Moon

The moon's astronomical nature also reflects its corresponding astrological and depth psychological concepts, which is why it should be briefly described here. The moon closely orbits planet Earth—as the latter orbits the sun at a distance—and it receives its light from the sun, just like the Earth. In contrast to the sun, which gives birth to its own light from within, the moon does not shine by its own power, but reflects the light of the sun. In this process, only half of the moon gets sunlight at any given time. The other half remains shrouded in darkness. This relationship between the sun and moon provides a wonderful analogy for the relationship of consciousness to the unconscious, except that the proportions are different in this regard.

The moon changes its shape every night when seen from the Earth since it orbits our planet once within just about a month—or more precisely, 29.5 days.[28] So we cannot see the new moon, but we observe the moon's growth to its full shape, the full moon, and then in turn its decline into the new moon or empty moon. It also rotates in synch with the Earth so that we always see the same side of the moon. The moon phases, and particularly the full moon, play an important role in the emotional world of human beings, especially for loving couples.[29]

Just as the concrete planet becomes visible at night and in the darkness—it unfolds its magic and bathes the familiar surroundings of the day in its mysterious light while everything that lies in the shadows becomes impenetrable for the light-dependent eye—the *Moon* in astrology is associated with the unconscious, nocturnal side of the psyche. The Moon symbolizes the individual's emotional, receptive, and impressionable side that is rooted in the darkness of the unconscious. Our emotions and feelings come from the unconscious sphere, from the darkness. So we may also be surprised, blindsided, or flooded by them and then behave very irrationally—in both beneficial and destructive ways.

Our ability to genuinely relate to others is rooted in the Moon quality. If we are empathetic, sensitive, and also sense or intuit what moves others, what they need, and how they feel beyond what they say, the moon is constellated within us. Our emotional intelligence enables us to grasp non-verbal processes and react adequately to them.

The Moon's world includes the realm of sleep and dreams. The latter is accompanied by all types of fantastical and moving images, as we know them from our nightly dream activity. In addition to nightly dreams, which rise up from the unconscious while we sleep and may be remembered and captured after we wake up, daydreaming and imagination[30] also belong to the Moon's world. In all spheres of fantasy, the unconscious shows itself in all of its colorful variety, even if our awareness of it is fleeting and fragmented.

The Moon, therefore, also symbolizes the soul in its changing and fleeting manifestations—in its metamorphoses and transformations that are inherent to the processes of life itself. This decisively includes the ability to adapt to the changing conditions that life brings with it.

So it is no surprise that the mother and child are associated with the Moon principle, since the child is what grows and becomes—changing constantly throughout their development—which happens more in secret during the prenatal stage and becomes visible after birth. The relationship of feminine-maternal rhythms to the Moon can also be seen in the menstrual cycle[31] and the average length of a pregnancy.[32]

Every child should have a mother who cares for, nourishes, and cherishes them by recognizing and responding to their changing needs. Depending on the placement of the moon and its relationship with the other planets, it may be relatively easier or more difficult for a woman to grow into the role of mother and care for her child with the necessary empathy.[33] The younger the child—for example, the newborn who cannot speak yet and therefore is unable to verbally express their needs—the more intense the dependency on the mother to correctly understand and respond to their alternating emotional states and physical needs.

In the life of every human being, the mother is an extremely important figure and experiences with her largely affect the individual's ability and the manner in which they relate to themselves and their fellow human beings. Relationship problems, either personal and professional, are among the most frequent reasons for starting psychotherapy.

When a woman becomes a mother, two factors come into play: her own structural dispositions (Moon constellation) for mothering and what she internalized about mothering through experiences with her own mother and other important female caregivers. The complex interplay of these two factors is often experienced as fateful, since much of it is concealed from the individual and beyond conscious understanding. The more comprehensively and adequately a mother is able to relate to her child, the more successfully her child—in the case of a girl—will be able to act in her own role as a mother. Each child absorbs a great deal from their mother, including atmospheric factors, and unconsciously reproduces this. In the case of a boy, his own maternal qualities and perception of the other gender, as well as his choice of a partner, are also considerably influenced by his own Moon constellation and experiences with his own mother.

The fateful character that the relationship with the mother has in the life of every human being becomes strikingly apparent time and again in psychotherapeutic and psychoanalytic practice. As stated above, the way mothering is imprinted on us depends on the two factors of disposition and influences from the surrounding world. So the determining factor is not just the actual mother's behavior and nature, but also the Moon in its overall constellation in the individual's birth chart. In the Moon constellation, the effectiveness of a certain expression of the mother archetype can be seen starting at birth. It makes a big difference for children and their environment whether they are born with more life-promoting or life-inhibiting structural dispositions—whether they are dominated by a Mary or a Kali, so to speak.

The various children of the same mother can therefore experience and describe her in completely different ways, even though she is the same woman. This is due to the different positions the Moon takes in each of their lives—the different positions activating specific qualities each child will perceive in the mother. In turn, this has an influence on the mother's reactions to the child. The interaction between a mother and her children is varied. For example, one child can develop a positive mother complex and the siblings a rather negative one, since each child projects his or her maternal archetypal disposition onto the actual mother. This projection becomes effective in the encounter with the mother and has a substantial influence on the concrete mother-child relationship. Whether there is a positive primal relationship depends on a sufficiently good constellation of the mother archetype and adequately good experiences with the actual mother.

As described in the previous section, the growing child feels safe and secure if the mother succeeds in perceiving their various needs in the different phases of development and satisfies them to an adequate degree. In this fortunate case, children not only feel safe and secure, they also get to know and appreciate themselves. Their future ability to take care of themselves in all aspects of their life is dependent on the Moon constellation and the care that they have experienced from the mother. Whether human beings maintain a good relationship with their body, and therefore also with all their needs, becomes apparent by the way in which they nourish themselves—if they get enough sleep and the appropriate amount of exercise, how well they protect themselves, and how they express themselves through adequate clothing, and so forth. Their ability to relate to others and the way in which they do so also depends on the above-mentioned factors of disposition and experience.

Analogous to what has been said and established about the Sun and certain differences between men and women—that women must live their own masculine qualities in the form of courage, determination, thinking power, and so forth instead of being content with projecting these abilities onto men—also applies to men with regard to the Moon. They should become familiar with and also live out their own feminine, emotional side and not just be content with projecting it onto women and relating to it indirectly. Instead, men should be in personal contact with it. The Moon and Venus symbolize the anima in the male psyche—the Moon qualities are connected with the mother and his own maternal qualities, while Venus is connected to romantic love and expressed in relationship to a woman as his beloved—but on a deeper level is expressed in his love for his own anima, his own soul (see the statements about "Venus" in the following section).

However, many men find it extremely difficult to know their own feelings, appreciate them, relate to them, and reflect on them. Nevertheless, the man must accomplish the same developmental task as the woman—even though the two feminine planets of the Moon and Venus may be more basic to her conscious identity and therefore her self-image as a mother and lover. In this process, the Moon element in the female psyche tends to symbolize the maternal and receptive qualities and the Venus element tends to represent the erotic aspect of the woman (see below under "Venus"). So, in order to achieve the greatest possible state of wholeness, she should also develop her Sun and Mars qualities. For the sake of his own wholeness, the man should also live out the qualities of the Moon and Venus. When he does so, this will be rewarded by the major gain of an improved ability to have relationships with others and himself. Working on his own ability to have relationships usually has a very positive effect on the man's life as a friend, lover, and father—as well as on his extended social and professional life.

Problematic Moon constellations in any gender can lead to a rigid emotional attitude or to overactive, compulsive fantasies and emotions—accompanied by an insufficient sense of reality.

The Moon in the body: fluid balance, glands, and stomach.

☿ Mercury

Communication is the domain of Mercury, as well as the exchange of goods. This is connected to our intelligence, our capacity to observe and appraise, and our ability to think economically. The utilitarian logic that exists with Mercury can also be expressed in a trickster-like way, as shown in the story of the god Hermes, the Greek equivalent of the Roman god Mercury.[34] The Mercury world is a counterpart of the above-described emotional world of the Moon.

Mercury symbolizes our interest in the world, our curiosity to know what goes on, and our ability to find a name for and communicate what we have experienced—whether this relates to everyday circumstances or events in the larger world. There are almost unlimited possibilities for trade and exchange since the process of exchange is the basic principle of Mercury. This can occur in both the good and the bad sense, because Mercury is not only viewed as the god of merchants but also of thieves and deceivers.

On a more concrete level, Mercury rules the exchange of goods such as raw materials, semi-manufactured goods, or finished products, and therefore the realm of trade in the classic sense. The exchange in culture, research, and development of new techniques occurs through personal cooperation, as well as in written form with the help of the written or printed text, or the Internet. There are now also various electronic media available for the verbal exchange. In any case, finding new means of communication is also part of the inventive and imaginative Mercury principle.

The handling of money, and along with it the entire economic world, has become so complex and multi-faceted that understanding its laws now requires special training. This also belongs to the realm of Mercury.

For people with a strong Mercury disposition, the focus is on utility and not on the ethics that Jupiter brings to a situation. People with a Mercury emphasis often learn easily and eagerly because they are thirsty for knowledge and open to everything that is new. They are frequently also very talented with language, which applies to both speaking and writing. This is usually already expressed in childhood at school—and such gifted children often develop and share their facility with words and writing in adulthood as journalists, authors, politicians, lawyers, teachers, or professors.

Even the manual dexterity that is typical of many people with a Mercury emphasis can already be seen in the way children pick up toys, colored pencils, paint brushes, scissors, or other tools. Talented artisans also owe their dexterity in handling the tools and materials that they work with to an emphasized Mercury disposition. There is often a double disposition in which intelligent people are also skillful with their hands and know how to create something out of everything that they touch.

Problematic manifestations of the Mercury disposition can be found in the abuse of intelligence, such as in spinning tales of gossip and intrigue. Fraud in both little ways and on a very grand scale is also part of its abuse. There are practically no limits to the illegal, asocial, and unethical application of intelligence and inventiveness.

Mercury in the body: nervous system, arms and hands, and respiratory organs.

♂ Mars

We owe our ability to be active, to move forward, and to be in motion—as well as our drive and assertiveness—to Mars. It symbolizes our fighting power, courage, and aggressive ability that faces obstacles and wants to eliminate them.[35] This is the impulsive side in us that can suddenly break out. It is impatient, wanting to see immediate actions and results.

This forward-pushing energy can—like every other energy—be used either constructively or destructively. Whether this warlike energy works to the benefit or detriment of individuals and their environment depends on many dispositional factors and experiences.

As an example, athletes and professional dancers have a great deal of Mars energy since movement is genuinely a part of Mars. However, the desire and urge to move is not enough to be successful: The joy of movement must be directed toward a meaningful goal (in which the Sun and Jupiter are primarily involved), and this goal can often only be achieved with great endurance and sometimes even toughness (Saturn) through years of effort.

Heroes and heroines, fighters and warriors, as well as courageous, industrious, hard-working people, are usually quite familiar with the energy of Mars and use it deliberately and intensively. If courage and fighting power are to serve constructive goals, which may occur in the physical or mental areas, this energy must be mastered. Championing an important idea also requires a great deal of courage and assertiveness, as shown by the history of intellectuals like philosophers and other scientists (including Marie Curie, Maria Montessori, Albert Schweitzer, and Pestalozzi) who are ahead of their time and challenge collective thought patterns by energetically and courageously opening new paths of thought (such as Kant, Freud, and Jung).

Courageous thinkers obviously also require Mercurial and other dispositions, but the courage and energetic implementation of their ideas indicate the strong participation of Mars. Politicians who fight against destructive ideologies and movements in order to protect and take care of their people have the Mars energy, as do those participating in political resistance to a tyrannical regime—who often endure years of imprisonment in the most difficult conditions for the sake of values such as democracy. The ideas of humanity, democracy, and so forth for which they fight may not be correlated with Mars but with other archetypes; however, Mars is what actively fights for them. It is also obvious that religious convictions have always had an action-taking effect. Unfortunately, this is often reflected in fanaticism.

If we allow ourselves to be blindly controlled by our impulses, we behave in arbitrary and unpredictable ways. This problematic expression of the Mars energy can be seen well in pathological conditions such as mania, borderline personality disorder, and in sociopathic individuals—whose Martian impulses often break out unchecked and lead to the harming of individuals and/or the social environment. Both the criminal acts of the common man and the dictator's commitment to brutally exterminate those who think differently or who are members of certain ethnicities are among the destructive manifestations of Mars energy. History shows that there have repeatedly been cruel and sadistic rulers who senselessly tortured and harmed their people instead of allowing them to flourish.

Male sexuality belongs to Mars. In this area as well, courage is required when it comes to pursuing relationships. Whether a man maintains his courage and continues to search for a romantic partner or gives up after the first rejection, and becomes an inveterate old bachelor is largely related to Mars energy.

In the woman's horoscope, the Mars constellation indicates the type of male lover she will find attractive. As mentioned earlier, Mars determines the image of the animus together with the constellation of the Sun.

Some things have already been noted about problematic expressions of Mars energy. It turns out that the aggression principle per se cannot be easily cultivated and that derailments happen quickly and frequently. Unfortunately, this destructive side of Mars constellates very easily not only in the individual, but also in the collective—as is shown by both the predictable and the unexpected wars that flare up time and again around the world.

Mars in the body: gallbladder and male sexual organs.

♀ Venus

Even for people who are not familiar with astrology, the name "Venus" will immediately evoke her Greek form—Aphrodite as the Goddess of Love—and her main attribute of beauty. The planet Venus in the horoscope is associated with the topics of love, eroticism, and beauty according to the myth of Aphrodite/Venus. Venus is also present in the search for harmony and balance—when a feeling for proportions is needed. This especially comes into play in the areas of art, culture, and aesthetics, even though the criteria we use to define them are changing and variable. Instead, the standards used express and adapt to the prevailing spirit of the age. So the voluptuous figures painted by Sir Peter Paul Rubens were seen as beautiful at that time, but now we tend to view them as rather corpulent and unattractive. Toward the end of the 20th century, the rotund human figure's opposite pole triumphed in the form of the gaunt and emaciated ideal that countless young women tried to achieve through mercilessly starving themselves. However, today the two extremes hardly meet the collective taste that no longer idealizes the very voluptuous or thin, but rather the relatively slender body with a defined musculature as beautiful.

So collective aesthetic norms change over decades and centuries, and the same applies to individuals of a certain time who do not experience the same things as beautiful. This is due to the dispositional character of Venus, which can be located in very different signs of the zodiac and also have entirely divergent aspects—i.e. it can have diverse relationships with the other planets. This situation can be seen in very specific stylistic preferences with regard to what we experience as beautiful and harmonious. On the other hand, whether the sense for what is beautiful and harmonious has been cultivated or not by the surrounding world plays a considerable role for the individual. Enjoyment can be modest or excessive—in the sense of too much or too little—and, depending on the aspect, the tendency manifests as wholesome or unwholesome. So not every astrological placement of Venus can contribute her qualities of balance equally well.

There is a Venus in every woman! All women have the archetype of Venus/Aphrodite within them. However, even if this archetype is not a predominant force in a woman's birth chart, it can also be cultivated. In any case, Venus is integral to a woman's self-image as a lover—as a sexual and erotic being who can seduce and can open herself up to being seduced or shut herself off from it. The woman's activity in matters of love also obviously depends on the constellation of other planets and their interaction. If a woman has enough Mars energy or her Venus is in a fire element (see Chapter 2 for the elements), she behaves more actively than when she is more strongly influenced by Saturn.

If the Venus component is impaired or exaggerated, the ability to be selective or behave appropriately toward potential lovers is disturbed. On the one hand, such extreme deviations can be seen in the woman who is compulsively sexually active; on the other hand, there is the woman who has turned her back on everything that is erotic and sexual. In earlier times, these two extreme types of women were quickly devalued and called either "nymphomaniacs" and even "whores," or "spinsters" and "old maids."

Astrology can create tolerance by showing that there are very different dispositions, which make it easier or harder to behave moderately in terms of enjoyment and devotion based on the manifold possibilities of Venus. Venus also governs the entire context of fertility, but this is also co-determined by other factors.

Of course, individuals also make conscious decisions about how the aesthetic principle will be expressed in their lives. The sublimation of erotic-sexual energy can lead to creative achievements in art and culture; instead of actual children—or in addition to them—works of art and other creative products can also be born.

In a very general sense, a strong and well-integrated Venus disposition usually appears in both genders as a groomed and tasteful appearance, as well as in a pleasant, friendly, and charming behavior toward others within relationships.

In the man, the Venus constellation corresponds with his anima image that he projects onto a woman when he is in love. As with the woman, the Venus component in the man is associated with the sense for what is beautiful, coherent, and harmonious. Depending on the degree of integration, he is more or less balanced in his choice of lover, his outer appearance, and how he behaves in relationships.

Professional preferences for artistic design and expression, or a profession that brings them into contact with works of art, dominate among people who are highly influenced by Venus. Collectors, gallery owners, art dealers, art experts, art restorers, employees of art museums, or cultural policy-makers usually enjoy works of art.

Problematic manifestations of Venus energy in the woman and man may show up as the idolization of opulence and materialism, or as devotion to pleasure at all costs. It can also be seen in an inflated desire for harmony or harmony at any price, which can escalate into a true addiction to harmony. This manifests in the suppression of reality, which is perceived as unpleasant, and any associated conflicts that should be resolved instead of ignored. This tendency to suppress can be seen in many areas of life and ultimately has a destructive effect on the individual and his or her surrounding world.

Venus in the body: kidneys, glands, and female sexual organs.

♃ Jupiter

Expansive, vast, reaching into the distance, taking future possibilities into account, a great need for freedom, optimism, and high ideals— these are important key words that relate to Jupiter. Travelling and getting to know people of other cultures are therefore part of the entirely natural behavior for people with an emphasis on Jupiter. There is often an actual longing for distant places, a type of wanderlust that Jupiter people are especially familiar with. However, this wanderlust and longing for what is foreign can also be partially satisfied at home: through contact with people from other cultures and different parts of the world, the exploration of different worlds of thought and imagination, or learning about religious ideas from various cultures and eras. Getting away from what is accustomed, everyday life, the here and now, as well as departing for new shores whether within or without— express the disposition of those with a strong Jupiter constellation in their birth chart.[36]

Belief in new possibilities plays an essential role for individuals with an emphasis on Jupiter and characterizes their ineradicable optimism about their ability to achieve the goals that they have set. This buoyant, basic mood is closely linked with questions about the meaning of life. These are often related to religious concerns, which can include the search for the sacred and an ultimate reason for our existence.

Questions of justice, excess, and sensible moderation are also Jupiter's themes. A good example of this is found in Bertolt Brecht's play *The Caucasian Chalk Circle*. There is a war. The governor's wife has fled and left her child behind. A maid rescues the boy, keeps him alive with great sacrifice on her part, develops a deep relationship with him, and ultimately passes him off as her own child. At the end of the war, the governor's wife returns and reclaims the child as her own—not out of love but because he has the prospect of a rich inheritance. However, the maid does not want to give the child back to her. This results in a trial. The village judge, who is known for his wisdom, draws a circle and places the child in it. He announces that the true mother will be able to pull the child out of the circle. Both women grab the child. While the governor's wife tries to yank the boy toward her, the maid lets go because she doesn't want to hurt him. As a result, the judge concludes that she embodies true motherly love. He declares that the child is hers and sends the governor's wife away.

Jupiter stands for high expectations and demands. Depending on the constellation, this may be directed more inward or toward the outer world. Those with Jupiter natures are quite often obsessed and driven by a need for "more and more" or "always better." This is a type of striving for excellence, which—depending on the relationship of Jupiter with other planets—can have an effect in the most diverse areas of life. This is often particularly dominant in younger years and leads to a considerable lack of freedom, which is tantamount to an actual reversal of Jupiter's concerns of extending the radius of freedom and experience in order to discover meaning in the process. Such a less constructive approach to Jupiter qualities can be corrected relatively easily by asking the question: Is this meaningful? The question about meaning can work wonders since it usually conjures up the right answer. Consequently, the demand that something must be ideal, which can never be satisfied, can be replaced by a striving for the optimum state. This implies an attitude that is balanced and takes into consideration the question of meaning.

If the Jupiter energy is not balanced, it may be expressed in hedonism and wastefulness, pomposity and boasting, insisting on being right, and missionary fanaticism.

Jupiter in the body: liver function and lipid metabolism.

♄ Saturn

Saturn is often associated with the restriction of life, and so, with death: Saturn metaphorically eats his own children, as is described in Greek mythology. The Grim Reaper, as we know him from fairy tales and the visual arts, also symbolizes Saturn. Death is the last, final boundary in life; its reality is inevitable. So Saturn also symbolizes the principle of reality and our transience in view of death.

Reality with the limitations in places on the individual and the collective are Saturnal themes that involve external facts, and our own physical, emotional, and mental reality—including our financial means and abilities to secure our own existence.

The Saturn side within us is pragmatic and realistic. Saturn makes us take responsibility for our thinking and acting, and for its impact on ourselves and on those around us—particularly our partners, children, and other family members. This also ultimately includes responsibility for the larger collective such as private and state institutions. Collective culture, with its laws, norms, and rules—together with its conventions and traditions—represents important Saturnal qualities. Saturn-influenced individuals are distinguished by their seriousness toward life, which is why they also take their professional obligations seriously and often hold themselves and others to standards of perfectionism and integrity. The superego with its demands for perfection has Saturnal qualities. Their faithfulness to a task once they have taken it on and their reliability enable people associated with Saturn to hold corresponding positions in the private sector and the state.

Among Saturn's strengths are his perseverance and endurance, which enable us to accept the delays and resistance that generally also accompany the performance of obligations.

Saturn is the master of concentrating on the essential, especially when the task at hand involves orders, structures, forms, and formal elements. This ability is crucial for practicing many professions. However, a strong Saturn disposition is especially desirable, and actually often exists, in philosophers and successful leaders. Architects rarely get very far in their profession without a corresponding Saturn disposition.

All of the experiences we've had—beginning in the prenatal state—get stored away in the unconscious, and can only be consciously accessed to a limited degree. Instead, they exist for the most part in the dark, where they influence our feelings, thoughts, and behavior. Saturn corresponds to this reservoir of experience. Positive experiences and successful achievements strengthen our sense of self-worth and self-confidence, while failures and traumatizing experiences can evoke guilt and fear, that we can experience as cramps that literally grip our intestines. They can trigger inhibitions and blockages that restrict our behavior. When people are controlled by such guilt for and fear of failure, they neglect to do much of what they should actually tackle.

Finally, Saturn is often connected with the term *fate*. However, we should differentiate between the factors that we are subjected to in life, but are not our fault—such as the milieu, the state, or the part of the world that we are born into—and the experiences for which we are responsible that result from our own behavior. Saturn is the ruler of the relentlessly ticking clock and governs how we deal with time—since it runs out whether we use it or not. This brings a fateful component into each individual's life. Unutilized time in life usually leads to feelings of guilt and can also trigger depression. These problematic Saturn correlations manifest in the restriction of life, in rejecting everything that is luxuriant, nurturing, flourishing, cheerful, and light. It can sometimes lead to an unnatural ending of an individual's life: suicide. Infirmity in old age, illness, and death set limits to life in an entirely natural way without the effects of violence. This is where Saturn acts as the Grim Reaper.

People who are influenced by Saturn tend to be cautious and careful with their resources. But when thriftiness becomes stinginess and austerity leads to physical, emotional, and mental starvation, the danger of emotional and mental atrophy is joined by social isolation, and even physical illness. Stingy people suffer on various levels from an obsession for restraint, which makes an exchange with their fellow human beings impossible. When we can only take but not give, we lose the flow of life that only occurs through give *and* take. Stingy people are often driven by a fear of impoverishment. They scrimp and save, even if they are rich and affluent. One extreme of this can be found in severe depression, where the impoverishment dominates in a compulsive way. The miserly are often presented as haggard and wrinkled figures since their stinginess is not only directed against others, but usually also against their own needs.

Social isolation is often the consequence of such a joyless existence since compulsively withholding energy—whether of an emotional, mental, or financial nature—scares away fellow human beings.

Saturn in the body: bone system, joints, teeth, and skin.

♅ Uranus

Intuition and an eye for new possibilities are genuine Uranian qualities. This intensive energy, which is unpredictable and suddenly comes to life is turned toward progress. It loves to burst the basic Saturnal attitude of preserving what is traditional. As if from the heavens, Uranus takes a bird's-eye perspective from an airy height, from where it has an immediate overview of the circumstances. It can therefore implement innovations, restructurings, and mutations in the right place and initiate fast and far-reaching changes. The archetypal human need for freedom is profoundly connected with Uranus, and the Uranus constellation shows the areas of life to which this striving for freedom extends. If the Uranus side feels restricted in its need for freedom by outmoded traditions or a dictatorial regime, it may take up the cause of rebellion and opposition. Revolutionaries are classic Uranians, but they still need the help of Mars (courage and energy) for the realization of their ideas.

When we feel restricted in our freedom, we may exhibit restlessness and nervous irritability—like a freedom-loving animal that is locked in a tight cage.

♆ Neptune

Neptune is expressed in the dissolution of boundaries, premonitions, extrasensory perception, sensitivity, clairvoyance, visions, aura, atmosphere, and musicality, as well as in wishful thinking, illusions, obfuscations, ambiguities, disorder, and chaos. It is immediately apparent that Neptune (like Uranus) is a great antagonist of Saturn, the keeper of order and ruler of reality. Neptune is the principle that breaks down boundaries and is therefore capable of eroding order, structure, and form. It overcomes barriers and penetrates walls. The Neptunian energy is embodied in a "symbiosis between various species and types of being," making it possible to have a "reciprocal reconciliation in an overarching harmony" and "transcendental vision."[37]

People with an accentuated Neptune constellation have major problems when it comes to setting boundaries against outside influences. Not only are they emotionally and mentally very receptive to elusive atmospheric energy, they often are also susceptible to infectious diseases on a physical level. But this not only involves the lack of boundaries toward the surrounding world, it is also expressed in a lack of boundaries with the powers of the inner world. It includes wallowing in wishful thinking, in aimless fantasies, and escapist daydreams—which can easily devolve into experiences of inner chaos.

Yet, constant and continuous work with fantasies and dreams has a cultivating effect on the Neptune energy. The dream world has its own structure and contours, and unfolds in its own way, as we encounter living beings, landscapes, colors, and sounds in the realm of imagination that cannot be experienced in the reality of the Saturn world. In depth psychology, Neptunian terrain is particularly fruitful for personality development.

Sensitivity, a fine intuition, and an unmistakable instinct are Neptune qualities that function without words. Neptune energy can be cultivated through meditative techniques and is indispensable for musicians. For example, Leonhard Bernstein fine-tuned his musical genius by meditating on a regular basis. Mystics also search for the connection to a world that lies beyond the consensus reality of Saturn.

But if it is not possible to tame the wandering fantasies and make them fruitful in the above-mentioned way, the result is the domination of illusion, seduction, and corruption. It becomes difficult for the real world to reach people who slip into addiction and get lost in fantastically beautiful delusions or horrifying realms of paranoia.

♇ Pluto

Pluto symbolizes a powerful, unconscious, and superior energy that requires transformation through making it conscious. Or, in the words of Thomas Ring, it requires a "radical transformation of form."[38] When we encounter a person with a strong Pluto constellation, we may be confronted with an energetic force that is overwhelming. This energy, which goes beyond the human dimension, must be transformed so that it does not have a destructive effect on the affected individuals and/or their surroundings. Pluto is about the themes of violence, power, and transformation. Like a nuclear power plant, Pluto constantly supplies all of the associated planets with energy and amplifies their respective typical dispositions. This force beyond human measure deprives people of freedom when they are subjected to it, and can seriously harm or even kill them—just like nuclear energy. On a psychological level, this corresponds to unconscious compulsions. These cannot be controlled by human restraint and or be judged by human standards. Such compulsions can stop people from developing a fruitful life.

A little example will illustrate Pluto's power a bit more vividly: If there is an analytical[39] Pluto-Moon contact in a child's horoscope, the human mother is never enough—even if she has an exemplary relationship with the child—since they will hold unrealistically high expectations of what the mother should provide. The child plagues the mother with an ever-present demand for more attention or a different type of attention that exudes a quality of insatiability.

Conversely, a mother with such a constellation exclusively devotes herself to her child, which leaves no space for anyone and anything else—not even her own husband. Of course, a woman who is obsessed by her mother role does not help her child to have a natural and undisturbed development since she—when acting unconsciously—is not capable of granting the child necessary freedom. This excessive Plutonian energy can impact all areas of professional and private life. In order to become fruitful, its compulsiveness must be subjected to the principle of metamorphosis—of death and rebirth—which creatively expresses the transformative essence of Pluto.

Synopsis: Images of the Gods Within Us

These brief and compact sketches of the planetary principles are intended to give an impression of their archetypal characteristics. As already established in the introduction, these archetypal principles as symbolized by the ten planets affect all human beings, but are expressed individually. It is helpful to imagine an inner life stage where various characters act out plays comparable to the manifold performances that occur on stages of theaters and opera houses around the world. Depending on the person's developmental phase and life circumstances, the actions can be differentiated in terms of key themes and styles of expression: Is this about relationships, love, eroticism, sexuality, jealousy, rivalry, or hatred (with Venus and Mars as the main actors)? Or is it about power or money (with the Sun, Saturn, Mercury, or Jupiter as the main actors)? Perhaps it is about various conflicts, between reality and illusion (Saturn, Neptune, or Mercury), honesty and deception (Mercury), courage and cowardice (Mars, Mercury, or Neptune). Or various questions could take center stage around problems of identity in all phases of life: Who am I? Who do I want to be? (Sun, Moon, Jupiter, or Saturn).

There are infinite variations of these archetypal themes that are reflected in the horoscope on the one hand and expressed precisely as particular dispositions on the other hand. The question of synchronicity, or the specific qualities constellated at certain times, also plays an important role here. We are faced with different development tasks during childhood, adolescence, mature adulthood, and old age. This is why different archetypes play a dominant role at different times and in different people, and why transits or moving planets become significant. They activate certain themes during the various phases of life, and these must be dealt with.

One of the main problems that most people face throughout their lives is their relationships with other people, whether professional or private. Unfortunately, the relationship we have with ourselves (which is a decisive factor in our relationships with others) remains unconscious for a very long time. It is often treated as an afterthought and only addressed when there is no other choice. The archetypal relationship specialists are the Moon and Venus, as well as Neptune; Mercury and Jupiter can also help.

How completely we are able to develop our personality in the course of our life involves complex factors. Whether we view life as a drama or a light piece, a tragedy or comedy, a shallow production or one with depth, an exciting or boring one, and whether it plays at a fast or slow pace, and so forth, depends not only on our disposition, but also our level of development. The signs of the zodiac in which the planets stand also play an important role here.[40]

The two "main lights"—the Sun as the central, driving life force and the Moon as a relationship function—should be given the most attention within this context. It is important to also consider both of them in their significance as archetypal expressions of the paternal and maternal, which govern our experiences with actual mothers and fathers, or other caregivers. Both the radiating Sun and the orbiting Moon tend to focus on expansion and enrichment, which is supported by Jupiter and Neptune, but restricted in turn by Saturn and partly by Venus, while Mercury contributes its cleverness and Mars its performance power and zeal.

Of course, Saturn's constricting and life-negating power can also dominate to the extent that expansive forces do not develop enough, and we cannot awaken or realize our deepest potentials. In the worst case, disease and death can occur—even in the young years.

As previously discussed, the Sun and Mars symbolize the animus in the female psyche.[41] Women have the deepest experience of the animus' power, the archetype of masculine power, when they fall in love. When projecting on the opposite sex, the animus corresponds with the ideal image of the man. When the woman encounters a man who appears to embody this inner image, the woman falls in love. Because an archetype comes into play through the projection of the animus, this infatuation can be absolute and bring with it not only joy and fulfillment but also forms of unhealthy dependence.[42]

With the woman's increasing self-perception and knowledge about her actual father and the real-life partner, she succeeds in becoming conscious of her own animus qualities, as well as becoming aware of, cultivating, and developing them. From the perspective of individuation as the human being's life-long psychological growth and maturation process, it is necessary and beneficial that increasingly fewer women want to, or have to, limit themselves to projecting their animus—demanding the animation of these animus qualities from men. Increasingly more women want to and can develop their own masculine abilities—their Sun and Mars qualities.

Even a woman's level of self-confidence is partly dependent on the animation and vitality of her own masculine dispositions and abilities. The more naturally a woman actively lives her Sun-like nature and translates it into reality (which in turn is the task of Mars), the better she will succeed in remaining true to her own life plan, whether within a partnership, or by living out her spiritual or even artistic interests on both the private and professional level.

The Sun and Mars, as representatives of masculine qualities, correspond to the two feminine planets of the Moon and Venus. Within this context, the Sun and Moon form a couple[43]—the king and queen. Mars and Venus form another couple, which is well known from Greek mythology.

The same task required of women in relationship to the animus, applies to men in relation to their anima qualities, which are astrologically symbolized by the Moon and Venus. The man also has the life-long developmental task of becoming familiar with his inner femininity and living it for himself instead of seeking and delegating away all emotional matters and competences by projecting them onto women in the outside world.

Planetary principles in keywords

⊙ **The Sun:** Main driving force in life, essence, development of the personality, creativity, vitality, will, consciousness, personal responsibility, self-esteem, self-expression, fatherly, inner image of the father, and the animus.
In the body: heart and circulation.

☽ **The Moon:** Emotion, unconscious, dream, imagination, soul, receptivity, variability, adaptation, and change, motherly, mother-child relationship, inner image of the mother, and anima.
In the body: fluid balance, glands, and stomach.

☿ **Mercury:** Communication, exchange, intelligence, intellect, rational mind, language, word, writing, interest, trade, and economy, manual dexterity.
In the body: nervous system, arms and hands, and respiratory organs.

♂ **Mars:** Driving force, assertiveness, activity, impulse, will, fight, aggression, courage, the instinctive and compulsive, inner image of the man as the lover, animus.
In the body: gallbladder and male sexual organs.

♀ **Venus:** Harmony and balance, sense of proportions, beauty, aesthetics and art, love, eroticism, fertility, and love of pleasure, inner image of the woman as the lover, anima.
In the body: kidneys, glands, and female sexual organs.

♃ **Jupiter:** Expansion, optimism, faith, religion, justice, reason, high expectations and demands, giving everything 100%, striving for the optimum state, and the question of meaning, compensatory principle.
In the body: liver function and lipid metabolism.

♄ **Saturn:** Reality, limitation, experience, and old age, norms ("people should"), convention and tradition, form and structure, conscience, obligation, responsibility, law, time, delays, resistance, harshness, concentrating on what is essential, fear, cramping, negation of life, disease, termination, death, and fate.
In the body: skeletal system, joints, teeth, and skin.

♅ **Uranus:** Intuition, bird's-eye perspective, overview, progress, the unpredictable, the sudden, the surprising, changes, innovations, restructuring, mutation, striving for freedom, need for freedom, desire to oppose, restlessness, and nervous irritability.

♆ **Neptune:** Dissolution of boundaries, premonitions, extrasensory perceptions, clairvoyance, visions, aura, atmosphere, imagination, wishful thinking, dream world, instinct, intuition, music, meditation, mysticism, illusions, obfuscations, ambiguities, disorder, chaos, seduction, infection, and addiction.

♇ **Pluto:** Superior energy that needs to be transformed, excess, lack of moderation, violence, power and helplessness, compulsion, guiding principle, principle of metamorphosis, dying and rebirth.

2
A Typology of Depth Psychological Astrology

The Four Elements in Astrology: Fire, Earth, Air, and Water in the Twelve Signs of the Zodiac

Just like the planets, the signs of the zodiac (also called "star signs" or "Sun signs," see below) are also archetypes and therefore subject to the law of polarity. There are twelve signs of 30° each, which together form the entire zodiac of 360°.

It should be emphasized right at the start of introducing the twelve signs, that all have an equal value and a certain function within the entire zodiac that will be explained in the following section.[44] There are no "good" or "bad" or "better" or "worse" zodiac signs, since each of the twelve has its specific strengths and weaknesses. Whether a certain sign tends to be lived more constructively or destructively is strongly dependent on the level of individual development and consciousness.

When people say: "I'm an Aries" or "I'm a Libra," they mean that the Sun was located in the sign of Aries or Libra at the time of their birth. This is why the signs of the zodiac are also called "Sun signs."

Ill. 2: The Zodiac. Miniature by Giovanni Battista Agnese (16th century)

There are a total of twelve zodiac signs or Sun signs, which are divided into four groups of three—each group of three is associated with one of the four elements of *fire, earth, air,* and *water.* So there are three fire signs, three earth signs, three air signs, and three water signs. The fire sign of *Aries* (fire) starts off the twelve, followed by *Taurus* (earth), *Gemini* (air), *Cancer* (water), *Leo* (fire), *Virgo* (earth), *Libra* (air), *Scorpio* (water), *Sagittarius* (fire), *Capricorn* (earth), *Aquarius* (air), and *Pisces* (water).

The twelve zodiac signs result in six axes with two poles each that are created by the two respective signs that are opposite each other at 180°. These are Aries (fire) – Libra (air), Taurus (earth) – Scorpio (water), Gemini (air) – Sagittarius (fire), Cancer (water) – Capricorn (earth), Leo (fire) – Aquarius (air), Virgo (earth) – Pisces (water). Illustration 3 shows this arrangement.

The two zodiac signs that are directly across from each other on an axis have a complementary relationship in terms of the elements they are associated with. They can reciprocally correct and supplement each other in their extremes, which not only makes them more moderate but also more complete.[45]

Before the various zodiac signs are introduced individually, it is important to understand another dynamic that differentiates them: the three basic energetic attitudes of the cardinal, the fixed, and the mutable. This distinction allows the individual signs to be depicted more comprehensively in their archetypal character.

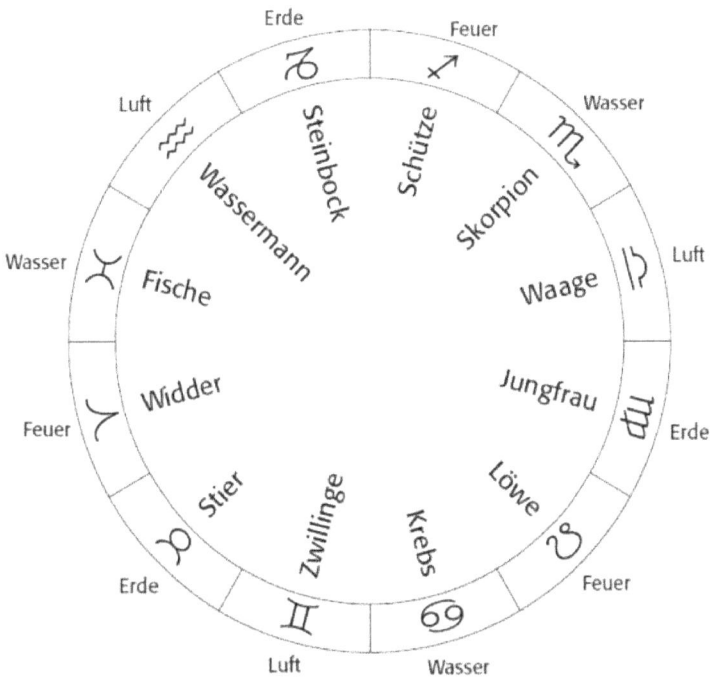

Ill. 3: The Zodiac with associated elements of the signs

[Text from the left, clockwise:
Fire - Aries / Water - Pisces / Air - Aquarius / Earth - Capricorn / Fire - Sagittarius / Water - Scorpio / Air - Libra / Earth - Virgo / Fire - Leo / Water - Cancer / Air - Gemini / Earth - Taurus]

43

Cardinal, fixed, and mutable signs of the zodiac

The zodiac signs are not only associated with the four elements, but can also be differentiated according to their basic energy style—which may be *cardinal, fixed,* or *mutable.* All three styles exist in every element: fire, earth, air, and water.

a) The cardinal signs are Aries ♈ *(fire), Cancer* ♋ *(water), Libra* ♎ *(air), and Capricorn* ♑ *(earth).*

What these otherwise very different signs have in common—since various elements belong to cardinal signs—is that they are always willing to start new projects, set new things in motion, or cultivate initiative. They are not only interested in new projects, but are directly and actively committed to them in keeping with the different corresponding elements. Above all, Aries and Capricorn are undaunted by obstacles of any kind that may arise along the way, while Cancer and Libra are less direct as they move forward in a more hesitant, fluctuating, and circuitous approach. Cancer can sometimes even move backwards, which is aptly expressed by the term "backing out," but this is followed by once again moving forward. This style of Cancer clearly differentiates it from Aries, which only knows how to move directly, persistently forward.

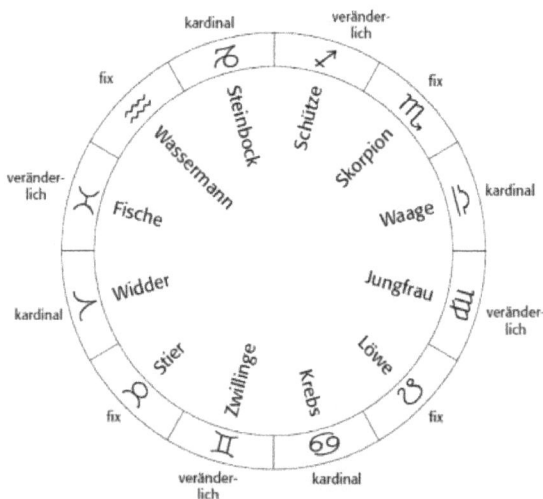

Ill. 4: The Zodiac with cardinal, fixed, and mutable signs

44

[Text from the left, clockwise:
Cardinal - Aries / Mutable - Pisces / Fixed - Aquarius / Cardinal - Capricorn / Mutable
- Sagittarius / Fixed - Scorpio / Cardinal - Libra / Mutable - Virgo / Fixed - Leo /
Cardinal - Cancer / Mutable - Gemini / Fixed - Taurus]

The cardinal signs are not satisfied with what they have previously achieved. When one thing has been taken care of, their attention quickly moves elsewhere. They never feel more alive than when they are striking out into new territory, and can fully concentrate and dedicate their energy to the current project. This can occur on the level of fiery action (Aries), creative imagination and feelings (Cancer), aesthetic experiencing and relationships (Libra), or the pragmatic striving for career success and collective, tangible accomplishments (Capricorn). But what they all have in common is that once they have finished a task, they keep moving forward. They are driven to follow their energy for initiative and are therefore oriented toward the future in the sense that there is always more to be experienced and achieved.

b) The fixed zodiac signs are Taurus ♉ (earth), Leo ♌ (fire), Scorpio ♏ (water), and Aquarius ♒ (air).

Despite all of the differences between these zodiac signs due to the various elements to which they belong, they are all involved with expanding what has been achieved and enriching what already exists. Not only can material goods and physical well-being (Taurus) be gained and cared for, but everything that elevates self-expression and can expand their kingdom of influence (Leo), metaphysical perceptions and power (Scorpio), and ideas in service to humanity (Aquarius). This expansion and increase develop from the inside out in concentric circles. It is a persevering attitude that allows for slow, organic growth.

The main emphasis is different in each of the elements. For example, the Taurus principle strives for the accumulation of possessions. securing of its own space, and bodily self-care, the Leo principle in heightening the meaning of its own significance and expression, the Scorpio principle in the search for and deepening of truths that extend beyond individual interests and connect us to the governing, sacred powers at work in the cosmos, and the Aquarius principle in the systematization of ideas and theories that can better the world. Everything that has already grown and been accomplished in the past serves as the basis for steady, future expansion.

c) The mutable zodiac signs are Gemini ♊ *(air), Virgo* ♍ *(earth), Sagittarius* ♐ *(fire), and Pisces* ♓ *(water).*

These four signs react very sensitively to the quietest of changes, glide quickly on from one moment to the next, do not get bogged down anywhere, and quickly lose interest in the face of resistance. Each of the four signs does this according to their element characteristics: Gemini (air) moves from topic to topic, since everything new is interesting; Virgo (earth) analyzes the problem and searches for appropriate possibilities to resolve it; Sagittarius (fire) demolishes old bridges and builds different ones that lead to new shores; Pisces (water) slips silently into the infinite world within, the watery depths of the soul and the world—but where they are headed remains a secret to the outside world and often also for them.

All four mutable signs are considerably different from the cardinal signs' enjoyment of taking initiative, and the persistent tenacity of the four fixed signs. The mutable signs simply let go and turn to the next possible project—until any difficulties arise, which will prompt them to quickly move on to another.

The three fire signs of Aries ♈, Leo ♌, and Sagittarius ♐

Comparable to actual fire that can glimmer, burn, or blaze in the outside world or on the inside of a wood-burning stove, human beings have an inner fire of varying degrees that can inspire them to accomplish concrete deeds or pursue their spiritual ideals. People with a pronounced fire disposition are more spontaneous, impulsive, and fiery than others. They present a strong contrast to the earth and water elements.

Just like the fire in nature or civilization can be helpful or rage destructively—which can happen spontaneously or also occur on purpose—this fire energy is seen in human beings. People with an intense fire disposition are quite strong-willed and often very passionate in this regard. When the fire energy is constellated in individuals, they feel courageous, self-confident, and self-reliant. They are freedom-loving and assert their freedom against all resistance, whether or not this is justified from other people's perspectives.

Fire people virtually burn others down with the fire of their affectivity. They cultivate a constructive approach to it when they use the fire energy to not only assert their personal freedom against other people's rights and claims, but can tame their own fire by allowing companions the same liberal rights. As a result, they embody true tolerance and generosity. If this is not the case, they can act indiscriminately, becoming unpredictable and aggressive individuals—only obeying their own narcissistic impulses. As in the activation of every disposition, the constructive or destructive expression of the fire element in any person depends on their level of maturation and development.

♈ Aries: 1st fire sign

Cardinal sign, associated planet: *Mars* ♂. "The willful driver"[46] is a fitting characterization of Aries.

Their guiding principle is "I want" since they are attuned to conquering the world. Aries is the archetype of the warrior or the hero.

People with an Aries emphasis are optimistic. They express strong emotions and are supported by an impulsive, action-oriented basic attitude that is courageous and combative, direct and honest. They are stimulated by resistance and will mobilize all of their energy to overcome it and achieve the goals that they have set. They are driven by a constant pioneering spirit, like to start new things, and often use their razor-sharp intellect to find innovative, creative paths. Their fire makes them fast, and they are talented when it comes to creating the quickest and shortest routes to solutions for problems. Their main strength is putting new projects together—but carrying them through requires the abilities of the Taurus.

Aries' shadow: When people characterized by Aries live unconsciously, they ram their heads against the wall—or other people. They are headstrong and want to assert their will against any resistance. When they do so, they can be very despotic and brutal. They impatiently and ruthlessly overrun those who think differently. Their lack of patience in carrying out and finishing a task or an obligation can lead to them ultimately not achieving any of the goals that they strive for.

Aries in the body: head.

♌ *Leo: 2nd fire sign*

Fixed sign, associated planet: *the Sun* ☉. "Consolidating through will"[47] is a fitting characterization of the Leo. Their motto is "live and let live—as long as my preeminent position is not threatened." Leo is the archetype of the ruler or king.

Monarchs normally have a court, and feel that their rightful place is at the head of it. So they are full of self-confidence regarding their own value and significance. They enjoy letting their light shine and can also radiate warmth and cheerfulness. By nature, they are most comfortable when they are the focal point and center of their respective environment. They obviously demand to be treated in keeping with their rulership of their domain. They have deep passion and strong drive. On the whole, they feel that they are powerful and that this power will always be available to them. People characterized by Leo can be distinguished by generosity and high-mindedness toward weaker people. They like to support these individuals through their own self-reliance and basic attitude of confidence. Leos enjoy resting in their environment as the radiant and all-dominating center, but also want to be acknowledged as such by others.

Leo's shadow: Individuals who are unconscious of their Leo aspect stand out due to their imperial, controlling impetuousness and demand to be the center of attention. They act dominatingly and like to exercise power over their fellow human beings instead of exhibiting control over themselves and their instinctual nature. Their pronounced lack of self-reflection and self-criticism makes it difficult for them to accept criticism from their surroundings, since they consider any criticism to be a seditious and malicious attack. Wherever people put on sovereign airs, present themselves as vain and dress accordingly, while acting conspicuously pompous, an unconscious Leo archetype is probably present. This can also include extravagance, sluggishness, and laziness— because work is for lesser people, since the ruler sits enthroned over others and is served by them.

↗ Sagittarius: 3rd fire sign

Mutable sign, associated planet: *Jupiter* ♃. "Willful determination"[48] is an apt characterization of the Sagittarius. Their guiding principle could be: "I believe in eternal ideals and strive for them." This is the archetype of the visionary.

Sagittarius-influenced people have a pronounced capacity to be enthusiastic for high goals. They believe in ideals such as freedom and justice. They often include the surrounding world and society in their vision. When an ideal affectively appeals to them, they commit themselves to it with an enthusiastic furor—whether it's a political or religious cause, or simply something they experience as just or meaningful. They will also attempt to convince others to join their cause— Sagittarian optimism is very contagious.

Good and lively teachers and speakers usually have a Sagittarius disposition. They are often in motion and so also like to do sports, anything with a fast tempo. Their speed is accompanied by impatience, and they can hardly tolerate when their momentum is slowed down by others who have a more leisurely pace (the earth elements of Taurus, Virgo, and Capricorn). However, their enjoyment of movement is not limited to the physical, but also extends to emotional and mental levels. It is easy to spark their enthusiasm for a political or religious idea.

It is vital for Sagittarians to always set their sights on a meaningful goal to pursue that lifts them out of the everyday routine. Their drive for spiritual ascent, which they can satisfy in philosophical and religious systems, is accompanied by an urge for expansiveness that can turn into true wanderlust. They fulfill this wanderlust through concrete travel to far-away countries or even by reading about foreign cultures, or even by exploring religious, philosophical, or political perspectives.

Sagittarius' shadow: People with a Sagittarius disposition can exhibit an idealism that is far removed from reality. This makes it impossible for them to see and respect reality. Insisting that they're right—when their opinion is only partially based on actual facts and often involves fanatical or quixotic ideas—is one of the most difficult traits in people who unconsciously live out their Sagittarius side. Even the best ideas, believed in and advocated for with missionary zeal, can provide no benefit if the boundaries and rules of reality are not considered.

Underestimating our personal reality, the reality of fellow human beings, the current situation, or the political state of affairs inevitably results in disappointment. This causes people characterized by Sagittarius to seem imbalanced since they—while clinging to their idea like a dogma—fall into the deepest despair from their elevated mood time and again, until they are lifted off by the next flight of fancy. Sagittarians can behave in a grandiose and jovial way, even without any reason for it. They tend to avoid conflicts and do not commit because they fear that they might lose some of their freedom if they are restricted to one particular path. In problematic cases, entering into relationships is difficult.

Sagittarius in the body: hips and thighs.

The three earth signs of Taurus ♉, Virgo ♍, and Capricorn ♑

The Earth supports and nourishes us. People like to use the phrase "Mother Earth," which expresses the female aspect of the earth signs. With this earthiness, the focus turns to the concrete world in all of its materiality, with its manifold limitations, and with the necessity of mastering everyday life—including the need for physical pleasure, bodily well-being, and other earthly joys. Earth-accented people tend to be slow, at least much slower than those with a fire emphasis, because taking material facts into consideration requires a lot more time. Our body is also earthy, and we know how long we need to feed and dress ourselves, as well as to recuperate. We spend about one-third of our lifetime sleeping. Physical health also depends on a regular and healthy diet, as well as adequate and moderate exercise. In turn, this has a very strong influence on our emotional and mental state.

Establishing a good relationship with the material world is a talent of the earth signs. They proceed step by step, if they move forward at all—which is not always so obvious for Taurus as it is for the diligent Virgo, and ambitious Capricorn.

☿ *Taurus: 1st earth sign*

Fixed sign, associated planet: *Venus* ♀. "The material basics"[49] is a fitting characterization of the Taurus. Their motto could be: "Enjoyment in harmony is everything." They are the archetype of the hedonist.

After Aries individuals have conquered the world, Taureans mark off their territory and build their house on it. They surround their garden with a fence so they can live undisturbed. After conquering the world, they are allowed to take a long rest. There's no rush! Things should be leisurely and unhurried. Earth's gravity and the slowness of the bull are among their main characteristics, as well as the corresponding need for regularity in schedule (notice how days, seasons, organic processes follow precise timetables) conformity to tradition (if it's not broken, don't fix it). The plant world is close to the Taurus essence, which is why this principle is very nature-oriented and can be compared with a houseplant in its pot: It can thrive within its protected area when there is no need to fight for its space and food. The beneficial amount of sun and rain, and perhaps some fertilizer, ensures that the plant feels good.

Orality and assimilation are the main keywords that characterize the primordial Taurus principle in its basic attitude toward life: having everything that they need available to them—food, drink, and sleep—plus all the things that make life more beautiful. Taureans feel attracted to the beautiful things and material possessions that make life more comfortable and enrich it, which is why they collect and surround themselves with them. Individuals characterized by the Taurus principle feel best in circles of like-minded and sympathetic people who enjoy the beautiful aspects of life with them. Wallowing in problems, stirring up conflicts, and over-exertion are definitely intended for other people! Only when pleasurable sensations appeal to the Taurus principle are they set into motion. Then they can stubbornly stick with a task. People with an accent on Taurus can have much endurance in doing things, just like they also tenaciously hang onto their existing resources. This already provides a transition to the problematic aspects of the Taurus principle.

Taurus' shadow: Taureans can be distinctly sluggish and lazy since they are only interested in what gives them personal benefit. So they may stew in their own juices and their unlived life can manifest as depression. The lack of flexibility and openness for different and new things shows a problematic side of the Taurus principle's fixed quality. They are masters at blocking out and ignoring everything that doesn't suit them. Even non-astrologers are familiar with their unreasonable stubbornness and bullheadedness.

Because anything unfamiliar initially disturbs the conservative nature of the Taurus, it will be rejected and suppressed. Suppression is definitely one of their pronounced shadows sides. When they feel pushed into looking at unpleasant things against their will, their peacefulness can turn into a raging, blind anger in which they smash everything to pieces—verbally or also physically. Some people like to whitewash this furious behavior by interpreting it as "righteous rage." However, this is still based on the above-described suppression strategy that avoids what is unpleasant—in this case, honestly acknowledging their own shadow side. Another problem may occur when people live their Taurean aspect one-sidedly in the form of materialism, so that their emotional and spiritual qualities are completely stifled by material excess.

Taurus in the body: throat and neck.

♍ *Virgo: 2nd earth sign*

Mutable sign, associated planet: *Mercury* ☿. "Boundary-setting on the material level"[50] is an apt characterization of Virgos. Their guiding principle could be: "The meaning is in the details." The archetype of Demeter is constellated in the Virgo principle.

The Virgo principle's main task is self-preservation, and its most conspicuous characteristic is being untiringly, attentively active. On the one hand, the Virgo disposition creates a need to make provisions or lead a healthy lifestyle in general, for which nutrition, sleep, exercise, and hygiene are the basis. On the other hand, Virgo is also connected with the need to simplify and cleanse—which can include their physical space and relational environment.

The maintenance of physical health is a natural concern of the Virgo principle. As a result, physical needs and functions are precisely registered as a matter of course and satisfied in everyday rituals. This quite obviously also includes hygiene and care of the body on a daily and regular basis. The concern for making provisions is based on a worry or even fear of not being adequately equipped for the uncertainties of the future. So the Virgo has a very careful and thrifty approach to dealing with all resources.

Valuing "order" is quite genuinely part of the Virgo principle; only by assigning the appropriate space and time to everything makes it possible for the Virgo to function well, by attending to their daily obligations and rituals without being disturbed. The regulated and thrifty approach to the personal resources and those of others is based on this fundamental ability to recognize, introduce, and develop useful organizing principles. No other sign of the zodiac has such a distinct love of detail, as well as the ability to recognize and consider every single factor, as the Virgo principle. This is evidence of an actual talent for becoming an expert and specialist.

The ability and necessity to process impressions and perceptions in a good way—the detailed "digestion" of the world—demands in turn a retreat from the surrounding environment and setting boundaries for it. However, the Virgo's self-preservation is not only accompanied by a proficiency in self-care, but also in caring for other people when it is transferred to the surrounding world. So Virgo-accented people can especially be found in all types of service professions. This includes the psychological and medical fields, where they conscientiously and carefully attend to the needs of those receiving services and ensure that the corresponding processes involved function smoothly.

Virgo's shadow: When the tendency for self-preservation takes on a life of its own, it can become an actual defense against everything that is unfamiliar. When this occurs, the individual immediately closes themselves off like a sensitive plant that can't be touched without wilting. This relates to being touched on the physical, emotional, and mental level. However, it also applies to the intake of foods and medications, where all types of intolerances and allergic reactions can occur. This makes it very difficult to live with other people.

When the Virgo's thriftiness is exaggerated, it becomes stinginess and miserliness both towards self and others. When order and hygiene become obsessions and occur in a one-sided way, become excessive, rule everything else, and leave no space for creative chaos or for new things to emerge in life, this healthy impulse turns ill, becoming compulsion and confinement. Another way the Virgo principle can go awry, is seen in the exaggerated use of analytic abilities: namely, when they focus on everything and everyone in everyday life with a hypercritical eye, complaining about everything that doesn't meet their exacting standards. The whole world meets with their disapproval. The result of this unconscious shadow of the Virgo can be complete social isolation.

Virgo in the body: small intestine.

♑ *Capricorn: 3rd earth sign*

Cardinal sign, associated planet: *Saturn* ♄. "The materially moving individual"[51] is a fitting characterization of the Capricorn. "You're doing it all wrong, let me show you how you *should,* how you *must,* do things" could be an appropriate refrain to characterize the principle of Capricorn. The Capricorn principle corresponds with the archetype of the senex or crone, the old man or woman.

As a cardinal earth sign, Capricorns are always active and laziness is a foreign concept for them. In their world, things happen in an earnest and serious way. They are devoted to reality—to things as they really are—and so can often be experienced as implacable and harsh. As pragmatists, Capricorns are masters at dealing with reality. People characterized by Capricorn, often already appear to be "old" as children and adolescents. Some even already seem old and serious when they are born. They frequently lack the playful, imaginative, and carefree qualities that are found in the opposing principle of Cancer. Aging, rigidity, frugality, and thriftiness fit with the Capricorn principle.

Capricorns are averse to every type of wastefulness. For the pragmatic Capricorn, reality with its adversities, complications, and limitations offers tasks for them to actively and seriously tackle. Their basic attitude is the recognition of facts, laws, norms, and rules, as well as conventions and traditions. For them, the focus is not only on the individual, but also the organized collective.

Like no other, the Capricorn principle is talented when it comes to understanding structure and therefore also how to structurally organize actual facts. The pronounced ambition of people with a strong Capricorn disposition for public recognition and awards—their need to achieve a high rank and good name and associate with people of high rank and a good name—is supported by their innate ability to recognize the entities, institutions, and persons who are important for them to do so. This allows them to plan their advancement long before it is achieved concretely. They climb the career ladder rung by rung in corporate and public organizations with seemingly unstoppable tenacity.

Their tendency to subjugate everything that is private to the common good[52] even applies to how they treat themselves. Capricorns set aside their individual well-being, their own physical, emotional, and spiritual needs to serve collective values. They virtually objectify themselves as people and make themselves fit for certain roles in their family, profession, and society. As a rule, they fulfill their roles with much reliability and a sense of responsibility. Capricorns can display a great deal of endurance—persisting through long stretches of bleak circumstances and navigating many kinds of hardships—because they see "people" as more important than the "self."

Capricorn's shadow: When people characterized by Capricorn have an exaggerated in sense of obligation, they can completely ignore their personal well-being and neglect their own spiritual, emotional, and physical needs—because they are not able to perceive them. However, they may not only objectify and ignore themselves, they may do the same to other people. The nasty expression "kiss-up-kick-down" reflects a problematic attitude certain individuals who are influenced by Capricorn can take. When the level of the individual's character is correspondingly bad, this can occur with calculating deceit, slowly, step-by-step, until the targeted position has been achieved. The presumed or actual rivals can be unscrupulously eliminated in the process.

When their sense of obligation turns compulsive, individuals who are characterized by Capricorn can become the prisoners of an obsessive-compulsive disorder. Another problem can be their fear of losing their livelihood and—even if they are rich—their fear of becoming poor, which makes their thriftiness turn into miserliness. This and the overload due to their sense of obligation can lead to depression, which can freeze the Capricorn in coldness and lifelessness.

Capricorn in the body: bone system, joints, teeth, and skin.

The three air signs of Gemini ♊, Libra ♎, and Aquarius ♒

Air means free space in which the laws of matter (to which the earth signs are subject) do not apply. Lightness determines how existence is experienced by the air signs, since no gravity keeps their feet to the ground—some have never even touched the earth. In the airy heights of thinking, speculating, and discussing, almost infinite possibilities are open, since there are no hard, physical boundaries that limit intellectual and mental activity.

No other element is as quick as air is in human beings. When earth and air encounter each other, conflict and friction can result. This applies whether the encounter is between two individuals with different characters or within one and the same person. Constantly occupied with knowledge and communication, the air element easily disregards the ongoing and rhythmic physical needs for nutrition, exercise, and sleep, simply because their relationship with the body is often very tenuous—and may even be split off from consciousness.

When it comes to their emotions, the air signs also experience them from a great distance. This is why they are often perceived as cool, coldly calculating, unpredictable, and superficial by others who are rooted in the depths of their emotions—as is the case for water signs.

This situation also involves differences in speed, since the slow and long-lasting emotions seem overlooked and cut off from the fast-paced interactions of the air spirits. These conflicts can also occur within a person's own psyche.

♊ *Gemini: 1st air sign*

Mutable sign, associated planet: *Mercury* ☿. "Mental fluctuations"[53] is an apt characterization of the Gemini. Their guiding principles could be: "Knowing about the latest news is the most useful thing for me today," "What is useful for me today may be useless tomorrow, and part of the past," "What is useful to me is good." The Gemini principle corresponds with the archetype of the puer/puella, the eternal boy or girl—the eternal youth.

The airy-exuberant Gemini is attuned to ceaseless changes. Everything new immediately stimulates their greatest interest. However, this quickly subsides as soon as the new has become old or is seen as old—then they move on to the next object that arouses their curiosity. Exchange and communication are the elixir of life for Gemini-accented people. If they have insufficient intellectual or mental stimulation, they feel bored to death and possibly depressed. However, they immediately revive when a new stimulus attracts their attention and invigorates them. They are usually not very aware of their quickly changing feelings.

Economics is everything. Those characterized by Gemini are ruled by utilitarian thinking. With the keen perception that belongs to the Gemini principle, they immediately comprehend and very quickly examine every idea for its usefulness. Depending on the result of this flash diagnosis, the thought is either put to use or discarded

The exchange of news and knowledge is important for people characterized by Gemini. They often have a pronounced language talent, in both speaking and writing. So it is not surprising that writers and journalists are usually blessed with a Gemini disposition. They easily learn foreign languages, write texts eloquently, and give speeches effortlessly. But the Gemini talent is not just limited to this skillful and diverse approach to words and texts—it also finds a fertile field of activity in the financial world and trade. In addition, a technical talent may also be present. This all-around disposition may also be accompanied by strong manual dexterity that can be used on all types of materials.

Gemini's shadow: Especially the extensive flexibility and mobility can become a major problem when it is not balanced and stabilized within the psyche by counter-tendencies. When lacking a stabilizing element, Gemini-accented people are flighty and fickle in their attitudes and approaches, like a weather vane that changes its position according to how the wind blows. In accordance with this, they are seen as people who cannot be relied upon. Everyday gossip and cheap journalism that only satisfies the desire for sensationalism can be preferred over serious research.

A nose for intrigue ultimately comes from the fear of boredom, which can be escaped when a drama is subtlety set into motion by misusing other people as playthings—whose feelings and reputation are harmed and unscrupulously ignored. Lies and deception in politics and the financial world also fall into the area of Gemini energy being used in a problematic way.

A Gemini disposition that has taken on a life of its own can have a harmful effect on individuals when they develop nervous tension or even fragmentation. This danger can manifest in all conceivable arenas of life, but especially in personal relationships, where they erratically move from one partner to the next.

Gemini in the body: nervous system, arms and hands, and respiratory organs.

♎ *Libra: 2nd air sign*

Cardinal sign, associated planet: *Venus* ♀. "The spiritual guide"[54] is a fitting characterization of Libra.

A guiding principle could be: "A harmonious relationship is everything." The Libra principle corresponds with the archetype of the Goddess of Beauty, Venus-Aphrodite.

Hardly anyone blossoms as much in the encounter with others as the person with a Libra disposition, since they are usually buoyant and joyful, cheerful, and carefree in relationships. In this process, they always seek a harmonious equilibrium and balance between the self and the other. However, their openness toward others is not limited to individual people, but also directed toward the creative expression that they can be found in art and culture. Many artists have a Libra emphasis of their own.

The Libra aspect in people shows a Venus influence and a corresponding sensual talent. However, this occurs in a refined way due to its combination with the element of air—in comparison to the earthier expression Venus found in Taurus. Libra, which has a refined taste and an equally exquisite sense of pleasure, is open and accessible to all that is beautiful, luxurious, and sophisticated.

Libras attempt to balance things that are in conflict by recognizing and considering all of the opposing, contradictory forces that play a role. Then they let themselves be steered by their sense for harmony, or steer things toward harmony. All of the diverging forces and individual expressions of will are brought into alignment with the direction of the guiding insight of the Libra principle, which always seeks equilibrium. The desire for balance and harmony is therefore not just limited to aesthetic concerns and talents, but is also reflected in distinctive diagnostic abilities. This is why the Libra disposition is required for all situations and professions in which balance, the ability to calm the waves, or take the sting out of conflicts play a role.

Libra's shadow: If the aesthetic principle develops a momentum of its own as the essential factor in life for Libra-accented people, it can dominate all other criteria in determining whether to open up to others, to objects, or to opportunities for experience. This can lead to a highly selective attitude that avoids everything unbalanced, ugly, and raw. Such individuals bury themselves in a world of beautiful appearances, pampering, and frivolousness. The shadow side also include superficiality in relationships and hedonism that may be focused on erotic experiences, as well as eating and drinking.

In conflicts, people with a Libra disposition find it difficult to take a stand and make decisions. There is nothing more agonizing for them than standing between the various options and having to decide on one. If they do not succeed in making a decision, Libras will ceaselessly vacillate as they remain in the midst of multiple, conflicting options. However, Libras often displace the agony of choice by very quickly and blindly doing or seizing the first best thing that comes to mind. This response corresponds to an unconscious and uncultivated shadow side, which has an Aries quality in the case of the Libra.

Another serious shadow side of the Libra is the unconscious compulsion to sow discord out of boredom. They may play people against each other so they can appear to create harmony between the antagonists—whom they have personally incited against each other—subsequently feeling great in their role as the agents of harmony.

Libra in the body: kidneys, glands, and female sexual organs.

♒ *Aquarius: 3rd air sign*

Fixed sign, associated planets: *Saturn* ♄ and *Uranus* ♅. "The mental organizer"[55] is an apt characterization of Aquarians. Their guiding principle could be: "Getting and keeping the highest, vastest standpoint is the most important thing." Aquarians correspond with the archetype of the Enlightenment philosopher.

Ideas and ideologies are the lifeblood of Aquarius-oriented people—in the sense of transpersonal ideas that fulfill and support their personal lives.[56] They try to understand the individual element and locate it within a larger order or system. Observing and systematically organizing the world and its activities in an equanimous, unaffected way based on a central idea gives them a sense of existential security. With this attitude, they can develop tolerance for the most diverse forms of life. This coolly observing and systematically organizing attitude gives them distance from the living moment with its affective colorings. It makes it possible for them to gain an overview that extends beyond the current situation. Wherever the reliability of a cool or well-tempered mind is required, an Aquarian disposition is advantageous. It plays the role of a lighthouse whose beam provides orientation.

But the head alone does not constitute a human being. So one of the main tasks in the life of every person characterized by Aquarius is uniting mind and matter, intellect and body—with its instincts and emotions. The Aquarian must bring them into contact with each other and cultivate this relationship. This is the only way that the light of understanding and tolerance can shine on Earth, and impact everyday life.

Aquarius' shadow: When people with an Aquarian disposition move too far away from tangible reality, and want to force their own unrealistic ideas onto it, they may (with the help of Saturn and Mercury) suffocate everything that has grown organically and individually with their rigid doctrinal grip. History shows this problem time and again in the cruel actions of despots.

But not every Aquarius is a statesman or stateswoman, and—fortunately—not every statesman or stateswoman is a misanthrope. However, people characterized by Aquarius should make sure that they do not exhaust themselves in bloodless doctrine and abstract schematism. This would be an indication that they have failed in their life task of bringing together mind and matter.

Aquarius in the body: calves and nervous system.

The three water signs of Cancer ♋, Scorpio ♏, and Pisces ♓

There is an entirely different atmosphere in the airy heights, than the one that prevails in the depths of water. In contrast to the weightlessness of the air, water is heavy. But similar to the air, it is also formless and can flow everywhere when not held by a container. In order to experience boundaries, water also requires a container that gives it support and form. This means that water-accented people react with much sensitivity to atmospheric conditions. Depending on how the surrounding world behaves and what it spreads in terms of mood, receptively gifted individuals with a water disposition feel invited to get involved to various degrees.

♋ *Cancer: 1st water sign*

Cardinal sign, associated planet: *The Moon* ☾. "The emotionally creative"[57] is a fitting characterization of Cancer. Its guiding principle could be: "Security and warmth are the most important things in life." Cancer embodies the archetype of the child.

Cancer-accented people can only be emotionally creative when they have found their own life melody. This is the main task for those conditioned by the Cancer sign, since they live in fantasies and dreams that are guided by their emotions. Every domain of the imagination belongs to the Moon,[58] and Moon-imprinted Cancers live quite naturally in the imagination and dreams. So they are close to the unconscious in its entirely colorful, but often fleeting and fragmentary expressions. The soul in its living river of changes, in its floating and fleeting manifestations, genuinely determines the attitude toward life of people characterized by Cancer—who like to allow themselves to drift in the life processes that are rooted in the darkness of the unconscious.

Whether Cancers can develop the ability to adapt to and actively participate in the changing conditions that life brings with it—instead of just allowing themselves to passively drift—is a decisive factor. When Cancer-influenced people succeed in translating their passive receptivity, wishing, and dreaming attitude into determined practice— concentrating on and realizing their talents in the process—they may become creative designers. Their strong tendency for reflection is a gift, but it may bear the danger of questioning every possible direction and getting stuck in the world of possibilities.

Individuals with a Cancer disposition blossom when they find atmospherically favorable conditions that support them. Like the child, this aspect in people makes them feel like their entire life, in all of its abundance, still ahead of them. This allows them to always continue searching, since dreams and fantasies have no limitations. In their hunger for life, emotional Cancers are virtually always on the move. In many cases, they seem to be driven more by the unconscious than any conscious desire to ultimately find their own life melody—and with it their own motivation in life that brings them closer to wholeness.

Their love of their own home and family, as well as their often pronounced joy in children— and in positive relationships with them—seem to contradict the wandering instinct that Cancers are distinctly subject to due to their hunger for life. Some Cancers remain stuck in this for their entire lives. In many cases, their roving spirit and family life are only seemingly at odds since their unsettled nature usually dominates during the first half of life, while the wish to establish a family becomes more pronounced in the mature years. Once the family exists, it represents an anchor for many Cancer-accented people that becomes a center for their lives. Many Cancers also feel strongly attached to their family of origin and are therefore oriented toward the past.

Also typical of the Cancer's experience, is the fear of starting something new when faced with a more or less unfamiliar situation, which completely dissolves once the threshold is crossed.

Cancer's shadow: Their sensitivity and vulnerability move Cancers to quickly retreat. Then they close themselves off to the surrounding world in a very specific way: by sulking. A wonderful portrait of a sulker has been drawn by the Cancer-accented Swiss poet Gottfried Keller in his novella *Pankraz, der Schmoller* (Pankraz, the Sulker).

When people with a Cancer emphasis do not find their own life melody, they remain imitators. In the male variation, such an uprooted individual is often a driven person who cannot commit in love relationships. In women, the immaturity that accompanies a lack of attunement to their own song, can often be expressed by wanting to remain in the status of a child—with a partner who takes on the parental role and therefore largely assumes responsibility for their mutual life together. Such a woman-child usually does not want children, because she would feel that they are competitors. In the mother role, she would have to bear responsibility as an adult. But she feels justified to mostly evade responsibility in the child role.

Cancer in the body: fluid balance, glands, and stomach.

♏ *Scorpio: 2nd water sign*

Fixed sign, associated planets: *Mars* ♂ and *Pluto* ♇. "The emotional tension-bearer"[59] is a fitting characterization of Scorpios. Their guiding principle could be: "The eternal search for the truth is my elixir of life." The archetypes of Scorpio are Hades and John the Evangelist.

In keeping with their associated planet of Mars, people characterized by Scorpio are combative and courageous when it comes to defending important values and uncomfortable truths. With reference to Pluto, the second associated planet that symbolizes the principle of metamorphoses or dying and becoming, those with Scorpio dispositions will live and die by their guiding principles. Current circumstances are rarely satisfactory to Scorpios, so they are oriented toward transforming existing conditions in all of their shortcomings. This implies a critical attitude toward life and simultaneously a constructive vision for how conditions can be improved. The question of moderation is always present in this process, since skepticism toward what is superficially visible determines the basic attitude of people with a Scorpio emphasis.

Since Mars in Scorpio is introverted (compared to the extraverted Mars energy in those with an Aries emphasis), they sometimes turn their piercing doubt primarily against themselves. There they usually take a fearless and radical approach, because they want the relentless truth.

Scorpios are in danger of living constantly in the extremes, or falling into a state of irritated ambivalence or defeatist indifference. The extremes can range from the inhuman to the superhuman, depending as always on the level of development and genetic constitution. But if those characterized by Scorpio succeed in keeping their extremism, ambivalence, and indifference in check, they are able—like no other sign—to reflect on themselves and their motives critically. Thanks to their Plutonian abilities, they subject themselves to a radical purification that can extend to a complete transformation: the catharsis, as found in Greek theater. When this succeeds, they can develop superhuman qualities that they place in the service of society.

In addition to their usual state of self-doubt, the outer world is also subjected to this critical gaze. In contrast to the family-related Cancers, Scorpios are interested in how people co-exist in larger groups and social organizations, as well as in the dominant moral and ethical values of justice and truth. With great tenacity, they uncover the problems that they have found and attempt to subject them to reform. It is no wonder that there were and are so many talented discoverers, researchers, criminologists, psychotherapists, and reformers (such as Martin Luther) with a Scorpio disposition, since this sign is equipped like no other with a necessary dual ability—namely, with a "eagle's eye" for the clear and unembellished problem on the one hand and the perseverance to endure conflicts and tensions until a solution arises for it on the other hand.

Scorpio's shadow: Whether the above-mentioned ability to look at things critically, to doubt appearances, is put to constructive or destructive use depends very much on the genetic make-up and the milieu of the individual. In the problematic case, no moderation is found. This may relate to self-doubt or doubts toward the outer world, but in either case, Scorpios will tend to one-sided extremes. In the worst case, this can lead to never-ending doubts and merciless, destructive self-criticism that can prevent individuals from developing and having confidence in themselves. This can apply to both private life and professional life.

If the criticism is exorbitantly directed toward the outer world and everything is negatively excoriated, being perceived as valueless and hopeless, annihilation is all that remains. This can assume a great many different forms: from notorious nagging, to always being ready to jump into destructive sarcasm, to querulous behavior that tries to sabotage the collective's constructive efforts. Because it is solely destructive, it is also a problem when people only criticize and offer no suggestions for something better, when the "dying" is not followed by a "rebirth."

Scorpio in the body: large intestine and sexual organs.

♓ *Pisces: 3rd water sign*

Mutable sign, associated planets: *Jupiter* ♃ and *Neptune* ♆. "The spiritual participant" [60] is an apt characterization of Pisces. The Pisces motto could be: "My fantasies carry me above the ugly realities into better worlds." The archetype of Pisces is the mystic.

People imprinted by Pisces (like the other two water signs of Cancer and Scorpio) are extremely sensitive and react unconsciously to what is atmospheric and unspoken. But in contrast to the first two water signs, Pisceans resonate with moods, immerse themselves in their surrounding influences, and absorb their melody and color.

Everything that is dreamlike and imaginative fulfills those characterized by Pisces. Their Neptunian side allows them to penetrate and see through all of the concrete, hard facts with their boundaries and limitations, which melt away and virtually dissolve themselves.[61] So Pisces-imprinted people do not allow anything to get in the way of their boundless empathy with the surrounding world. This is usually felt in some kind of suffering, which allows them to mobilize their willingness to help. In this process, they are second to none when it comes to completely becoming absorbed in helping, relieving suffering, and supporting other souls since this is precisely where they find their actual elixir in life. However, their strength—as can easily be read in this statement—is usually less in concrete actions than in empathetic resonance. Their compassionate, tender, and emotional attunement is boundless. And the same applies to the tears that quickly flow for these delicately strung souls. The musicality that often exists in Pisces is based on this ability to understand without words.

People characterized by Pisces have a natural access to all realms that lie beyond ordinary reality, which include the world of spirituality, mysticism, and meditation. Like the quality of Neptune, the Jupiter side of the Piscean individual also finds it extremely difficult to find and set boundaries.[62] Based on the combination of these two rather boundary-eliminating archetypes of Neptune and Jupiter, the question of moderation arises in particular. Where no boundaries are seen or just serve to be penetrated, dissolved, or overcome, there is an eternally constellated longing for dissolution into the cosmic reality of oneness. When constructive, this can lead to deep mystical experiences—even to experiencing oneness with the divine.

Pisces' shadow: When the boundaries between the self and the surrounding world become completely blurred or dissolve entirely, and when there are no supportive and protective vessels for this eternal longing for the dissolution of boundaries through meditation or genuine religiosity, the situation can become dangerous for Pisces individual. Then they can no longer distinguish between themselves and others, virtually melting and therefore sinking into chaos. The longing for merging and entering into a world of dream and imagination, where no angular realities disturb, also brings many types of dangers with it. Besides adopting sanctimonious attitudes and getting lost in all kinds of cults, drugs of all types (alcohol, medications, soft drugs, and hard drugs) become very attractive. It is often not clear whether those characterized by Pisces are the seduced or actively seduce others—the boundaries between active behavior and passively slipping into something are often unclear.

Pisces in the body: feet.

The twelve zodiac signs in their functional sequence

As already established at the start of Chapter 2, the twelve signs of the zodiac correspond with twelve archetypes. These should be understood in a functional sequence. They belong quite naturally to human beings, and the more fully we have these twelve archetypal functions available to us, the greater opportunity we have to develop wholeness.

The twelve archetypal qualities of human existence appear in an astro-psychological sequence. However, this is not a linear progression from one sign—with its specific qualities and tasks or functions—to the next, but the representation of a wholeness that can be attained more or less completely over the course of life. So some people come into the world with an overly mental disposition and fight for many years to become anchored on the material level, in their body with its instincts and feelings. Others are so earthy that it takes a great of effort for them to think in abstract or symbolic terms. So the sequence of the zodiac signs is about the archetypal human themes that are relevant to every individual in a unique way. The more complete our disposition is, the more "whole" we become in the course of our life—provided that we work on ourselves and the challenges that life poses for us, with its developmental tasks.

The order for the signs of the zodiac is as follows: Aries, Taurus, Gemini, Cancer, Leo, Virgo, Libra, Scorpio, Sagittarius, Capricorn, Aquarius, and Pisces.

The previous section covered the twelve zodiac signs under the aspects of the three energetic characteristics of cardinal, fixed, and mutable—as well as their association with the four elements of fire, earth, air, and water—the functional sequence of the signs can now be explained.

Ill. 5: Anatomy of Man. French book painting by the Limburg brothers (around 1416)

The aim of this section is to provide a sketch of the twelve archetypal aspects of the entire zodiac with their individual elements (signs of the zodiac). The objective here is to reveal the distinct talents and weaknesses of the successive signs. Since popular astrology still differentiates between "good" and "bad" zodiac signs (and astrology is abused and harmed at this level), the aim here is to counteract this perspective and show that all signs of the zodiac have specific functions that are necessary for the whole. Each of us has a special function, and the more completely we bring it to life, and develop it during the course of our lifetime, the more holistically our personality can develop. This is accompanied by a growing sense of authenticity.

The zodiac signs are therefore twelve elements of a functional whole, which also includes their respective special dynamic and relationships with the adjacent signs. So an arc should now be traced from the first to the last signs of the zodiac, which starts with the energetic beginning in Aries and ends with the gentle dissolution in Pisces.

♈ Aries (March 21 to April 20)

The entire zodiac begins with Aries. The Aries principle is the initiating, fiery, cardinal, and Mars-accented sign of the zodiac.

The following applies to Aries' impulse-driven zest for life: "In the beginning was the deed!"[64] When an idea ignites in the mind of Aries-accented individuals, they immediately want to implement it in reality. Their strength is in stimulating and initiating, so they are the trailblazers and pioneers. They have a spirit of optimism and embody Spring's awakening. Even an image from the plant world can illustrate this: namely, the delicate snowdrop that sprouts from the darkness of the soil—through the still hardened and often snow-covered terrain— toward the light and the sun.

Forward movement is a genuine part of the Aries principle, since it is life-affirming and courageous. Their thirst for action and vigor are unstoppable and unbeatable. According to their guiding principle of "I want!," their basic motive is to assert their own will and own ideas, which they do against all forms of resistance. People characterized by Aries do not allow themselves to be distracted in their forward movement and can often ram their heads against the wall in the process.

Their headstrong opinions with which they impatiently, vehemently, and impetuously enact, can also intensify into despotism. They literally have no time to lose, and nothing makes them more impatient and irritable than having to wait. Their flag is raised toward the conquest of the world. Since the world is large, there is always something to initiate, fight for, and achieve. So it is no surprise that this will-oriented sign with its attunement to immediate implementation is also affected in the head on the physical level—since this is the seat determination (as a result, there is a frequent correlation between the Aries disposition and head injuries).

☉ Taurus (April 21 to May 21)

Taurus is the earthy, fixed, Venus-accented sign of the zodiac and follows the action-hungry Aries principle.

A Taurus individual takes an entirely different approach compared to an Aries-accented person who tirelessly pushes forward. After the world has been conquered by the force of Aries, individuals characterized by Taurus first take a rest and settle on the conquered territory. They build their houses and want to secure them by building a fence to protect the property against intruders.

Taurus-accented individuals want to inhabit their own space and enjoy a peaceful and contemplative life in harmony with their surrounding world. Slowness is the order of the day, since the first earth sign of the zodiac is devoted to the material level of actual, everyday life. Earth is solid, heavy, and hard to move. Our body can be seen as an example of this: If we want our organism to function in good health, we must make an effort on a regular basis to attend to nutrition, sleep, and exercise. All of this requires sufficient time. So it is no wonder that, among other things, there is also a marked difference in pace in Taurus, when compared to the activity-oriented Aries disposition in an individual.

In the Taurus principle, as the first earth sign, the material world moves into the spotlight. Together with it, the focus is on all organic processes—which cannot be accelerated beyond their natural pace. Patience and time are necessary to ensure that the physical needs of the Taurus are addressed, since physical well-being is the basis for a good life. However, allowing ourselves enough time can become exaggerated, and turn into sluggishness on a psychological-spiritual level. It can lead to stagnation or a standstill, the Taurus individual becoming inactive—their entire energy flow coming to a stop.

But if the pleasure principle is activated, the Taurus side can be set into motion. If the pleasure of a task that has been started is maintained, the Taurus cannot be slowed down and develops a great stamina. The Taurus element is the master at holding onto and carrying out tasks that have been started. It brings with it a persevering ability that the Aries principle is lacking.

The basic oral constitution of the Taurus principle makes it easier to understand their explicit enjoyment of pleasure, as well as their passion for collecting. It is easy for them to take, but they find it more difficult to give—which is exactly the opposite for the countersign of Scorpio, which is found in the shadow of Taurus. So the Taurus side in people finds it difficult to let go at the right moment or at all. This often results in stubborn adherence to outdated things, which can be old clothes and objects or outdated emotional patterns and mental attitudes.

On the physical level, the neck and throat can be associated with the Taurus principle.

♊ Gemini (May 22 to June 21)

Gemini is the airy, mutable Mercury-accented sign of the zodiac.

After time at home, resting in the sign of Taurus, the Mercurial, curious, communicative, and quicksilver Gemini aspect pushes its way out into the world again. In this respect, Gemini-accented individuals are like adolescents who want to get to know the world. So they often actually have something youthful about them throughout their lives. They travel with light baggage and are immediately at home wherever they go due to their adaptability.

As its name implies, the Gemini principle is based on duality—they are divided within themselves and live in contradiction within themselves. Exchanges and communication with other people are their elixir of life. People with a pronounced Gemini disposition want to have new experiences and catch a glimpse of the latest news. Their curiosity and hunger for information lead them into manifold situations. The danger of fragmentation into many different interests must be taken into account because their thinking is as fast and light as the movement of air. And just like air, it can constantly change its directions.

Gemini-accented individuals are very quick in comprehending situations and facts. No one likes to tell stories as much as they do, and their imagination is a never-ending resource for them. Their mental activity always searches for new food. In order to banish the specter of boredom, they are perfectly capable of debating for the sake of debate and can maneuver their opponent into the position of a foil for their intellectual game. They are also true masters at spinning intrigues since they have a pronounced eloquence. They can definitely use this skill for their own benefit at the cost of others.

This ease and agility give the Gemini's puckish mind its fickleness, as they adopt a standpoint that virtually changes with the wind—re-orienting itself in every new situation and temporarily adapting to it.

People with a pronounced Gemini side tend to be in a lively and cheerful mood. They can easily be inspired by new things and are at home in the realm of thinking. Precisely this strength is also their weakness because their superficial, fleeting, and agile thinking—accompanied by a dispersion of concentration and activity in all directions—causes them to easily lose contact with all slower, developmental processes. So they are often far removed from their own emotional and physical processes and needs—the latter of which were very much in the foreground for the Taurus principle. If they dissociate entirely from their bodies, this can easily lead to specific somatic disorders: namely, nervous overstimulation and diseases of the respiratory organs.

Cancer (June 22 to July 22)

Cancer is the watery, cardinal, and Moon-oriented sign of the zodiac.

After extensive exploration of the surrounding world, which occurs in the previous air sign of Gemini, the path leads back home—into the individual's own atmosphere and privacy. Moods, feelings, fantasies, and dreams define those who are imprinted by Cancer. They like to spin their own emotional space into a cocoon. Trusted people and the four walls of their home offer them the sense of emotional security, intimacy, and protection they desire. However, their passive nature that tends toward comfort and easily becomes absorbed in pleasure allows itself to be activated by external influences. But they need repeated goading, encouragement, and assurance to move toward a specific objective.

Without the constant pull from the surrounding world, the emotional and sensitive Cancer personalities indulge in imaginative dreams about possibilities that they fulfill in their splendid seventh heaven. Cancer-accented individuals recoil from the hard facts of reality. After a hesitant step forward, they easily take two steps back into the protection of their shell. They love to look at the world in a holistic and relaxed way. However, it is difficult for them to note and consider the individual details. This weakness in terms of the details is then compensated by the talent of the Virgo principle.

People with a Cancer emphasis are driven by many different longings. But thanks to their hunger for life, they eventually find their own way on many circuitous paths and byways over the course of their lives. They mature slowly, only gradually and hesitantly taking root within their own personal qualities. If they succeed in this, they achieve a security in later phases of life that is based on the authenticity that they have gained. Otherwise, they adapt to their circumstances, lean on those who have a stronger purpose, and participate in projects that are defined by others.

The receptive nature of this principle is reflected on the organic level in relation to the stomach.

♌ Leo (July 23 to August 23)

Leo is the fiery, fixed, and Sun-accented sign of the zodiac.

In strong contrast to the sensitive, yielding, easily influenced, and adaptable people characterized by Cancer, the Leo personality wants to make the decisions, rule, and have the say. It is very natural for the self-affirming and self-confident Leo personality to exercise dominance. They are born with the feeling of being the center of the world, around which everyone else must revolve.

Many people with a pronounced Leo disposition are entirely naive in their belief that it is a benefit for the surrounding world to stand in their shadow and the Leo's splendor shine on them. This can actually apply to weaker and insecure people around them. A Leo disposition can actually work wonders to balance timidity, insecurity, or even despondency. People with a Leo disposition certainly do not lack in courage and strength.

Individuals characterized by Leo have a basic sense of power. As a result, they believe that this means they have an everlasting abundance of power and always can live drawing from full energy stores. Aging Leo-accented personalities usually have a difficult time in acknowledging their dwindling powers and the need to slow down a bit like everyone else as they get older. In contrast to individuals with a hesitant, soft Cancer disposition, the power-charged Leo principle approaches its goals in a straightforward and direct way. With a natural carefreeness, they reach for their desired prey without any doubts about having priority over others.

People with a Leo disposition love pleasure and also like to live the high life. No one can accuse them of petty miserliness. Generosity can ultimately be seen as resulting from their feeling of living in abundance, which is the trademark of those imprinted by Leo on all levels. However, this can easily escalate into waste, gluttony, and even boasting. The joy of being seen can culminate in blatant vanity, and their radiating, warming self-assurance can lead to scorching, burning heat. These attributes of the Leo that place them at the center of things, can also be associated with the organic center: the heart.

♍ *Virgo (August 24 to September 23)*

Virgo is the earthy, mutable, and Mercury-accented sign of the zodiac.

After the big party, where only the best has been enjoyed in abundance, it is time to return to everyday life, and therefore also to work. The well-structured, ritualized working day is the biotope of the Virgo disposition, which also includes a healthy and moderate diet. For the continually active Virgo, wise self-care that includes moderation serves them well in the mastering of their busy everyday lives. In contrast to the Leo disposition, Virgos take into account the infinitesimal specifics and notices every shade of distinction. They register the slightest changes and deviations, since the detailed analysis of facts and events is their major strength.

Virgo-accented personalities are masters in precise, highly detailed perception. Nothing escapes their analytical minds. Wherever the greatest precision is necessary, this is an indispensable talent. This love of detail is also accompanied by an appreciation of it. This is probably also associated with Virgo's aversion to wasting resources of any type. Their appreciative and economical use of resources is not as pronounced in any other sign of the zodiac. However, the question of moderation also arises within this context. If thriftiness is exaggerated, the result can be stinginess. This can be expressed toward individuals, the outside world, or within a person's psychological system—on the inside, where generosity or some form of wastefulness are in conflict with the thriftiness or even miserliness.

The thrifty attitude of those with a Virgo disposition is probably closely related to the principle of self-preservation. Resources must not only be sufficient for today, but also for tomorrow—so that life is not threatened in the future either. As already mentioned, this healthy concern—namely, a reasonable and economical approach to given resources—can become exaggerated in certain cases and result in stinginess. This especially applies when the Virgo is experiencing fear and losing trust in life.

Like every other ability, the Virgo's minutely precise perceptive faculty has its light and shadow sides: It is not uncommon for people with a Virgo disposition to approach social situations with analytical acumen and possibly ruin them when a cheerful, relaxed, and casual interaction would perhaps be more appropriate. In terms of bodily functions, this good relationship with their own bodies, and the associated precise perception of the smallest health fluctuations, can also be exaggerated to the point that hypochondria eventually develops.

The small intestine as an organ for the precise breakdown of foods embodies the detail-oriented Virgo principle.

This completes the first half of the zodiac. These first six signs are about subjective and personal necessities in human life: The determined movement into life, and the conquest of opposition to it, is the strength of the Martial, fiery Aries; the protection and closure of personal space reflects the Venusian, earthy Taurus principle; the exploration of the immediate surroundings and establishing communicative links with it are the special talents of the Mercurial, airy Gemini disposition; and the return to and immersion in the home, and the soul with its dreams and wishes, corresponds with the Moon-like, watery Cancer principle. The sunny, fiery Leo disposition enjoys its full power, stands at the center of life with self-confidence and trust in the world, celebrating it to the full;

the Mercurial, earthy Virgo principle ensures the well-being of everyday life, and for the future, by wisely allocating resources. The first six signs in the zodiac therefore serve the self and represent the six archetypal preconditions that prepare us to turn from the self to others, which becomes the main theme in Libra.

♎ Libra (September 24 to October 23)

Libra is the airy, cardinal sign with an emphasis on Venus.

In Libra, the focus shifts to the self and others, which means the entire world with its beauty and possibilities for pleasures. Following the careful, task-oriented, reserved, modest, and detail-focused Virgo principle, there is now an expectant opening to the world as a place offering refined sensual pleasures, dance, play, and other amusements under the erotically-imprinted Libra principle.

Aesthetics, art, and culture—enjoyment, luxury, and love—are main themes in the life of people characterized by Libra, which can tend toward hedonism. The search for harmony between the self and others is the main driving force in all of their feeling, thinking, and acting. Their high level of interest in others implies that they would like to harmoniously attune to every other person, in order to create the best-possible balance between themselves and others.

This behavior is equally evident in both private and professional areas. However, as soon as Libra-accented personalities must relate to not just one individual counterpart but several people or a group with various attitudes, they get into a conflict. Which person with which attitude should now be given preference? The determined emphasis on the will by countersign of Aries lies in the Libra's shadow. This means that the Libra individual has no will of its own to take the lead—which is in complete contrast to the diametrically opposite Aries principle, which is able to naturally express its own will. If Libra personalities succeed in integrating more decisive personality components, they can become brilliant diagnosticians. This is especially due to their talent of simultaneously comprehending the different facets in a number of attitudes, facts, and circumstances.

However, if there is no possibility of comprehending a given multiplicity, bundle it, and make it into something of their own as a result, personalities characterized by Libra remain trapped in a back-and-forth vacillation and constantly change their attitude—again, entirely in contrast to Aries-accented people who sometimes cling to their position to the point of stubbornness, depending on which influences from the surrounding world are affecting them.

Individuals with pronounced Libra qualities often believe that they are directing the course of destiny, but they have actually just assumed other people's views and allowed themselves to be defined and controlled by them. This situation is completely different for signs of the zodiac that insist on a certain attitude—whether this is based on a combative will set towards attaining a goal at any price (Aries), a personal striving for dominance (Leo), or defending the personal territory (Taurus)—the Libra-accented reaction achieves a momentary attitude via complicated mutual influences, whereby it is always important to keep a sense of proportion. This is a strong contrast with the impulsive Aries principle that does not shy away from any conflict in order to attain the set goal as quickly as possible.

In an unfavorable case, personalities characterized by Libra appear to be lukewarm, lackadaisical, and avoid conflicts. People pleasing and a craving for admiration also belong to the chapter of less developed Libra attributes. The indecisiveness of Libra-accented people also creates a lot of suffering in their love lives, because wavering back and forth between different romantic partners often leads to Libra's ultimately remaining alone. This is quite ironic because they are so focused on love and partnership.

Suffering due to love can also get to the Libra's kidneys, the organ that is associated with it.

♏ Scorpio (October 24 to November 22)

Scorpio is the watery, fixed sign that is characterized by Mars and Pluto.

Scorpio expresses the counter movement that comes after the cheery and playful Libra, who is devoted to refined pleasures as well as beauty and harmony—stylistically confident on the parquet of the outer world with its possibilities for enjoyment—and has the weakness of avoiding conflicts. In Scorpio, things get serious. The focus here is on recognizing the deepest background, the motives, and the ultimate truths that are active beneath the surface of beautiful, external appearance. Their courage lets Scorpio-accented people unswervingly stand up for uncomfortable truths and reject pseudo-solutions, even if they must sacrifice something personal.

The Scorpio principle is committed to the "death-and-rebirth" principle, which is why they have the task of uncovering everything that is illusionary and wrong, spoiled and sick, so that the true, genuine, and healthy can be brought into life. The Scorpio principle extends between heaven and hell. As if on a ladder, it can move up and down between these two extremes. It does this fearlessly, because it takes upon itself the task of bringing the highest ideals of truth and justice that flourish in heavenly heights down to the Earth. It is not afraid of descending into the deepest abysses of human and social hells in order to expose all kinds of grievances that are hostile to life—saving whatever is worthy of life from them. The lie must die so that true life can blossom.

This obviously creates conflicts with the signs that have a different interpersonal or intrapsychic orientation. The preceding Libra (which prefers not to look so closely and turns a blind eye due to an aversion to conflict or need for harmony for the sake of peace) feels its aesthetic sensibilities especially disturbed by the ethical approach of Scorpio, which uncovers all illusions and falsehoods instinctively.

The Scorpio side in individuals is committed to questioning and saying "no" to everything superficial, which is examined with x-ray vision to uncover more stable values. This "no" should ultimately lead to a new "yes." In view of society, this is about exposing and eradicating corruption, social grievances, and injustices—whereby no abysses are shunned. When it comes to collective renewal processes, Scorpio-accented people are at the forefront, because they embody the steadfast champions of human rights.

This is in diametrical contrast to the Taurus principle, which lies in the shadow of Scorpio, and is aimed at increasing and defending private possessions. Accordingly, Taurus has a difficult time giving up something that is familiar or a personal possession, so the ability to let go is one of the pronounced Scorpio skills. While the Taurus principle is a master at holding on, the Scorpio principle is a master of transformation, of "dying and becoming"—which also implies letting go.

However, letting go can also be exaggerated, namely when too little has been integrated from the countersign of Taurus and a waste of resources occurs. In contrast to the Taurean tendency, which specializes in defending personal space, the Scorpio principle sees social symbiosis and good, just, and humane coexistence as a major concern. This is what they are committed to. Their ability to "smell" a problem and maintain concentration on it, as well as tolerating the tensions that come with it, predestine them for mastering complex, difficult to see, problems.

However, if the Scorpio principle lacks something relevant to fight with their restless, martial, water energy, their skeptical attitude, doubts, and sometimes corrosive criticism can become mis-directed at either themselves or any other person or situation. This is then judged and virtually analyzed or criticized "to death." People who act out their Scorpio side in such a merely corrosive way are feared due to their destructivity. The Scorpio can experiences the saddest existence, caught in frustrations and nagging resentments, due to a lack of meaningful life tasks. In such cases, criticism for the sake of criticism dominates the Scorpio, without the second step of constructing new possibilities and promoting their development.

The themes of purification and detoxification in the depths of one's own soul, as well as in the group psyche or social and societal systems, are important here. It is therefore appropriate that the large intestine is associated with Scorpio.

♐ Sagittarius (November 23 to December 21)

Sagittarius is the fiery, mutable Jupiter-accented sign of the zodiac.

People with a pronounced Sagittarian disposition are easily and quickly enthused when their quest for meaning is fed. Their fiery spirit reaches into the transcendental heights; they are carried forward by ideals, which they often pursue and express with a real fervor. While on their hunt for ambitious goals, they feel inspired. However, it is not uncommon for them to be stopped in their fiery flight of fancy. This may occur by running into the hard facts of reality, with which they are confronted by in the following sign of Capricorn, in the inertia of the Taurus, or in the thorough, detailed consideration of the Virgo. If they are slowed down, the furiously fast Sagittarians can fall into desperation and depression. But they just as quickly become optimistic again when they see a new meaningful goal that they can pursue with renewed vigor.

Unlike the earth signs, they are not interested in what *is* but in what *should be*. So everything related to everyday life bores them to death. They quickly feel confined in routine processes, in complete contrast to earth signs, which need a certain regularity. By contrast, everything extraordinary awakens and animates all of the Sagittarian senses and their spirits.

The Sagittarius side in human beings is devout and optimistic, carried forward in the search for meaning. This expansive disposition transports these individuals on both concrete and spiritual journeys into the remotest places—whether to foreign cultures, religions, or philosophies. The Sagittarian disposition is different from the previous Scorpio principle in as far as its doubts are not so dominant and it lacks the sustained determination with which the Scorpio side faces conflicts when the defense or implementation of important values (such as human rights) are involved. Although those who are characterized by Sagittarius pursue their goals without any concessions and are not weakened by any doubts, they avoid direct battle and search instead for peaceful solutions.

Unlike the Gemini disposition (which lies in the Sagittarian shadow with its strength for utilitarian thinking), values and therefore ethics are the territory of the Sagittarian principle. As a result, the enthusiastic Sagittarius side is idealistic. However, Sagittarius-accented individuals prefer to leave the laborious, detailed implementation of these ideals in everyday reality to others (like the pragmatic earth signs of Virgo and Capricorn)—since they prefer to conquer and improve the world through spiritual vision. Everything narrow and petty restricts the Sagittarian disposition, which is attuned to an untiring expansion. They require vastness and heights, together with a great deal of space, to develop.

A constructive realization of the Sagittarius principle can be seen when tolerance is actively lived, when reason is the measure of all things, when value judgments are made with a sense of proportion instead of immoderation, and human reality with all of its weaknesses is taken into account instead of being skimmed over. This requires both a spiritual vision, which is the result of a comprehensive education, and taming the wild, fiery energy that blazes in people characterized by Sagittarius.

If the latter does not occur, Sagittarians can become individuals who "sit on their high horse," put themselves above their fellow humans, because they feel that they are better or "nobler"—without having earned their claimed superiority, since it has no basis in reality. Lecturing, know-it-all, or even missionary behavior can often be observed in such cases. Such self-awarded prestige is sometimes accompanied by boasting, a waste of resources, or even becoming an imposter.

Since the sign of Sagittarius is associated with the search for meaning and their need for moderation that provides balance, the liver with its regulatory function is addressed on the physical level.

♑ Capricorn (December 22 to January 20)

Capricorn is the earthy, cardinal, and Saturn-accented sign.

The Capricorn focuses on reality with its limitations, norms, and structures—including time, which runs in an unstoppable and unrelenting rhythm, and so should be treated as a precious commodity. In keeping with this, Capricorn-influenced people usually treat time with great care. These individuals are sometimes true masters of concentration and consolidation since each moment becomes a precious jewel. The Sagittarian's wild blazing, impetuous flight, and yearning for distant goals is alien to the Capricorn, since they are devoted to creating results in the here and now and getting things grounded. Everything must hold water.

The Gemini principle's flash-in-the-pan mentality that chases new things is alien to the Capricorn. Instead of the personal or the specific, the latter sign places value on what is general and enduring that has been built into solid forms, rules, and structures. This is what they like to stand up for. Spontaneous ideas and impulsive actions are therefore also foreign to them since they prefer to implement their own deliberate life strategy, which includes long-term planning. In doing so, they persistently, slowly and, continuously move forward. They can endure long dry spells, and always have their goal in mind. Cool tenacity and ambition are their faithful companions.

It almost goes without saying that the impulsive approach of the Aries element, the flaming enthusiasm of the preceding Sagittarius principle, and the constantly changing interests of the Gemini principle are all alien to Capricorn. In their opinion, only well-planned and continuous work on a project will bear the corresponding fruit.

With their well-planned approach, they also stand in marked contrast to the Cancer principle, which is easier to impress, and can be retuned and steered in a different direction when its emotions are appealed to. The sign of Cancer—with its seeking and open attitude that always has something momentary and provisional attached to it—is Capricorn's shadow. If the latter succeeds in integrating something of the flexibility from the emotional Cancer element, a sense of humanity comes into play that knows not only the demands for performance and the fulfillment of duty, but also leaves space for leisure and pleasure.

If little or no balance is achieved through the more spontaneous and pleasure-loving signs of the zodiac, the sense of obligation and loyalty to tasks can become so rigid that individuals characterized by Capricorn plod along on their arduous path as if they were clamped in a yoke—looking neither to the left nor the right. In doing so, they ignore not only their own needs, but also those of others. Such a one-sided attitude that objectifies and suppresses life, as well as the accompanying constant overload, can express itself in problems with the skeleton; above all, this means the knees and back since the skeleton as the structure-giving principle or framework that carries the body is associated with Capricorn.

Aquarius (January 21 to February 18)

Aquarius is the airy, fixed sign that is accented by Saturn and Uranus.

The duality embodied in the opposition between Saturn and Uranus, as well as the combination of "air" and "fixed," create a complex archetypal structure and reflect the difficult task of Aquarius-imprinted individuals in bringing together the body and the mind. There is quite frequently a type of split that occurs in favor of the mental realms and at the expense of physicality.

With its Uranian side, a very specific face of the Aquarian principle emerges: namely, their intuitive, creative, and inventive abilities with which they break out of Saturnal limitations. With their spontaneous ideas and notions, they burst Saturnal structures with relish.

The Saturnal qualities of the Aquarian disposition are generally different than that of the earthy Capricorn principle, which is exclusively ruled by Saturn. While Capricorn-imprinted individuals suffer from the severity of implacable Saturn and (especially in the younger years) are often burdened with serious obligations—the airy Aquarian dispositions look at their Saturn side with a wink. A playful component enters that takes away the absolute harshness of the Saturn principle.

However, there are also Aquarius-accented people who show a tendency to simultaneously think in bizarre and rigid ways, which can both be dogmatic. They may cling to a system of thinking regardless of its impact on their health and instincts, and so can become hostile toward life. Consequently, their mental side will contradict their physical, affective, and emotional necessities. In such a case, the physically attuned Leo principle opposite from Aquarius has been split off instead of integrated. If it is not possible to come into contact with the living, organic Leo components, quixotic and utopian worlds of ideas may be born that can lead Aquarius-imprinted people into a state of mental and social isolation, into loneliness. Then they rule their realm of ideal possibilities and dogmas in a castle in the air. They remain at this great height, far away from the Earth's warmth and its inhabitants, trapped in a spacious, cold bubble.

However, the true function of the Aquarius sign within the zodiac is to reform institutions and society (which are often hardened and rigid in the previous Capricorn attitude) with new, larger, and more inclusive ideas, which can make the world more humane. If this succeeds, spirit and matter, ideas and reality are connected with each other, and life flourishes.

The calves are associated with the Aquarius principle.

♓ Pisces (February 19 to March 19)

Pisces is the watery, mutable zodiac sign with a Jupiter and Neptune emphasis.

The Pisces principle represents the end of the zodiac, since it involves the dissolution of all structures. The atmosphere here is completely different from that of the previous Aquarius air sign. From the airy heights, there is a descent into the depths of the emotions. A pronounced delicacy of feeling and sensitivity characterize the Pisces principle. Resonant, compassionate, and empathetic behavior comes naturally to Pisces-imprinted individuals. The dissolution of their own boundaries and those of fellow human beings allows Pisces-accented people to intuitively know how others feel—even if neither are aware of the exchange. While the Capricorn principle is a master in setting boundaries, the Pisces principle is a master of dissolving limitations, allowing things to flow into each other, mixing them, and empathizing with them. Especially because people with a strong Pisces disposition participate so easily and deeply in the misery of others, they are also willing to help wherever they can. This high level of responsiveness quickly brings the danger of overexertion and excessive strain with it.

While the preceding sign of Aquarius dwells in its light, orderly mental world and attempts to spread the light of reason and humanity evenly from its spiritual overview, Pisces-imprinted people float in feelings, dreams, and fantasies that can assume a cosmic expansiveness. In the emotional Pisces principle, there is no point in searching for clear concepts as in the Aquarius principle—the latter defines concepts as clearly as possible and distinguishing them from each other since clean conceptual distinctions and definitions are the preconditions for functioning thought processes. So the thinking of those imprinted by Pisces is often diffuse, but this should not be confused with a lack of intelligence (a good example here is Einstein, whose Sun sign was Pisces!). Pisces has a talent for sensing and intuiting layers of affective impact and nuance in any perspective. For a well-structured and organized intellectual approach, these frequently fall through the gaps.

Love and sympathy are the magic words for people imprinted by Pisces. But because of their openness to the atmosphere around them, they are also easy to influence and affect. This can especially bring difficulties to love since seducibility and seduction can lead to relationship problems with existing partners.

Another problem can result from the dissolution of boundaries characteristic of the Pisces principle: the desire to dissolve and escape hard reality with the help of various addictive substances such as alcohol and drugs. Meditation and music are examples of an entirely different possibility for dissolving the boundaries of earthly encumbrances. These strengthen and enrich the personality in its sensitivity and permeability without dissolving the necessary personality structures required for healthy functioning on the planet Earth.

Perhaps because getting a foothold in reality is not a simple task for Pisces-imprinted individuals, the Pisces principle is associated physically with the feet.

The Four Functions of the Self According to C. G. Jung: Thinking, Feeling, Sensation, and Intuition

The interaction of the four psychological functions of the self is clearly illustrated in a simple sketch by C. G. Jung's colleague Jolande Jacobi:

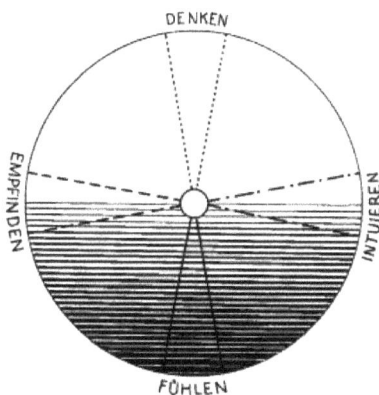

Ill. 6: The four functions of the self
Jolande Jacobi, Die Psychologie von C.G. Jung
© *Patmos Verlag. Verlagsgruppe Patmos in der Schwabenverlag AG, Ostfildern, 2. Auflage 2012*
www.verlagsgruppe-patmos.ce

[Text from left, clockwise: Sensation / Thinking / Intuiting / Feeling]

85

This sketch clearly shows that thinking and feeling, as well as sensation and intuition, are respective opposites. Jung speaks of the *primary function*, which is at the top of the vertical axis and most accessible to consciousness, and therefore lies opposite to the so-called *inferior function*—which is placed at the bottom of the vertical axis and is essentially unconscious. The two *auxiliary functions* are polar opposites on the horizontal axis. If the main function is extraverted, i.e. directed outwards, the inferior function is introverted and vice versa.[65]

So what is the meaning of these four psychological functions and the corresponding four function types: thinking type, feeling type, sensation type, and intuition type? Jung established that four different orientations to acting and reacting in various life situations are available to human beings—to help them cope with and shape their lives. These are *a priori*—present and active in us whether we know it or not—and therefore have an archetypal nature. These basic functions of thinking, feeling, sensing, and intuiting are also called "functions of the self" because they enable the self to become oriented and find its way around in the world. These are innate abilities of human beings that exist at various distances to consciousness, allowing people to immerse themselves in life and have experiences.

Jung noticed that these four approaches to the world differ to varying degrees in individuals, so that some people always initially respond to what they encounter with their thinking, while other people habitually feeling things out. Other individuals mainly participate in life through their intuition or sensations, and the latter are based on tactile, sensual perceptions that should not be confused with feeling. According to Jung, most people end up showing a certain one-sidedness in how they adapt to their environment during the first half of life—by preferring to use their most strongly developed function (the primary function) in every aspect of their life.

An essential criterion for defining the primary function is that it can be used consciously and deliberately. Jung wrote, "The products of all functions can be conscious, but we speak of the 'consciousness' of a function only when its use is under the control of the will and, at the same time, its governing principle is the decisive one for the orientation of consciousness."[66] So only one function primarily conscious, while the least developed function—the so-called *inferior function*—lies in the unconscious and contributes less, and can subvert, our attempts to cope with reality in comparison to the three other functions.[67] The two other functions can serve as auxiliary functions.

Auxiliary function is the term that Jung uses for a function that is not as conscious as the primary function, and does not have as much of a determining effect on how a person lives as the primary function. But it is also relatively conscious and can support the primary function, from which it is essentially differentiated by its additional qualities.[68] For example, students with a primary function of intuition or sensation also require a well-developed ability to think if they want to be successful. A reliably available thinking as the first auxiliary function is necessary for both an intuition type and a sensation type in that it complements and supports the primary function. In some cases, the second auxiliary function can also be quite well-developed (this would be the feeling function in the above example). However, it often tends to be less reliably available to conscious control than the primary function or the first auxiliary function.

According to Jung, the inferior function is the least developed and correspondingly archaic or autonomous in the sense of being distant from consciousness and beyond restraint. Because of its tendency to be unconscious, it largely eludes conscious control. The more unconscious it is, the more autonomously it becomes involved and can make itself felt in a very unpleasant way against the affected person's will. Within the scope of a Jungian analysis—the aim of which is to achieve the greatest possible wholeness and therefore also become aware of unconscious traits and abilities—this can involve working with the inferior function that is found in the shadow, in order to be able to use it as a resource.[69]

Jung differentiates all four function types according to *extraversion* and *introversion,* a subdivision that will also be discussed in relation to the astrological houses in Chapter 4.[70] In short, people with an extraverted attitude are oriented toward the outer world and highly value it as a result. Extraverted people have the task of making sure that they do not completely lose their subjective standpoint under the influence of external objects.

On the other hand, introverted people (who are oriented toward the inner world) do not directly perceive external object as such, but mainly experience the world through their own subjective reaction to it. According to Jung's conceptions, this is tantamount to a devaluation of the object in question. However, this approach serves introverted people by grounding them in their own subjective experience.[71]

But turning attention to the inside does not necessarily mean that this is just about personal and subjective themes. Instead, it quite often involves coming into relationship with an objective *inner* reality and inner objects such as images—best known from the dream world. These can also be visions or feelings, sensations, and ideas. Their objective character is especially obvious when they have a collective nature, which means that they originate from the collective unconscious. For extraverted people, there is a danger of losing themselves in the outer world and dissociating from inner reality in the worst case. By contrast, introverts can sink completely into the inner world and therefore lose their relationship with the outer world.

The focus of this section is to present the four functions of the self in their role as primary functions—along with their extraverted and introverted expressions—as briefly and comprehensively as possible. At the same time, we should also keep the other three functions in mind.

Just as the twelve zodiac signs in astrological typology should always be understood merely as functional facets of the personality and never be identified with the individual, whole, self, Jung's typology must also be understood correctly. In practice, these types are hardly found in a pure form. Instead, all of these types have a typical trait, which is emphasized disproportionately while their other individual traits are relegated to the background.[72]

A typology emphasizes the type and does not describe the respective individual, who always uniquely shows certain typological traits in a more pronounced way and less of others. As a result, the function type and the individual person should not be equated with each other.

Thinking in the extraverted and introverted attitude: The thinking type

Logic, consistency, rationality, critical thinking, and judging (in the sense of evaluation) are some of the important attributes of the "thinking function." The ability to think logically and understand the surrounding world, as well as ourselves by using our intellect—which means all of our cognitive abilities—is necessary for each individual to successfully adapt to environmental conditions. Jung describes a person as a "thinking type" when thinking is more strongly developed than the three other functions and "when the life of an individual is mainly governed by reflective thinking so that every important action proceeds, or is intended to proceed, from intellectually considered motives."[73]

Thinking can be related to objects and ideas from the outer world (as is the case of extraverted thinking) or directed to the inner reality of a person, and therefore also to ideas that are turned into objects for reflection. This is the case in introverted thinking.[74] Extraverted thinking is strongly in demand in scientific research, where the goal is objective and rationally comprehensible thinking, while introverted thinking, according to Jung, refers to subjective, i.e. inner processes.[75]

The *extraverted attitude* of thinking types is therefore also shown in that their thinking and judgments are based on objectively, externally ascertainable data, to "something borrowed from outside," and is oriented toward the outer world throughout their entire life. However, the object that is the focus of interest for the thinking type can be a concrete object or a concrete situation or condition—as is the case in the natural sciences and medical research. But these can also be abstract ideas, found within the framework of a current philosophical discourse,[76] in politics, or art and culture. The main criterion for Jung's definition of extraverted thinking is that its object—or what the thinking is concerned with—is related to the outside world.[77] It does not matter whether this object is concrete or abstract. Of course, not only thinking on a high intellectual level belongs to the field of extraverted thinking; practical thinking is indispensable in many professions, whether for the businessperson or the technician. The ability to think practically can also be advantageous for all private individuals who want to keep an eye on their household and budget.

In principle, the outer world in all of its diversity can stimulate extraverted thinking types to think. However, thinking is less concerned with the pure factuality of concrete objects and situations, and more with how they can be grasped and evaluated through thinking. Beyond concrete reality, universal ideas are important, especially in the current age of technology and digitalization.

On the one hand, the highly impersonal nature of extraverted thinking types means that their unconscious personal and emotional side is usually correspondingly archaic, infantile, and sensitive. This can create a double problem for their surrounding social environment. The first can occur when extraverted thinking types set standards for correct thinking and behavior for their partner or children based on their own rational-intellectual attitude. They can dogmatically insist that only logically stringent speech and actions are "right" and totally terrorize their family with their rationality—because they see this as an irrevocable law of reality to which not only they but everyone else must submit.

On the other hand, extraverted thinking types often exert pressure on other people in their surrounding world through their lack of affective sophistication and the sensitiveness of their inferior emotional side. This forces others to strongly restrain themselves and adapt to the moods and sensitivities of extraverted thinking types, if they want to avoid unpleasant consequences. The reason for this situation is that, "The more the feelings are repressed, the more deleterious is their secret influence on thinking that is otherwise beyond reproach."[78] Thinking then becomes rigid and dogmatic. It is easy to comprehend the futility of having a discussion with someone who inflexibly insists on their own world view and is unable to allow space for other opinions or feelings.

Another ugly form of the thinking type is the complainer who believes that no one else does anything right—or stringently and effectively enough—unaware that others perhaps may follow different standards of life in order to stay true to themselves. When rationality is the supreme law and absolute value, much living and creative potential is suppressed and cut off, making life shallow and banal. A funny example of such a stale, querulous thinking type can be found in the figure of the Scribe in Novalis' *Heinrich of Ofterdingen* novel. The character writes and writes, but when Sophia (the personification of wisdom) occasionally dips his pages into the water of wisdom, hardly a word remains to be seen on them.[79]

It is easy for these individuals to label others as "stupid"—whether family members, partners, friends, or colleagues—who tend to be strongest in one of the three other functions. Above all, conflicts are inevitable with feeling types, since their thinking function is inferior according to Jung's view. The thinking and feeling functions differ diametrically. A thinking type is has a weak, unconscious feeling function. A feeling type has a weak, unconscious thinking function.

In the encounter between a feeling type and a thinking type, the respective inferior functions of each are reciprocally triggered. This can often lead to an chaotic and futile quarrel—or at least to a profound experience of not being understood. However, extraverted thinking types can develop their qualities in a very constructive way. For example, when they integrate them professionally in planning and organizing, which is essential for all well-functioning institutions.

In contrast to extraverted thinking, which is directed outward, *introverted thinking* turns inward to form its judgments. According to Jung, it can (like extraverted thinking) also be "concerned with concrete or with abstract objects," but always orients around the "subjective factor."[80] The strength of this attitude lies in the development of questions, views, and theories based on a subjective idea. Jung describes the accomplishment of introverted thinking as an actual creative process in which it is capable of shaping "the initial symbolic image hovering darkly before the mind's eye . . . into a luminous idea."[81]

This type of thinking strives to create a suitable abstract expression for creative ideas, which is not found in external facts. While extraverted thinking types are in danger of getting lost in a purely empirical, senseless accumulation of facts, introverted thinkers risk sinking into the inner images and symbols, obscuring external facts as a result. If powerful inner images (the more archetypal, the more powerful) captivate introverted thinking and cast a spell over it while the relationship to outer reality is simultaneously lost, adaptation to the outer world can be threatened. Introverted thinking can then become "mystical and just as unfruitful"[82] as extraverted thinking if these exclusively objective facts are not taken into consideration.[83] Darwin and Kant, to Jung, are two very prominent representatives of the two thinking types. He called Darwin the extraverted and Kant the introverted thinking type.[84]

In contrast to extraverted thinking types, who become absorbed in contemplating the outer object, and in extreme cases, completely forget themselves in the process, introverted thinking types neglect the outer object because it distracts them from what is essential to them—which can ultimately only be found within themselves.

Concerning the latter, Jung notes: "This negative relation to the object, ranging from indifference to aversion, characterizes every introvert and makes a description of the type extremely difficult. Everything about him tends to disappear and get concealed. His judgment appears cold, inflexible, arbitrary, and ruthless, because it relates far less to the object than to the subject."[85] However, Jung does not exclude the possibility of an introvert also being polite, amiable, and kind. But if the object is not an idea but a fellow human being, this person will always feel a slight devaluation.[86]

When introverted thinkers pursue an idea and would like to bring it into the world, this is usually more difficult for them than for those who are extraverted and more adept at relating to actual, external conditions. Accordingly, introverted thinkers often show a lack of skill in choosing partners or companions. As Jung wrote, "he is taciturn or else throws himself on people who cannot understand him, and for him this is one more proof of the abysmal stupidity of man. If for once he is understood, he easily succumbs to credulous overestimation of his prowess."[87]

Due to their weak relationship with external reality, as well as their undifferentiated feeling function, their interpersonal relationships often present all kinds of stumbling blocks for introverted thinking types. If they are male, they often become the victims of women who—because of their emotional naivety and childishness—have an easy time with them and take advantage of them. This may go as far as driving them into the gutter, as depicted in Heinrich Mann's novel about Professor Unrat called *The Small Town Tyrant* and in its film version *The Blue Angel*. Others become misanthropic and socially isolated bachelors, vividly described in the novella *The Bachelors* by Adalbert Stifter. A current popular example for the (extroverted) thinker would be Dr. Gregory House, the brilliant diagnostician in the American television series *House*.

As a conclusion to the description of the introverted thinking type, Jung's own summary in his essay on the "General Description of the Types" (especially §§ 620 to 637), rounds off his extensive portrait of this type and is very worthwhile to read.[88]

Feeling in the extraverted and introverted attitude: The feeling type

Feeling, emotion, empathizing, "appropriate emotional judgment," "evaluation," and "adaptation" are key words for this function.[89] According to Jung, feeling is one of the *rational* functions. In the introduction to Jungian typology, what Jung meant by the feeling function being "reasonable" has already been briefly mentioned and described in more precise terms: "Their rationality . . . accords with what is collectively considered to be rational."[90] However, this does not result in a very clear impression of the feeling function. In his efforts to define the feeling function, Jung seems to confront a much greater mystery than what he encounters in the thinking function. Perhaps this is because feeling was not his great strength, and he looked at it through his own inferior emotional lens?

The extraverted feeling function is oriented toward the outside, which means outer reality—its objects determine what is felt. Accordingly, extraverted feeling is oriented around values that come from the outside.[91] The value judgments of extraverted feeling types always adapt to what feels right for the respective situation. Jung uses the example of a painting that the feeling type cannot openly call "ugly" because this could possibly insult the host and owner of the picture. Feeling types cannot behave in such a tactless manner; instead, they are interested in producing a pleasant emotional atmosphere so that it becomes a cozy, sociable, and harmonious evening.

For Jung, extraverted feeling attunes to collective values and causes, to why people "flock to the theater or to concerts, or go to church, and do so moreover with their feelings correctly adjusted"[92] in order to share emotions in the community. As in the case of every extraverted function, the affected feeling types are also in danger of succumbing to the influences of the external world, and therefore of becoming co-opted by the object. The authenticity of the personality and therefore the living naturalness of feeling can be lost. Since feeling can wholly adapt itself to a given situation, the individual can seem like they're acting, to fit in, which ultimately becomes cold, objective, and unbelievable. Such arbitrary adaptation to changing conditions carries the danger of dissociation and can ultimately result in hysteria.[93]

According to Jung's view, the extraverted feeling function (which is responsible for the individual's adaptability to the outer world) is compensated by an introverted, undifferentiated, archaic, and infantile thinking. This is correspondingly expressed in opinionated, prejudiced, and—due to its proximity to the collective unconscious—is mixed with fantastic projections. When the inferior function (introverted thinking in this case) gains the upper hand, the collective unconscious is constellated with its archetypal images. If this is made conscious, there is the possibility of processing and differentiating the unconscious side; if not, it can lead to dissociation and/or hysterical neuroses.[94]

Jung mainly describes *introverted feeling* as being determined by the subjective dimension that has already been mentioned—in contrast to the extraverted feeling type's orientation toward outer circumstances and values. Introverted feeling people are less interested in the outer than inner or subjective objects. The value of these inner objects is correspondingly high for them since their energy is directed toward and revitalized by inner reality.

Jung also associates introverted feeling (like introverted thinking) with the collective unconscious: "The primordial images are, of course, just as much ideas as feelings."[95] Just like the introverted thinking types are concerned with the wealth of the inner object world as ideas and concepts, introverted feeling individuals approach it correspondingly with feeling.

According to Jung, introverted feeling types can have difficulties in adequately communicating their internal emotional world to their surrounding environment:

> It is principally among women that I have found the predominance of introverted feeling. 'Still waters run deep' is very true of such women. They are mostly silent, inaccessible, and hard to understand; often they hide behind a childish or banal mask, and their temperament is inclined to be melancholy. They neither shine nor reveal themselves. As they are mainly guided by their subjective feelings, their true motives generally remain hidden.[96]

However, this description reflects the superficial impression that feeling types apparently made on Jung, and is less about their actual experiences and way of functioning.[97]

So introverted feeling do not come off well in Jung's characterization of it. Those encountering introverted feeling types, receive "no touch of amiability, no gleam of responsive warmth, but are met with apparent indifference or a repelling coldness . . . Any stormy emotion, however, will be struck down with murderous coldness, unless it happens to catch the woman on her unconscious side . . . by arousing a primordial image. In that case she simply feels paralyzed for the moment."[98]

Since the coldness and reserve that is presented to the world could lead to the superficial impression that introverted feeling types have no feelings at all, Jung ultimately adds a different side that he considers to be characteristic: namely, the intensity of feeling that compensates for the outward inexpressiveness: "They develop in depth."[99]

Using the example of how the two feeling types deal with the feeling of sympathy, Jung attempts to illustrate their differences. The extraverted feeling types can adequately express their compassion and then free themselves of it again, while the introverted feeling types sense such an intensive compassion that they are not capable of expressing it. Instead, they freeze. "It may perhaps break out in some extravagant form and lead to an astounding act of an almost heroic character, quite unrelated to either the subject herself or to the object that provoked the outburst."[100]

In contrast to Jung's association of the introverted feeling type with women, here is the example of two men in their prime. Out of the blue and on the open street, both of them propose marriage to a young woman with whom they have fallen in love with from a distance— during an advanced training course. Both were introverted feeling types and had nourished their love for this young woman in the depths of their souls until they had to burst out with it in her presence. This comes as a complete surprise to the woman in question, since she had no idea about the existence of these two men or their increasingly strong feelings for her. The entire situation (on the open street) illustrates the lack of adaptation to the external world of the two men who were hopelessly in love. All of this sounds quite tragicomical. One wonders, who would want to have this as their primary function?

However, as with all introverts, introverted feeling types also have the potential to deal creatively with their own emotional depths. Through a creative examination of their depth of feeling, the difficulties of introverted feeling types, of their emotional world, and their movements within their environment, can handled in an adequate and even constructive way. Jung mentions the composition of poetry as a possibility for self-expression. For example, if the above-mentioned unfortunate lovers had attempted to approach the young woman through emotional letters or poems—to which she could have responded—one of them may even have had a chance to be heard.

Marcel Proust is a compelling example of an introverted feeling type. He spent fourteen years writing his world-famous novel *In Search of Lost Time*, in which he recalls his childhood memories. In a well-known section, he brings to life the scent of freshly baked madeleines from his childhood.[101] This shows that the inner world of introverted feeling types can be shared with their fellow human beings, even if this usually happens in a much simpler manner in everyday life than what is expressed in the rich and talented way of this ingenious writer.

If the thinking function is so inferior in feeling types that it is completely suppressed and therefore entirely unconscious, it is projected onto an object in the outer world. These projections are correspondingly dark and antagonistic. According to Jung, "all sorts of mean things" are projected on others who are seen as "scheming evil, contriving plots, secret intrigues, etc."[102] This creates a vicious circle, in which the introverted feeling types respond with counter-intrigues and suspicions: "Endless clandestine rivalries spring up, and in these embittered struggles she will shrink from no baseness or meanness, and will even prostitute her virtues in order to play the trump card."[103] The consequences for the affected people are severe exhaustion and neurasthenic neuroses.

Jung's critical description of feeling types is one-sidedly disparaging in places and reveals his own typology. By devaluing the feeling function, which was intended to be equivalent to the three other functions of the self, he contradicts his own concern for depicting the four functions as equally adaptative mechanisms for coping with life. As interesting as this approach may be, it requires a balancing revision—though Adam[104] has already achieved much in this direction.

Sensation in the extraverted and introverted attitude: The sensation type

Thanks to our natural senses of touch, taste, smell, sight, and hearing, we have innate abilities for connecting with the world. The basic psychological function of sensation is therefore especially pronounced in young children.[105] Like intuition, sensation is one of the irrational functions. In contrast to the two rational functions (thinking and feeling), these do not primarily evaluate but simply observe and perceive.

The more pronounced the sensation function and the weaker the contrasting thinking and feeling function, the more extensively the outer world is grasped through hearing, seeing, touching, smelling, and tasting. Like any extraverted function, sensation is also determined by external objects. Those that trigger the strongest sensory impressions create a distinct *sensuous* tie. Jung defines extraverted sensation as "a vital function equipped with the strongest vital instinct."[106] If extraverted sensation is the primary function, the persons concerned are only interested in the strength of the sensation.

When people mainly relate to the world in the above-described manner, we can regard them as *extraverted sensation types*. Their strengths are their realism and objective sense of facts. Jung considers it to be a widespread error to classify such a pronounced orientation to concrete fact as *rational*, since extraverted sensation types do not care about the reasonableness or unreasonableness of a sensation. Only its intensity is important to them. Ranging from eating good food while wearing beautiful clothing at a stylishly set table, to erotic-sexual enjoyment with a correspondingly attractive other, sensual intensity is rarely lacking in their life.

In his description, Jung shows how much he is influenced by the spirit of his time, and primarily relates the extraverted sensation type to men. This may particularly apply where sexuality is concerned, in addition to aesthetics.[107] However, an examination of whether there are actually more men than women who correspond with this sensation type would be necessary—especially in current times.

For women, the importance of the outer world may not always appear in the same way. Sensual pleasure may not have as strong an accent on sexuality, but on a luxurious or at least a qualitatively impeccable everyday lifestyle. This ranges from living comfortably to culinary enjoyment, extravagant clothing and jewelry, to cultural interests. Some of these aspects may be more in the foreground and others less.[108] Of course, male sensation types can also enjoy the same things. Jung describes the entire range of expression extraverted sensation types can take, from the refined aesthete to the crude pleasure-seeker— the latter "ruthlessly exploits and squeezes dry" the pleasure-bringing object "since now its sole use is to stimulate sensation."[109]

As for every extraverted type, the externally oriented sensation types also risk losing themselves to the outer object: namely, when they "disappear behind the sensations."[110] An obsession with the object means loss of freedom for the subject. Then the affected individuals attempt to gain pleasure in a compulsive and unrelated way. But blind enjoyment goes hand in hand with the total devaluation of the pleasure-giving object. So the previous high valuation of the object turns into its opposite: "The bondage to the object is carried to the extreme limit. As a consequence, the unconscious is forced out of its compensatory role into open opposition."

Above all, the repressed intuitions begin to assert themselves in the form of projections on the object. The wildest suspicions arise; if the object is a sexual one, jealous fantasies and anxiety states gain the upper hand."[111] The easy-going attitude toward mere sensation can develop into compulsion.[112] The results can be depression, phobias, and compulsive disorders. However, these are often very difficult to treat because the analyzing functions (feeling and thinking) are at best only available as auxiliary functions in this type—which means that the ability for self-reflection tends to be unconscious and therefore often undeveloped.

Even in the *introverted attitude*, sensation is focused on objective stimuli. However, this changes considerably since the subjective factor once again plays the decisive role here. Jung explains this with the example of the fine arts. The same landscape or person, drawn by various painters as objectively as possible, will still look different in their diverse artistic reproductions, and this is not only due to the various talents of the artists, but also results from their different ways of seeing. The subjective factor can even be so strong that the object may be grasped, but no longer recognizably depicted. The object only serves as a stimulus for subjective impressions.

So this is where introverted sensation types are considerably different from those with an extraverted attitude. "Introverted sensation transmits an image which does not so much reproduce the object as spread over it the patina of age-old subjective experience and the shimmer of events still unborn. The bare sense impression develops in depth, reaching into the past and future, while extraverted sensation seizes on the momentary existence of things open to the light of day."[113]

For the extraverted sensation types, the strength of the effect that an object has on them is the determining factor. But introverted types are oriented towards the intensity of the subjective sensation that is triggered by the objective stimuli. There is not even a need for a proportional relationship between the object and its perception. A certain kind of arbitrariness arises since others can never know what will make an impression on an introverted sensation type, how they will process the impression, and how they could express it to the outside world in turn. Like all introverts, they cannot be easily assessed in terms of their reactions to stimuli from the outside. Outer circumstances only serve them as catalysts for their own subjective reactions.

According to Jung, this results in the devaluation of these objects since they are not seen in their own value. In pathological cases, this can go as far the persons no longer being able to distinguish "between the real object and the subjective perception."[114]

Jung strongly emphasizes the irrationality of these types, although this may be difficult for others to recognize—precisely because of the innocuousness that is accompanied by an attitude of calmness, passivity, and "rational" self-control. Their outer environment only gets acquainted with the irrationality of introverted sensation types when their inner world is so intensively touched and activated by an object that they act out an unconscious script that has been brought to life,[115] also showing their true nature to outsiders in the process. An example from everyday life could be a stalker who stubbornly pursues a young woman to whom he is sexually attracted and obsessed with. He thinks that this is love without noticing that he is only harassing and hurting her.

On the other hand, introverted sensation types can also quite easily become victims themselves. On the outside, this type shows little affective reactivity, but a rather neutral attitude—always striving for balance "in order to keep the influence of the object within the necessary boundaries."[116] However, their harmless appearance causes them to "easily become a victim of the aggressiveness and domineeringness of others. Such men allow themselves to be abused and then take their revenge on the most unsuitable occasions with redoubled obtuseness and stubbornness."[117]

The intuitive function is suppressed in this type and expresses itself in a correspondingly archaic manner when it breaks through. Jung describes how the archaic intuition sniffs out ambiguous, shadowy, sordid, and dangerous scenarios. Instead of premonitions, distorted and delusional unconscious perceptions occur that are in no way connected with reality. This is in total contrast to the highly differentiated intuition that has accurate, i.e. reality-related unconscious perceptions.[118] However, when the introverted sensation types begin to take a thorough look at their archaic shadow side, they will gradually get to know their unconscious depths and ultimately balance out their conscious naiveté and gullibility. But if the inferior extraverted intuition remains split off from the conscious introverted sensation function, which is the primary function, the result may be obsessions that can develop into an obsessive-compulsive disorder.

Jung provides a beautiful comparison between the extraverted and the introverted sensation types, which uses the example of perceiving a red flower mentioned in the definitions[119]: He differentiates between "sensual" or "concrete" and "abstract" sensations. The "concrete sensation" that is mixed with ideas, feelings, and thoughts appears to be entirely fitting for the extraverted sensation types. After all, they are completely oriented toward the factuality of an object. They perceive the red flower in its wholeness as a botanical organism, including the stalk and petals. Its appearance awakens within them feelings of desire or aversion, as well as the perceptions of smell, and they may even develop a few thoughts on its botanical classification.

On the other hand, the "abstract sensation" is a differentiated form of perception. It follows aesthetic principles that are felt by the observer (who may be an artist) as subjectively important, and which he or she has abstracted from the concrete object and distilled into a "pure" form. Using the example of the flower, it could be the brilliant red that constitutes the main content of conscious perception, while all the other qualities of the flower no longer given attention. This kind of concentrated use of the object through subjective perception corresponds to the way that the introverted sensation types deal with outer objects.

Intuition in the extraverted and introverted attitude: The intuitive type

Premonitions, visions, new possibilities, direct and sudden knowledge, an eye for the whole, a wealth of inner images, imagination and creativity, mysticism and prophecy arise when dealing with the world of intuition. Jung introduces his definition of intuition with an etymological explanation, probably because this captures its core meaning. It comes from the Latin word *intueri*—"to look at"—which communicates the unconscious perceptions and views connected with intuition. These can appear in the form of finished pictures or as premonitions and visions. It is "a kind of instinctive apprehension"[120] and, like sensation, is considered to be an irrational function of perception. The perceptions gained through the two irrational functions of intuition and sensations are typically accompanied by certainty—as givens, they are simply there. The certainty that comes from direct perception differentiates the two irrational functions from the two rational functions of thinking and feeling which can only organize and evaluate content derived from the irrational functions.

What intuition perceives appears as a psychological fact which suddenly comes into view from the unconscious. From the perspective of consciousness, such a sudden knowledge cannot immediately be comprehended in a rational way. However, many intuitions can be subsequently broken down into their component parts and rationally understood through laborious, detailed work. The philosopher Spinoza considered intuitive cognition to be the highest form of cognition because of the direct assurance and certainty that comes with it.

Since intuition is mainly an unconscious process, its nature is also very difficult to grasp and define. So the following explanations from Jung are intended to shed some light on intuitive functioning: "The primary function of intuition . . . is simply to transmit images, or perceptions of relations between things, which could not be transmitted by the other functions or only in a very roundabout way. These images have the value of specific insights which have a decisive influence on action whenever intuition is given priority."[121] Jung also explains why intuition and sensation are polar opposites:

> Sensation is a hindrance to clear, unbiased, naïve perception; its intrusive sensory stimuli direct attention to the physical surface, to the very things round and beyond which intuition tries to peer . . . Hence, if intuition is to function properly, sensation must to a large extent be suppressed. By sensation I mean in this instance the simple and immediate sense-impression understood as a clearly defined physiological and psychic datum."[122]

In contrast to sensation types, for whom the strongest physiological stimulus is the most important, a different sensation that is difficult to define is unconsciously at work for intuitive types. Through unconscious subjective factors, it becomes the focus and trigger for their views. To intuitives, it "appears to be pure sensation. But actually it is not so."[123] In contrast to the sensation function, which is based on concrete sensory perceptions, intuition is namely an unconscious perception.

In contrast to a conscious comprehension of objective facts, the intuitive function very quickly grasps existing possibilities in an unconscious way. Intuitive types often experience premonitions about a future event that cannot rationally be predicted, but that usually turn out to be true, even if there are time delays. "When [intuition] is the dominant function, every ordinary situation in life seems like a locked room which intuition has to open. It is constantly seeking fresh outlets and new possibilities in external life."[124]

Intuition in the extraverted attitude is directed entirely at outer objects and circumstances—seeing through them (as a function of unconscious perception) to find their hidden possibilities. No one else has such a "keen nose for anything new and in the making."[125] So people with an extroverted intuitive attitude are always prepared to dedicate their entire lives to a new possibility. This applies all the more because they experience stable situations as a prison from which they must liberate themselves.

When the intuitive function is the primary function, thinking and feeling are less differentiated and therefore unable to temper intuition with other relevant information. The importance for extraverted intuitive types to acquire a capacity for judgment through the development of the two rational functions (which can set realistic limits to their thinking of possibilities), is shown when we look at the professions such people are found in with an especially high frequency. With their ability to sense external possibilities, they are successful as business tycoons and speculators, entrepreneurs, agents, politicians, and the like.[126]

Extraverted intuitive types are predestined to be initiators and promoters of important and promising social projects or champions of marginalized groups. Extraverted intuitives succeed in inspiring courage in their fellow human beings, kindling enthusiasm for unrealized possibilities, and motivating others to take action.[127] However, their untiring efforts to create new possibilities in culture and society can hold great dangers for these individuals since "all too easily the intuitive may fritter away his life on things and people, spreading about him an abundance of life which others live and not himself."[128] They are in danger of not benefiting from their own labors because they have already turned to new possibilities.[129] Their own unconscious can ultimately turn against them. To Jung, as with the sensation types, for the intuitive;

> Thinking and feeling, being largely repressed, come up with infantile, archaic thoughts and feelings similar to those of the countertype. These take the form of intense projections which are just as absurd as their own, though they seem to lack the "magical" character of the latter and are chiefly concerned with quasi-realities such as sexual suspicions, financial hazards, forebodings of illness, etc.[130]

In the case of extraverted intuition that is only lived one-sidedly, sooner or later repressed sensations appear. In combination with the inadequately developed emotional and thinking functions, this can also lead to selecting an inappropriate partner, because such choices will be based on projections. Extraverted intuitive types can gravitate toward *mesalliances*—relationships with partners who are often weaker in terms of education and social status. This can frequently be seen in public persons who play an outstanding role in culture, society, and politics, as well as having rendered great services in these areas.

As compensation for the neglect of the concrete world (which can come in the form of a partner or one's own body), intuitives fall victim to "neurotic compulsions in the form of over-subtle ratiocinations, hairsplitting dialectics, and a compulsive tie to the sensation aroused by the object. His conscious attitude towards both the sensation and the object is one of ruthless superiority."[131] This occurs because the intuitive simply cannot see the same thing "that everyone else sees and rides roughshod over it."

Much like sensation types—who have no eye for the object's soul in problematic cases, devaluing and exploiting it as a result—one-sided intuitives develop phobias and compulsions. However, these have a hypochondriac nature and the unconscious archaic and indefinite sensation function takes revenge through "every imaginable kind of absurd bodily sensation."[132]

In contrast to extraverted intuition, introverted intuition is directed toward inner objects. In this case, these are "the elements of the unconscious."[133] In the introverted attitude, the intuitive function shows its openness to all emerging possibilities in the psychic inner world, in the world of the imagination, and its accompanying inner images. Like the external world, the inner world is much older than the individual human being. Jung connects this ancient inner cosmos to his concept of the collective unconscious and the archetypes, which are the innate structural possibilities of experience. By means of perception, introverted intuition finds access to the world of *a priori* archetypes— the forms of all experiences that have ever been had on our planet. In order to perceive and understand archetypal images as they appear in dreams and visions, introverted intuition is required.

The benefit of introverted intuition, according to Jung, is that it can supply certain data via its inner perception that is "of the utmost importance for understanding what is going on in the world. It can even foresee new possibilities in more or less clear ways, as well as events which later actually do happen. Its prophetic foresight is explained by its relation to the archetypes, which represent the laws governing the course of all experienceable things."[134]

Due to the relationship with the inner world of images, it is not surprising that there are often dreamers, mystics, and seers among introverted intuitive types, as well as visionaries and artists.[135] Jung also places misunderstood geniuses in this category. In any case, introverted intuitives are usually quite aloof from tangible reality, and therefore not very good at mastering everyday life.

Jung notes, however, that the purely aesthetic functioning intuitive, can achieves a certain degree of differentiation in their thinking. This is how they can arrive at moral judgment, question the meaning of a vision and face the responsibility that it brings with it for themselves or for the world. Without this, they deprive themselves and the world of the possibility of making a difference with their visions—in which case their lives appear to be purely symbolic, unadapted "to present-day reality."[136]

Why is this so? Jung thinks this is because their language is subjective in nature, and not generally understandable because it lacks rational justifications. "He can only profess or proclaim. His is 'the voice of one crying in the wilderness.'"[137] This image implies great loneliness, which is not surprising when we remember that introverted intuitives are the furthest away from the object, since they completely repress sensation. Therefore, they are also in danger of splitting off from the body with its needs. Their unconscious counteracts this in such a way that it compensates their pronounced conscious intuitive attitude by producing unconscious archaic and extraverted sensations. Like with everything strongly repressed, the unconscious sensation function is correspondingly excessive and instinctual, as well as strongly bound to sensual experience. The spiritual detachment of introverted intuitives is therefore compensated by the unconscious pull of the world of instincts, which brings this type into contact with earthly-animalistic realities. But if this compensation fails because the conscious attitude continues to be one-sided, an obsessive-compulsive disorder (OCD) can develop.

It should be noted, in conclusion, that all of the types and functions have an equal value, so none of the four functions or four types is "better" or more important than any of the others. We can only achieve an optimal approach to ourselves and the world when we function in a way that is as holistic and differentiated as possible. This means that feeling, thinking, sensation, and intuition—as well as the two attitudes of introversion and extraversion—are available to us. It does not matter which function is primary when it comes to achieving the greatest possible wholeness. However, it is eminently important to strive for a differentiation of the less conscious functions. This can be compared to astrology, in which none of the twelve zodiac signs is "better" than the others because each has a certain function within the whole. How we deal with our own disposition and whether or not we live toward a more comprehensive development—that also includes ethical action toward ourselves and the environment—is ultimately up to each of us as individuals. This approach is independent of the typological perspective from which we try to grasp it.

Synopsis: The Four Basic Characters (Fire/Intuition, Earth/Sensation, Air/Thinking, and Water/Feeling)

This survey of astrological and Jungian typology reveals the many similarities between the two—even if the question of introversion and extroversion has been left out in the typology of the planets and signs. But this will be covered in Chapter 3 in relationship to astrological quadrants and houses.

But even without including how introversion and extraversion work in astrology, certain parallels between the astrological characterization of the fire signs (Aries, Leo, and Sagittarius) and the descriptions of Jung's intuitive type are obvious. The same applies to the earth signs (Taurus, Virgo, and Capricorn) and Jung's sensation type; to the air signs (Gemini, Libra, and Aquarius) and Jung's thinking type; and to the water signs (Cancer, Scorpio, and Pisces) and Jung's feeling type. However, there is a very important difference in the degree of differentiation of the four Jungian function types and the astrological types. Without diminishing Jung's merits in creating his typology, it should be noted that astrology provides a more multifaceted set of characteristics for different types, by presenting every element in three specific variations—since each of the four elements have three distinct archetypal forms of their own. Every zodiac sign can also be associated with different aspects of the body, which is not included in Jungian typology.

The following presents the correspondence between the astrological types and the Jungian function types:

- Fire type (Aries, Leo, and Sagittarius): intuitive type
- Earth type (Taurus, Virgo, and Capricorn): sensation type
- Air type (Gemini, Libra, and Aquarius): thinking type
- Water type (Cancer, Scorpio, and Pisces): feeling type

A more extensive work that is specifically dedicated to the comparison of the two typologies in terms of their similarities and differences would be required to develop these concepts more precisely, but this is not possible within the scope of this book.

However, the above rough classification should at least be expanded by the following considerations. Astrology is an ancient and much more differentiated system with a very large number of possible combinations. In contrast, Jung's typology seems more preliminary and unfinished. This makes it difficult for many people to find themselves in his typology and better understand themselves on its basis. Perhaps this is also because, in comparison to astrology, Jung's typology is relatively young and must still continue to mature and/or be further developed.[138]

These are among the reasons why the above comparison can only be tentative within the scope of this chapter. Nevertheless, it seems important to expand on it briefly. For example, the three earth elements with their materialistic and fact-oriented attitude correspond with much of Jung's sensation function, but the two typologies are not congruent in all aspects. The sensation function does not appear to be limited to just the three earth signs of Taurus, Virgo, and Capricorn since planetary aspects—i.e. the relationships of the planets with each other—also play a big role in the birth chart.

In the section "The Ten Planets in Astrology" (Chapter 1), the characteristics of the individual planets as archetypes are thematized. Which of these "gods" play a main role in an individual's birth chart regardless of whether a person is a sensation type, intuitive type, thinking type, or feeling type. Astrological typology has many mixed forms.

However, there is only a limited amount of such mixed forms in Jungian typology, depending on how strongly pronounced the respective auxiliary functions are:

For all the types met with in practice, the rule holds good that besides the conscious, primary function there is a relatively conscious, auxiliary function which is in every respect different from the nature of the primary function. The resulting combinations present the familiar pictures of, for instance, practical thinking allied with sensation, speculative thinking forging ahead with intuition, artistic intuition selecting and presenting its images with the help of feeling-values, philosophical intuition systematizing its vision into comprehensible thought by means of a powerful intellect, and so on.[139]

Jung's thinking type has been assigned to the astrological air element. But it is also very important to consider in which element—and even more precisely, in which of the three possible signs of an element—the planet Mercury is located. The element is "colored" by the planet, which in turn strongly influences the respective style of thinking. From the viewpoint of astrology, various aspects determine the development of a specific mental disposition and intellect. In addition to the distinct styles of thinking found in Gemini, Libra, and Aquarius, the planet Mercury (the messenger of the gods) manifests its own manifold possibilities in relationship to other planets. Also, the twelve astrological houses give a person a different orientation in terms of interest depending on the planets that are in them, which is Mercury in our example. In addition, the astrological houses provide information on the question of introversion or extraversion (cf. Chapters 4 and 5).

To give another example, a person with a dominant Saturn influence will show characteristics of the sensation function; but the same applies when the earth element is especially pronounced in a birth chart. The earthy disposition or even a pronounced Saturn constellation corresponds with the sensation type. And as just mentioned, the composition of the houses can provide information on introversion and extraversion.

When discussing the topic of intuition, it should be added that the typical attributes of the intuitive function cannot be limited in their expression to the three variations found in the fire signs of Aries, Leo, and Sagittarius; they can also be found in horoscopes without a fire disposition. This occurs when the planets of Uranus and Jupiter (which also supposedly instill intuitive abilities) play a dominant role in a horoscope. Intuition is also often pronounced in people with an Aquarius influence, even though Aquarius is an air sign. Why is this so? Aquarius is associated with both Saturn and Uranus. If the Uranus component is more dominant than the Saturn component, the thinking of the Aquarius air sign is more strongly intuitive and animated with ideas than strictly logical and factual. This is probably why certain people do not feel correctly located in the sign of Aquarius when they hear that they are "thinking types"—when their thinking is actually more intuitive. Along the same lines, there is also a kind of feeling thinking, like when Mercury is located in a water sign—which certainly can be associated with the feeling type—or forms an aspect with the Moon, which stands for feminine and empathetic qualities.

Since it could fill an entire book of its own, this discussion will end here. However, there will be a more thorough look at the application of the astrological system in the combination of the Sun sign, the planets in the houses, and the planetary aspects in Chapters 4 and 5.

3
Inside and Out: Two Psychological Orientations

In his typology, Jung combines the four function types with the two attitudes by individually characterizing each of the function types in terms of its extraverted and introverted expression. However, the function types that result from the predominance of certain signs in the astrological system—as well as from the weight of specific planets and their aspects—are not directly connected to either attitude type. The question of extraversion and introversion cannot be as simply answered in astrology, since many factors influence which may be expressed. The involved signs, the type and number of planets in the quadrants of the circle and/or in the twelve houses, the aspects of the planets, and their forward or retrograde direction of movement are all relevant. For instance, retrograde planets have an introverted tendency in relation to their function, and in how they color the signs and houses that they invigorate.

All of these factors must be considered both individually and in their combinations when interpreting a birth chart. This process will be shown in a more detailed and comprehensive way in the eight horoscope examples discussed in Chapter 5.

The four quadrants with their respective three houses can also only give very general hints about an extraverted or introverted attitude. However, they become central in determining a tendency toward extraversion or introversion when they are "inhabited" by the planets—since these are ultimately archetypal forces that provide the quadrants and houses with energy. So the distribution of the planets in the circle plays an essential role. Based on the number and type of planets (essential forces), a tendency toward introversion or extraversion can be deduced.

Extraversion and Introversion According to C. G. Jung

Jung defines people with an extraverted orientation as those who are interested in the outer world[140] and therefore place a high value on it. According to Jung, the danger that can arise in this case is a complete absorption in external reality, resulting in the loss of the individual's own standpoint. This can go as far as dissociation.

On the other hand, introverted people are not interested in objective reality and "devalue" the outer world as a result. Jung writes that introverts are guided by the "subjective factor" and merely use outer objects to stir their own, subjective ideas. However, Jung's definition should be supplemented to the extent that the introvert does relate to highly valued objects, but those of an inner reality. For example, these can be ideas, feelings, sensations, or inner images that come from the collective unconscious and therefore also have their own kind of objectivity. Jung mentions this relationship with the archetypal depths in his descriptions of introverted intuition and sensation.

Within the scope of this introduction to depth psychological astrology, the essential criterion that differentiates extraversion and introversion is the direction their interest takes. Extraversion expresses the attitude that devotes its interest to the outer object as such, abstracting subjective impressions from it in order to experience the objective givenness of outer reality. Introversion expresses the attitude that is governed by subjective motives and realities found within, which makes outer objects secondary to the individual's inner world. However, this attempt at a definition in relation to astrology should be viewed with caution. Above all, this is due to the immense complexity of each individual horoscope. So only relatively general classifications are possible, which must always be carefully examined in each individual case. This applies all the more since both tendencies (an introverted and an extraverted attitude) can be found in different ways.

The Circle with Its Semi-Circles, Quadrants, and Houses in Astrology

Starting with Aries and ending with Pisces, the twelve signs of the zodiac form a ring in their counterclockwise sequence. Every horoscope is additionally divided into twelve segments called houses, areas of interest, or fields. They are numbered starting with the Ascendant, and also proceed in a counterclockwise manner, just like the signs.

The Ascendant (from the Latin word *ascendere*: "rising") is the constellation of the zodiac that is rising above the eastern horizon at the moment of birth. As Thomas Ring explains,[141] the Ascendant can be imprinted by each of the twelve signs of the zodiac. Each point on the ecliptic—which is the line of orbit for all astrologically relevant phenomena (signs of the zodiac and planets) from the perspective of the Earth—rises in the east above the horizon (Ascendant, AC), moves counterclockwise to the upper meridian or culmination point, which is called the Midheaven (Medium Coeli, MC), descends to the westernmost point (descendant, DC), sinks beneath the horizon to the lower meridian, which lies on the vertical axis opposite the MC, and is therefore the lowest point, marked as the Lower Heaven (Imum Coeli, IC). Then it begins to rise again and reaches the horizon at the easternmost point again in the morning.[142]

The Ascendant is the point of intersection between the eastern horizon and a certain point on the ecliptic, which is the sign of the zodiac rising there at the time of birth. It is calculated from the birth data. Each of the twelve zodiac signs can color the Ascendant and therefore also the First House, which starts at the AC.

Every house is normally associated with a certain sign, corresponding with the counterclockwise sequence of the zodiac. As already mentioned above, a house can be various degrees in size and comprise less or much more than 30°. It can also be imprinted by two or even three signs of the zodiac. As soon as we compare actual horoscopes, it becomes apparent that the houses can have entirely different sizes. Large houses can extend over two or even three different signs, while very narrow houses may be in just one single sign or even go through two different signs of the zodiac. The size of the house depends on certain astronomical factors, which cannot be explained within in scope of this book due to their complexity.

A birth chart with very large houses is illustrated clearly in the *Horoscope Example 1: Johannes*. His First House begins near 13° 52' of the sign of Aquarius. It includes the entire 30° of Pisces and only ends at 8° 40' of the following sign of Aries. The same applies for the Seventh House, which is the opposite in the circle of houses and starts at 13° 53' Leo, includes the entire 30° of Virgo and ends near 8° 40' of the sign of Libra.

This leads to the phenomenon of "enclosed signs," as seen in *Horoscope Example 1: Johannes*. His First House starts in Aquarius, encloses Pisces, and ends in Aries. The opposite Seventh House starts with Leo, encloses Virgo, and ends in Libra. The First House is associated with the first sign in the zodiac, Aries; the Second House with the second zodiac sign, Taurus; the Third House is related to Gemini, etc. The circle of the houses and the zodiac are only identical when the Ascendant is located in the first sign of Aries, which starts with 0° in Aries and corresponds with the signs of the zodiac attributed to the houses. In every other case, both circles are shifted against each other.

The four quadrants of the horoscope contain three houses each: Houses 1, 2, and 3 form the first; Houses 4, 5, and 6 form the second; Houses 7, 8, and 9 form the third; and Houses 10, 11, and 12 form the Fourth Quadrant (see Ill. 9). In a concrete horoscope, the 12 signs of the zodiac and 12 houses overlap to form various combinations that depend on the Ascendant.

The circle symbolizes wholeness. The four quadrants, subdivided into three houses each—i.e. constituting a total of twelve houses or fields[143]—stand for certain archetypal and therefore natural or motivational areas of human life. The more planets there are in a quadrant and its houses, the more energetically charged these areas of life are—in accordance with the respective characteristics of the related "gods" (which is what the planets are also called due to their archetypal quality). So more energy flows into the quadrants and fields "inhabited" by planets than those that are "empty." However, "emptiness" does not mean that these value dimensions and areas of interest are absent in the life of a particular person, only that energy is not especially directed toward them those areas.[144] They are less animated as a result.

The four quadrants and their relationship to extraversion and introversion

As a start, this little drawing will illustrate the circle with its quadrants:

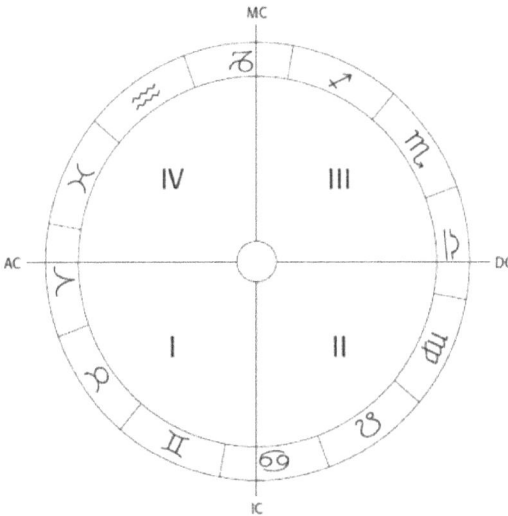

Ill. 7: The circle with the four quadrants as dimensions of life and value[145]

1st Quadrant   *AC – Ascendant,* 6 a.m. daybreak (time of the 1st Quadrant: between 12 and 6 a.m.).
Self quadrant, birth of the self, asserting the self against the world, and the "one against all" struggle for survival; Individuality, subjectivity, and the personal realm. Nutrition, property, and livelihood.
Associated zodiac signs: Aries, Taurus, and Gemini.

The association of a sign with a quadrant applies to the zodiac in general since it starts with Aries. However, there are a great variety of combinations and variations in an actual horoscope. Any of the twelve zodiac signs can be the Ascendant, which depends on various factors and must be calculated. In *Horoscope Example 1: Johannes* (see Chapter 5), Aquarius is the Ascendant and the First House includes Aquarius and Pisces, as well as a bit of Aries; the Second House is inhabited by Aries and Taurus; and the Third House includes Taurus and Gemini. This means that the Aries qualities of the First House, which is about self-assertion, are modified in keeping with the style of Aquarius and Pisces (and just a bit of Aries). This short explanation of how houses and signs are connected should suffice at this point. Chapter 5 will illustrate a few combinations of different ways signs relate to the 12 houses.

2nd Quadrant *IC – Imum Coeli (Lower Heaven)*[146]: 12 a.m. midnight (time of the 2nd Quadrant: between 6 p.m. and 12 a.m.).
"Family quadrant," private life, family, and blood relatives; Creatures of nature, emotional and physical intimacy, relationship to the unconscious, inner world, dreams, imagination, instincts, and emotions; Conception and care of new life; preservation of the species.
Associated zodiac signs: Cancer, Leo, and Virgo.

3rd Quadrant *DC – Descendent*, 6 p.m. evening, sunset (time of the 3rd Quadrant: between 12 p.m. and 6 p.m.).
Community quadrant, encounter with the other, familiar people, kindred spirits, friends and enemies, partnerships, and symbiosis; Wanderlust, travel, foreign cultures, and worldwide network of relationships; Spiritual vision, philosophy, and religions; Human progress and idealism.
Associated zodiac signs: Libra, Scorpio, and Sagittarius.

4th Quadrant *MC – Midheaven*, 12 p.m. noon (time of the 4th Quadrant: between 6 a.m. and 12 p.m.).
Humanity in general, collective norms and laws, the general public, society, the public, and public representatives; Politics, technology, and culture; Window to the world and world stage; Anonymity.
Associated zodiac signs: Capricorn, Aquarius, and Pisces.

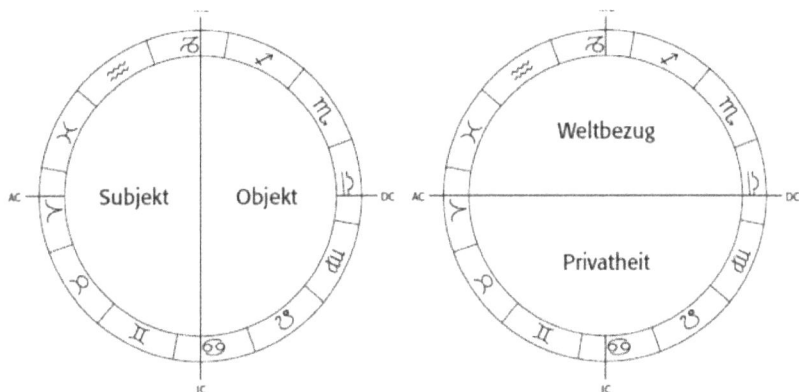

Ill. 8: The circle with left/right division and with top/down division

[Text in left circle: subject / object.
Text in right circle: top: relationship to the world; bottom: privacy]

In the above sketches, it becomes clear that there is a horizontal and a vertical axis that twice subdivide the circle into two semi-circles, and therefore also into four quadrants. The horizontal axis extends between the Ascendant (AC) on the left/in the east and the descendent (DC) on the right/in the West; the vertical axis runs between Imum Coeli (IC) below/in the north and Midheaven (MC) above/in the south.

Thomas Ring assigns the lower semi-circle (below the horizon) to the private areas of life and the upper semi-circle (above the horizon) to our relationship with the world. In view of the two sketches, the question arises as to whether the privacy of the lower semi-circle fits with Jung's description of the introverted attitude and whether the relationship to the world of the upper semi-circle can be equated with Jung's extraversion. Whether and to what extent the left semi-circle (which Ring calls "organic contactless"[147]) and the right semi-circle (defined by Ring as "organic contact"[148]) could be related to Jung's theory as explained in the following descriptions of the individual quadrants. In any case, it is very important when interpreting a person's birth chart to determine the location of the planets in the semi-circles and quadrants at the time of his or her birth.

1st Quadrant

Individuals with their existential needs are born and want to survive in the rough-and-tumble of the world. This is why the First Quadrant is about the will to self-assertion, the intake of food, and the assimilation of everything that people require to be strengthened and survive. This applies to not only the physical, but also the emotional and mental levels. People with a strong emphasis on the First Quadrant (many planets in the three first fields at the lower left) only express an interest in their surrounding world as long as it is useful in satisfying their needs and supporting their self-will. If this is not the case, they show that they are indifferent and block out the external world. Even little children command attention when they have physical and emotional needs such as hunger and thirst. The same applies when they want to be held, cradled, and cared for—or want some entertainment. The older children get, the more their thirst for knowledge awakens and they will also test and develop their manual and cognitive abilities.

This desire to learn new things and develop persists throughout life, even for adults—and this is often due to professional reasons. After all, adults must ultimately ensure their existence through their occupation. With the money that they earn, they can in turn afford material possessions and this is important for their sense of security in life.

People with a strong disposition in the First Quadrant act on the basis of subjective motivation and spontaneity to assert their momentary self-interests. This approach can easily change on an ongoing basis according to the First Quadrant rationale—"what benefits me is good." Such individuals use every opportunity to assert, feed, and enrich themselves. Because individuals with an emphasis on the First Quadrant view everything in terms of how it serves or relates to themselves and their subjective needs, Ring also calls them "organically contactless."[149] Since the self (the subject with all of its needs) is the focus here, it can therefore be seen as having a tendency toward introversion.

2nd Quadrant

Astrologers also speak of the family quadrant, in which themes of privacy and preservation of the species are equally addressed since children are usually part of a family. The family and life with it are one important aspect in the Second Quadrant; the relationship to one's own psychological-spiritual center with its creative depths is the other. The inner world, the unconscious with its emotions that are expressed in dream images and fantasies, the connection with the natural and instinctual side, can ground these people within themselves. The more securely individuals can root within themselves, the better they can integrate their emotional and physical intimacy within their family life and friendships.

This is a very important aspect for many people: that they can find rootedness in their lives together with their relatives and trusted people within a private setting. Living, feeling at home, and being settled in a nest of one's own—all of this is part of the private atmosphere and is always designed in a very personal way. The theme of intimate love and sexuality is also significant within this quadrant, including the topics of fertility and potency.

The warming nest and sense of being safe within one's own family obviously includes the necessary affection and care for all of the relatives. People with a domestic and private disposition can find their main meaning in life in their role as mother or father. However, there are also quite problematic forms this can take such as the "shrew" or the "household tyrant." For each of the respective expressions, the sign and especially the type of planets in their aspects play an essential role—as well as the personal experiences that individuals have within the circle of their family of origin.

In addition to family issues, private life also includes the cultivation of intimate friendships and sexual encounters, as well as all types of games and fun, sport, music, and other fields of creative activity. All of this can be done as a hobby or at a high artistic level. This is always about creative self-expression: As we know, not only biological children but also other forms of progeny such as works of art can be created.[150]

The focus on the private and the personal, together with the connection to the creative depths of the unconscious—and how this results in a particular kind of lifestyle—can indicate the presence of an introverted attitude. On the other hand, this also involves other people (family members, friends, and lovers) with whom individuals have a relationship. In keeping with this description, Thomas Ring describes the right semi-circle as "the contact direct."[151] This means that people with such a disposition have a direct and organic contact with their surrounding world. The focus is no longer on the subject with his or her own individual needs of self-preservation and self-assertion against the rest of the world, as in the First Quadrant. Instead, it is on individuals as beings of nature who have not only an intimate contact with their own emotional-spiritual depths but also with the environment of family and trusted friends. Their central life requirement is the preservation of generations.

These considerations show that although a clear tendency in the direction of introversion can be determined here, this applies when the focus is on the personal realm as the root of all being and doing. Depending on the type of signs and planets that have an effect in the Second Quadrant, certain extraversion tendencies can also manifest in this context. Perhaps Jung's theory of attitude types cannot be translated one-to-one for the Second Quadrant in astrology. This will be discussed in greater detail as part of the summary at the end of this section.

3rd Quadrant

In this quadrant, familiar people, what is foreign, and therefore the outer world, becomes the focus of the subject, attracting his or her interest. There are intensive encounters that often to lead to long-term and even lifelong partnerships, both professionally and privately. This is also about the coexistence of the self and other within an expanded, non-family context. An even-handed giving and taking, fair exchange, and mutual reliability and commitment are related to and can also be expressed by the concept of symbiosis. Living together in a social context has many facets. In addition to friends, it also brings enemies with it, and individuals must deal with them. Perpetrators and victims also form a kind of bond. This domain includes experiencing power and helplessness in encounters with others and dealing with these experiences.

This brief insight into the diversity of possible relationship patterns shows that both mutual support and fighting against each other can play a role here. People with an accented Third Quadrant usually have a pronounced sense for the conditions of the surrounding world. The family ties from the Second Quadrant are expanded in the Third Quadrant toward committed connections with other, non-familial, people—culminating in extended and even global relationships.

People with a strong emphasis on the Third Quadrant stand between the poles of ethical values and their violations. This is about their own rights and the rights of others, making questions of 'justice" and associated humanitarian concerns paramount.[152] The intense orientation of the fields of interest in the Third Quadrant toward the external world shows a strong parallel to Jung's concept of extraversion— the main characteristic of which is also a high level of interest in the external object.

4th Quadrant

In the Fourth Quadrant, people with the corresponding disposition are drawn to the world stage. In order to conquer a space in public life and also be able to stay there, the respective individuals must internalize collective norms and values. They are constantly guided by the principle of "people do this, but people should do that, and people must." The superego is strongly constellated in people with a distinct disposition in the Fourth Quadrant. This is accompanied by a great deal of self-control and repression of personal concerns, which can even lead to losing a living relationship with their own bodies and instincts—as well as becoming deprived of direct contact with the colorfulness of the emotional world. For the respective people, there is the danger of functionalizing themselves to meet the requirements of the external world and stopping at nothing to do so—not even self-destruction. This is because their personal wishes and needs, everything that is private, must be set aside in favor of objectification, and the general values and rules as they apply in respective public institutions or as required by the collective mood.

In contrast to the intimacy that determines the Second Quadrant, friendships are less personal and emotional in the Fourth Quadrant;

instead, they have a more objective character and serve a collective function. They develop through social and professional occasions at which (in addition to factual topics) small talk must also be mastered as a superficial art that creates relationships precisely for this reason.

It is typical for individuals with an accented Fourth Quadrant to also have abstract relationships to objects or other persons in which the contacts always have a certain impersonal character. This ability to objectify personal impulses requires them to develop from private persons into representative ones. In the best case scenario, this sacrifice of the private sphere is simultaneously accompanied by the development of the competence that is required in order to become a leader—whether in business, science, culture, or politics. Both humanitarian politicians and despotic dictators often have many planets in the Fourth Quadrant. However, sacrificing the private personality can also assume an entirely different dimension; for example, in the case of a mystic who becomes one with the cosmos—their individuality and subjective needs virtually dissolve.

This orientation toward the outside world with its collective values and norms suggests that the Fourth Quadrant should be associated with the extraverted attitude. Even though it belongs to the left semi-circle and is therefore defined by Ring as "organically contactless,"[153]—which tends to be expressed in a rather indirect, abstracting, and functionalizing relationship to the outside world—it can better be associated with a tendency toward extraversion than introversion. To the same extent, it can also make sense to associate the Twelfth House (located in the Fourth Quadrant) with extraversion instead of introversion since this involves the dissolution of the self into the greater whole. This is expressed especially well in mystics who overcome their selves and enter into a more comprehensive reality that transcends the human ego. At this point, the question of a clear connection of the Fourth Quadrant with one of the Jungian attitude types must be left open. Further considerations follow below in the summary.

Synopsis: Extraversion and Introversion in Jungian Psychology and Astrology

The question of introversion and extraversion in relation to the four quadrants is important, but can only be partially addressed here. In astrology, a personality structure can be represented in a very complex way due to the many combination possibilities of zodiac signs, quadrants, houses, and the planets. They show various aspects, so the typological parameters such as extraversion or introversion can only be applied in a general way to the individual structural elements such as the quadrants. Through the combination of the affected individual's structural disposition with their personal experiences and the influences of the surrounding world, there are additional differentiations and modifications. Once the individual case has been carefully studied, the attitude type can usually be recognized with relative clarity.

However, the following tendencies can be determined in summary. When we remember how Jung characterizes the introverted type as determined by the subject, this fits quite generally with the description of those with a First Quadrant disposition. In both systems, the subject and/or the individual person is the focus of interest and not the outer object. The latter is only shown a bit of interest that lasts as long as it is useful to the subject in the fulfillment of the person's own needs—and is not appreciated on its own terms. To use the words of Jung, the object is "devalued" as a result. So, the focus of interest is on the subject for Jung's introverted type, which also applies to people with a strong disposition in the First Quadrant.

The situation is exactly the other way around with the Third Quadrant as the polar opposite to the First Quadrant. The main characteristic of persons with a planetary disposition in the Third Quadrant is that they are interested in familiar persons, other people, everything foreign, and the non-I. This description fits well with Jung's characterization of the extraverted type, whose full interest relates to the factuality of the outer object.

The two other polar opposite quadrants of Second Quadrant and Fourth Quadrant cannot be classified as clearly and require a few additional considerations. People with a strongly accented Second Quadrant tend to be intensively interested in their own psyches, but as a creative, collective dimension. Artists illustrate this, for whom living out their own creativity in both the concrete and figurative sense is the main motivation in life. Although not everyone who works with dreams and fantasies is an artist, the latter must definitely have an authentic relationship with himself or herself and the archetypal depths of the psyche.

However, most people with an incisive constellation in the Second Quadrant are strongly oriented toward family matters, as well as their own rootedness in the family—and the possible problems that arise with their relatives. They are also preoccupied with their close circle of friends or even sexual love partners. At first glance, this could be related to an extraverted attitude. But the personal, inner dimension always plays an important role in the Second Quadrant, since this involves participating in an intimate experiences rooted in the instinctual and emotional world of those involved. Artists also express themselves creatively in their works, which requires self-reflection and authenticity, which suggests a more introverted attitude.

It is also necessary to mention the less positive forms that can be encountered in the Second Quadrant quite frequently, which also indicate introversion. Interest in oneself at the cost of the relationship with the partner especially comes to light when a narcissistic preoccupation with one's own erotic-sexual power of seduction, fertility, or potency moves into the foreground. This includes a focus on the subject's own sexual desires, vanities, and fears (and other narcissistic dispositions). Yet, not only the individual's self-dramatization as someone with irresistible sex appeal who needs endless the love partners as self-verification—devaluing them in the process—but also the exaltation of the father or mother as the center of the family devalues the other members of it. The children revolve around their parents due to dependence on them, and must adapt in order to receive a minimum of affection.

Although people with an accented Second Quadrant may have organic contact with the surrounding world, their motivation has a more personal and subjective nature. So the Second Quadrant could be associated with an introverted attitude—even if this is not as distinct as in the case of the First Quadrant.

So what about people who have a disposition dominated by the Fourth Quadrant? With their tendency to subjugate personal and private realms in favor of the greater whole, their orientation toward collective norms and topics, and their sense for the political and social spirit of our age—in short, with their entire orientation toward the outer world—they closely approximate Jung's extraverted type at first glance. This may even apply in special case of the Twelfth House in the Fourth Quadrant, with its dissolving tendencies that can be seen in individuals giving themselves to an object and becoming completely absorbed by it, even if this is an abstract object that can be given the name of "God," for example. This is what happens in the case of mystics.

According to Ring, people with a Fourth Quadrant disposition appear to be "organic contactless"[154] since outer objects—and therefore also fellow human beings—are not interesting to them for their own value and givenness, but become functionalized to serve the greater whole. This tendency is expressed with special clarity when the head of a state starts a war and accepts the death of thousands of people to serve a collective agenda. Another example is a venture capitalist who launches and shuts down companies, only hiring and firing people according to their functional usefulness for generating corporate profit.

We could say that the Fourth Quadrant is most closely associated with the extraverted attitude if we consider the following factors: sacrifice of the private, individual subject for the sake of adapting to collective requirements and customs; the intensive interest-related orientation toward society and public life—which includes the relationship with the object that may be functionalized but still exists.

However, the Twelfth House causes even further considerations since it is more frequently associated with seemingly introverted individuals than the two previous fields of interest, the Tenth and Eleventh Houses of the Fourth Quadrant. House Twelve is distinct in its contrast to the visibility expressed by Houses Ten and Eleven, which are associated with the spotlight of public life. The emphasis of the Twelfth House is realized largely in secret and mostly far from the eyes of the public. For example, we can think of the so-called "grey eminences" who stand in the service of a cause and can exert much power from the background without the public having any awareness of them. So this is essentially a rather invisible extraverted attitude.

However, more definite statements about how extraversion and introversion apply to each of the four quadrants is only possible within the framework of an individual horoscope.

The Twelve Houses as Archetypal Fields of Life

As already indicated, a certain house or area of interest is activated the energy of the planet that occupies it.

Here are two examples to make this less abstract: If this situation involves the Sun, the corresponding house or field focuses on our will to live, the development of our individual personality, and our creative energy, as well as a conscious approach to these themes. It relates to the topic of the "father." But if the Moon—which is associated with the "mother" and "child"—is located in this field, that relationship dynamic is constellated, along with feelings and unconscious forces that are revealed in dreams, for example (see Chapter 1, section on "The Moon" under "The Ten Planets in Astrology").[155]

The distribution of the planets in specific fields, or houses, reveals at first glance which of the twelve life areas are more important and which are less important to an individual. It also becomes clear where conflicts and blockages are inevitable and where life runs more smoothly.

Occupied and empty fields: As already described above, the houses occupied by planets have a stronger emphasis and are therefore more important than the houses that are "empty" and have no planets in them. But this does not mean that such "empty" fields cannot also be lived. For example, when a person's Fourth House—the house of the family—is empty, it is still possible to have a family. However, this will be expressed in a different way than for someone with a strong emphasis on the Fourth House.

The different sizes of the houses and enclosed zodiac signs: As soon as we have compared some horoscopes, it becomes apparent that the twelve houses can be very different in size—as briefly mentioned at the start of this chapter. A house can also be so small that it has less than 30°, which means that it is possible for two houses to start in the same sign of the zodiac. A very narrow field can obviously also start in one zodiac sign and end in the following one. As a rule, the zodiac sign at the start of a field is seen as setting the tone for the entire corresponding field or area of life. There are sometimes also very large houses that have far more than 30°, which can lead to the phenomenon of enclosed zodiac signs. This is the case in *Horoscope Example 1: Johannes* (see Chapter 5), in which the First House starts with Aquarius, contains the entire zodiac sign of Pisces and ends in Aries. Such an enclosed sign cannot adequately manifest itself—except when it is "occupied" by a planet like the enclosed Pisces is by Venus, the Goddess of Love, in *Horoscope Example 1: Johannes*.

Strength of a planet and field cusp: Planets that are located on the cusp of a field—which means at the beginning of the respective house—are particularly influential. This still applies when they are even 5° away from the line that distinguishes individual fields from each other. For the Ascendant, this can be expanded to 8–10°. For the other three lines of transition from one quadrant to the next—the Imum Coeli, Descendent, and Medium Coeli—the tolerance area is found between the two dimensions.

Here are two examples of this: When the Sun is on the Ascendant line or located up to 10° before or after it, a very strong disposition develops and leads to a personality that has its own powerful radiance. It expansively pushes its way out into life, conquers a place for itself, and creates a stage for itself there. However, if this is the antagonist of Saturn with its concentrative and rather life-inhibiting energy, we develop an entirely different basic attitude in our approach to life. This is characterized by reserve, pragmatism, and the difficulty of letting our own resources flow (cf. in Chapter 1, "The Ten Planets in Astrology").

Combinatorics: For the concrete understanding of a horoscope, it is very important to understand the way in which the planets (essential forces) can be combined with the houses (life fields) and the signs of the zodiac, as they reciprocally influence each other in their effectiveness. This corresponds to the aspect picture, which we can imagine as the conference of the gods. It will be discussed in greater detail in Chapters 4 and 5.

The twelve archetypal life fields and the twelve signs of the zodiac: The twelve houses or areas of interest are brought to life when planets occupy them. The more that the houses are activated in this way, the more multi-faceted and holistic a horoscope will be.

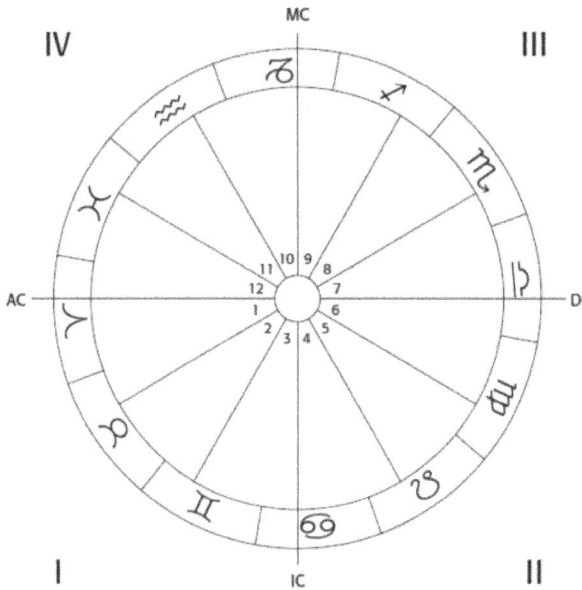

Ill. 9: The circle with the twelve houses.[156]

It makes sense when moving through the twelve areas of motivation—another way of describing the houses—to visualize the twelve zodiac signs and the zodiac in its functional sequence (cf. Chapter 2), since this specifies the qualities of the twelve houses in an exemplary way. For example, the First House is associated with the traits of energy-charged Aries, since this field always involves setting out and conquering the world—even if an entirely different sign is in the Ascendant. The style of stepping out into the world and self-assertion is imprinted and transformed by the respective zodiac sign in which the First House is located. In keeping with the twelve characteristic traits of the zodiac signs, this is different for each person.

1st House: Personality[157]

The First House introduces the First Quadrant and begins with the *Ascendant*[158]. The Ascendant is an essential point in every horoscope, and its importance increases when it is occupied by planets. Of course, it can also be quite easily felt and experienced when the First House is "empty"—when no planets are close to the Ascendant and it is only characterized by the zodiac sign in which it is located. However, its influence in a horoscope is understandably increased by the type and number of planets around the Ascendant—since planets are the energetic focus and bring their specific qualities into the houses that they "occupy."

Because the Ascendant actually shows our unconscious nature, it has an importance similar to that of the Sun in the horoscope. Since the Ascendant is close to and capable of consciousness, it should be included in the explanations of the First House. So this will occupy a bit more space than the descriptions of the other eleven areas of life.

The Ascendant line marks the start of the First House. Analogous to the zodiac that starts with the fire sign of Aries, Aries qualities are attributed to the First House (see Chapter 2, "The Four Elements in Astrology"). This even applies when one of the eleven other zodiac signs is the Ascendant. Depending on the zodiac sign that gives the Ascendant its color, the energy of departure in the first area of life expresses itself in a modified form that fits in with the elements to which it belongs: All three fire signs show an open stepping out into the world, but Aries and Sagittarius do this with much vigor. On the other hand, the earth signs prefer a slow approach, and so tend to show a certain level of hesitancy and reserve; furthermore, the third earth sign of Virgo tends to be fearful. In contrast, the air signs dance out into the world with ease and optimism. In turn, the water element tends to wait and conceal itself. This means that it is difficult to grasp.

A trained eye can recognize a person's Ascendant and the planets located in this sign of the zodiac based on certain physiognomic attributes[159] and an individual's immediate and instinctive reactions to environmental factors. This includes how they expression this through voice and movement.[160]

The Ascendant influences the way we relate to the world in an involuntary and unreflective manner—in contrast to how we might engage with the world under the influence of the Moon, which would tend to be more conscious. For example, a person with a fire Ascendant such as Aries and the Moon in Virgo in the 6th House will find that this involuntary stepping out into the world is spontaneous, courageous, and carefree. But the more conscious shaping of relationships through the Moon will be attentively approached. Every detail is taken into careful consideration and responded to. So the Ascendant and the sign in which the Moon is located do not need to coincide at all. They can be entirely different, as in the above example. These types of differences lead to the individual's colorfulness and challenge the person towards a more multi-faceted development, which isn't the case when just one element predominates.

The Ascendant or First House introduces the First Quadrant, above which the flag of the ego and egocentricity flies. The main focus is on one's own person. When people have a pronounced emphasis on the First House, they will look at everything through their subjective glasses and only recognize what serves their personal motivation. For example, if they also have the Sun in the First House, they will spare no effort in making themselves visible. They will adopt a style of clothing and behavior according to the effect that they would like to have on the surrounding world. People imprinted by the First House usually have an excellent understanding of how to present themselves in order to achieve their personal aims. This may be completely independent of (above all, this applies to people who have a fire Ascendant) or by adapting to the expectations of their social environment (especially for earth and water Ascendants).

The more planets are located in the First House or around the Ascendant—which is also called the "position of the self"—the more egocentric the individuals will be. In extreme cases, they may see themselves as the center of the world, around which everything else must revolve.[161] In any case, the subjective attitude is the measure of all things. The need to determine everything themselves and defend their own needs and interests, as well as their subjective view of the world, can come from a strong planetary constellation in the First House. Such people are only interested in their environment in so far as it is useful to them and serves them in pursuing their own interests. This leads to a perpetual struggle with the surrounding world and with fellow human beings—all of whom have their own wishes, ideas, and views. They may even pursue completely different goals than individuals with a different strong imprint by the First House.

2nd House: Property[162]

The Second House is related to the earthy and material Taurus principle, since it involves the accumulation and assimilation of building materials and means enabling the self to get a foothold in the real world and secure a place in it.

This begins with physical nutrition, which may not only be quite healthy, but also enjoyable. The instinct for quality food tends to be well developed here, as long as it is not disturbed by difficult constellations. Good physical health also requires enough sleep and moderate exercise, and securing a safe existence includes a having a place that offers protection. However, only ensuring that physical needs are met is not enough, because human beings also require emotional and intellectual nourishment. This already starts with the support received in the parental home.

The Second House is the first of three vocational houses, and the accent in the second field is on the profession as a means of securing one's livelihood. Depending on the characteristics of the Second House, the affected person's need for property can be very strong. The desire or need to have things can also manifest in the accumulation of money and all types of material things, and this includes the hoarding of personal property. Property ultimately represents a sense of security to people with this structural disposition.[163]

Primarily oriented toward the material world, this disposition results in an affinity for professions related to finance and financial management. But the approach is less like playing poker and more about looking for safe investments—whether this involves the buying and selling of securities, land and real estate, or similar products. In the second field, the topic of financial reserves is a main aspect. A regulated policy of tracking and planning income and expenditures is also important here.

The need for independence is also often pronounced for people with a disposition in the Second House. This is strongly related to the private property that they acquire on their own. Apart from real estate, this includes all types of valuable objects—furniture, works of art, jewelry, and much more. But the right to one's own body also plays a central role for their personal sense of independence: the body as an individual's private property.

Wanting to possess can also be taken in a figurative sense, which entails the hoarding and dogmatization of intellectual property. This may also mean claiming ownership of certain people and often controlling them with jealousy, in their everyday habits, or in using them for pleasure and personal satisfaction—everything becomes a "thing for me."[164]

3rd House: Career[165]

The third life field is associated with the air sign of Gemini, which sheds some light on the lifelong joy of learning and the untiring drive for further personal and educational development in this house.

Curiosity and enjoyment of communication develop in an entirely natural way during childhood, so the playful interaction with siblings and neighbor children is the first learning field in childhood. The thirst for knowledge can be satisfied in various ways: in the exchange of all kinds of news, reading books, or surfing the Internet. Systematically acquired, knowledge is further expanded through courses at school, apprenticeships, and other studies. This is supplemented by continuing education and all types of advanced training.

For people with an emphasis on the Third House, learning languages, reading, writing, and travel have a high priority. The training gained through formal, intellectual education is also important. In general, the third field characterizes the logical-rational type of thinking, which is why these individuals always raise the question of how useful their actions are.

In addition to developments that are linear, the Third House involves what can be learned through experiencing crises and new turns of events, as well as changes of positions. In summary, people with an accented third field can be described as always interested in their own life-long personality development, which also brings about many types of changes. The accent in the third field is on spontaneously seizing useful opportunities that arise in the daily flow of life.

4th House: Root cause[166]

The fourth field is related to the water sign of Cancer. With the Imum Coeli at its cusp, it introduces the Second Quadrant and its focus on how private life is shaped. In the Fourth House, the emotional interior becomes the area of interest: our own rootedness within it and anchoring in the family. The more planets around the Imum Coeli[167], the more important a personal and private framework becomes for individual development. The connection back to the parental home and the homeland, as well as the entire ancestral milieu, are central values here. Inherited possessions—especially houses and land—form a good biotope for the development of people with an accented fourth field. An intimate relationship with nature is the result.

Seen in archetypal terms, this is the mother's realm of home and hearth. However, we now know that this does not have to be restricted to women, since men can also show strong maternal qualities and an active interest in cultivating and maintaining the home. When things go well, each family member has an individual opportunity for development within the scope of the "family" as an organism. The precondition for this is a good atmosphere and specific rules in which a certain, limited space is given to the individual. The retreat to the private sphere makes it possible for people to come to themselves and find themselves.

Parallel to the development of the individual natural dispositions, those imprinted by the Fourth House acquire their own personal standards. Their basic nature with their early childhood memory images plays a central role in the fourth field. The unconscious with its various personal and the archetypal layers is the main source for self-discovery.[168]

Life begins and ends in the Fourth House. We are born as babies into a family context and reap in old age the fruits or problems that correspond with whether we have lived our self-realization or not.

5th House: Procreation[169]

In keeping with its association with the fiery Leo principle, the Fifth House involves all avenues of playfully self-expressing. This includes the sex drive both within the framework of love relationships and as a path of adventure. Potency, and the ability to conceive a child when there is a desire to have one, are also included in the Fifth House. When children are present, the issue at the forefront of how parents relate to the child is whether the child will serve as a bearer of hope for the parent's own ideas. Or, do the parents succeed in promoting the child's own dispositions and talents? The care and education of children—whether they are our own offspring or our students—always has something playful attached to it, which is why this field could also be called a playground.

In the case of planets in the fifth field, artistic talent may be constellated. In addition to conceiving children and giving birth to them, there are also figurative children in the sense of creative works or projects. In this process, all of the expansive planets such as the Sun, Mars, Jupiter, or even the Moon and Neptune—and obviously, the aesthetic principle of Venus—can support such a talent. Whether or not this talent is developed then depends on the training and promotion of it. The central point in every case is the possibility of sublimating the vital instincts and expressing them through creativity. Yet, very few people achieve a high aesthetic level in this process. It is much more common for them to exhaust the creative potential in dilettantism and in cultivating all types of hobbies.

Among the problems that may constellate in the fifth field and must be mastered are the lack of moderation in play and enjoyment, which can be manifested in eating and drinking, sexuality, gambling, and the speculative handling of money and other resources. The love of pleasure can easily escalate into addiction and waste. An example of this is when the Sun, Jupiter, the Moon, Neptune, or Pluto are located either individually or in conjunction with each other in the Fifth House. So the task of educating ourselves to be moderate on all levels is given in the Fifth House.

6th House: Work[170]

The house associated with Virgo is the second vocational house, and this is primarily related to service. The focus is on our own body, taking care of it, and keeping it healthy since only a healthy body can perform well. Themes such as a wholesome and regular diet, moderate exercise, sufficient sleep, and restoring the body's balance after an illness are important in the sixth field.

Analogous to the associated Virgo principle, this also involves the acquisition of manual and intellectual skills, as well as the specialization of services, and their methodical and technical application. This includes the consistent, proper care and maintenance of working materials, in addition to professional dealings with colleagues, employees, or bosses. If this is not accomplished and friction arises, work is disrupted and many resources lie idle or are wasted.

The last field of the family quadrant plays an essential role for all facets of household management, ranging from the procurement of everyday necessities, to the skillful and moderate handling of money. Keeping order in all areas of everyday life—at the job and privately— makes effective, uncomplicated work possible. Adequate clothing to adapt to the respective temperature and situation also belongs to the sixth area of life, as well as all questions of hygiene.

Depending on the type of planets and zodiac signs in the Sixth House, the individuals may succeed in leading a regulated and ritualized life, which benefits their health. For example, the Sun or the Moon makes it easier for people to have a healthy approach to their comprehensive physical needs. On the other hand, Saturn or the trans-Saturnian planets of Pluto, Neptune, and Uranus indicate problems with a regular, natural, and adequate relationship to everyday body care—especially in the basal areas such as diet, exercise, and sleep.

7th House: Living together[171]

This field introduces the Third Quadrant and is the House of Libra, the start of which is determined by the Descendent. This is the transition point from the subject to the object, where the other person enters the field of vision in his or her autonomy and confronts the subject as another to exchange or battle with.

If a horoscope has an accumulation of planets around the Descendent[172], which is also called the "you point," the outer world is very important for the development of individual. The topic of closeness and distance is always constellated in the seventh field. Here as well, the type of involved planets also plays a major role in addition to the zodiac signs present, since they provide indications as to whether the individuals live or block their interest in the world, with its people and objects. This shows whether they are open to influences from their surroundings—allowing themselves to respond and be guided by them—or whether they influence and guide their surrounding world or would like to shut it out. The main thing here is to perceive and recognize the other person's rights and personality, which requires intellectual and communicative involvement with whatever is other or foreign.

On the one hand, this is about the assertion of the subject against the outer world; on the other hand, it involves interacting and connecting with it. This is especially the case in a life partnership such as marriage[173] in which two individuals learn to bridge their differences time and again, achieving a hard-earned commonality and harmony in this way. However, when the other person's shortcomings and one's own weaknesses cause dissonances, misunderstandings and disappointments—and getting stuck in them—can result in conflicts and separation.

As already mentioned, the way in which people deal with the outer world depends very much on the respective planets around the Descendent. If expansive or belligerent forces are in effect—such as the two male planets of the Sun and Mars that constellate the issues of dominance and aggression—conflict often results in the encounter with the object, especially if Mars is located in the seventh field. Individuals behave quite differently when, for example, the two main feminine forces of the Moon and Venus are located in the Seventh House. They support an empathetic, adaptable, and charming attitude toward the surrounding world, which can make it easier to live in a relationship.

In contrast to the Fifth House—in which love and sexuality tend to be lived more freely, spontaneously, and related to the present moment—the seventh field often involves binding, long-term relationships and life-long partnerships.

8th House: Background of life[174]

The Eighth House is related to the water sign of Scorpio. This is about expanding the life interests to the extended social environment and participating in tasks that benefit the common good and collective resources.

As a result, many people with an accented disposition in the Eighth House can be found in social welfare and tax offices, wealth management, security agencies, and political parties of all kinds. In times of upheaval and crises, which can also be caused by wars, they are confronted with the depreciation of money on the one hand and economic growth and the establishment of prosperity on the other hand. Socially significant ups and downs of profits and losses, growth, destruction, and reconstruction also belong to the domain of the Eighth House. The qualities found in the Eighth House include the strong ability of the respective persons to attune to the tone of social and state institutions such as offices, ministries, institutes, etc. Such people become involved in administration and allocation of communal or similar public property.

The ambivalences of the eighth area of life can manifest in many ways. In addition to people who receive legal inheritances or even voluntarily contribute large donations to non-profit purposes, there are war and inflation profiteers who enrich themselves at the expense of the community. People who engage in tax evasion are also quite common. Even destroying social security can be fueled by various reasons. Either old political forms are to be dissolved in favor of new ones—in which case a will to reform is at work—or this happens for asocial motives.

As soon as human beings become socially and societally involved, they are confronted with the concrete conditions and contradictory tendencies of a community. They become affected by this and can either allow themselves to be carried away by the atmosphere of their social environment or they can be burdened by the tensions and conflicts between opposing camps. Both of these alternatives have an effect on the mental, emotional, and physical levels.

So the question of life-long physical and psychological exertion is especially present in the eighth field. On the one hand, this is accompanied by the topics of regeneration, but involves fatigue and wear, aging, and death on the other hand. In terms of the resilience that provides psychological elasticity, as well as the power of regeneration and resistance, the Eighth House with its planetary constellations and respective zodiac signs offer points of reference. For example, the zodiac sign of Scorpio and its associated planets of Mars and Pluto favor regeneration; however, the less elastic signs such as Taurus or Capricorn, as well as the planet

Saturn, tend to bring wear and tear with them (cf. the descriptions of the zodiac signs and planetary principles in Chapter 1 and 2).

The focus on the background of life—i.e. the realities concealed behind what is superficially visible or recognizable—usually creates an interest in thresholds of all types, which also include metaphysical issues. The theme of passing and rebirth, of transience and permanence, is also located in the Eighth House. This is where the Scorpio principle of "dying and becoming" is echoed in a very general way.

9th House: Key goals[175]

The ninth field correlates with the fiery Sagittarius principle, which expansively reaches out into the distance as it aims for both short- and long-term goals. If there is a strong emphasis on the ninth field in a horoscope, this favors exploration beyond the milieu of origin, together with the very general impulse to go beyond everyday life with its limitations. For example, people who are strongly influenced by the disposition of the Ninth House find it easy to emigrate and leave behind their origins without major problems.

They usually have much interest in different fields of knowledge and geographical, historical, legal, theological, ethnological, and mythological topics. Everything that broadens the mind becomes interesting to them. These can be the fruitful impressions gained from research and discovery trips abroad, enthusiastic participation in religious communities or political reform movements, and bigger economic and technical developments in areas such as world trade and international transport.

The entire world becomes an adventure. The best comparison for the orientation of this disposition is a tendency toward cosmopolitanism. Engagement in international organizations that unite nations and work for the common good or collaboration on interdisciplinary research projects, as well as on cultural progress on the whole, is relevant for people with an imprint from the Ninth House. They set far-reaching goals and strive for teaching positions at universities and other public educational institutions, for example. They also like to participate in scholarly and student exchanges.

The ninth field always involves superlatives. This means that a "selection of the immortals"[176]—which can be found among authors of world literature and other important thinkers, teachers, and leaders of humanity—are the major role models for people with such a house disposition. As a result, a philosophical inclination aimed at the "education of the human race"[177] and study of the last things, and what is eternal, are also very important here. Prophetic intuition and spiritual visions and dreams are sometimes also possible in this context.[178]

10th House: Public sphere[179]

People with a strongly emphasized Tenth House, the start of which is determined by the Medium Coeli,[180] feel vocationally called into professions in the public sphere. The Tenth House is strongly emphasized when the Sun or planets such as the Moon, Jupiter, Saturn, and Mars, or even Venus, are placed there. The tenth field is associated with the earth sign of Capricorn and introduces the Fourth Quadrant, which is characterized by anonymity and organic contactlessness. It contrasts with the privacy of the Fourth House at the start of the Second Quadrant.

While intimacy is lived out in the fourth field of life in the family quadrant, and addresses the private or inner depths of the human being, the polar opposite of the Tenth House calls for everything that is private to be set aside so that individuals with the corresponding disposition can develop into representative, collective persons. This means dealing with public reality, which in turn requires mastering outer structures. This applies to any public position and implies consideration of the predominate norms and views of the collective. The individual is ultimately supported through anonymous public opinion and promoted to public offices, which are usually linked with rank and prestige, power, and fame.

However, individuals can hardly achieve key positions of politics and the economy or even culture without urgent ambition. But pronounced ambition alone is not enough: The corresponding competences must also exist and the required services that appeal to the zeitgeist and the general public must be performed.

The rise and fall are close to each other, as the fates of politicians, financiers, and other public persons such as artists or scientists have shown time and again.[181] So it often happens that the polar opposites of private emotional and erotic-sexual needs – which frequently must be very much suppressed in a daily life that is subject to public observation – assert themselves at the most inappropriate moments and expand into scandal in the light of the public eye. This can wreck an otherwise glorious career. In addition, there are many other kinds of private interests for people in a public function that can cause conflicts with their roles and bring about their demise.

11th House: Spirit of the times[182]

The Eleventh House is characterized by the air sign of Aquarius. The eleventh field can be seen as a window to the world since people with a pronounced emphasis on this house have a sense for what currently interests and moves humanity. They easily grasp the prevailing Zeitgeist or spirit of the times, which makes it possible for them to always "have their finger on the pulse of society." Depending on the type of planets located in the Eleventh House, an individual can easily find patrons, advisors, and promoters, as well as the corresponding protection and support, for their planned projects. However, such individuals can also be misled into failure if these advisors and friends are not adequately in tune with the Zeitgeist.

Participation in the spirit of the times inspires certain people with an emphasis on the Eleventh House; in turn, they are also willing to promote blossoming talents. However, usually there is not enough effort given to become a patron, but sometimes just a party animal. When this is the case, it is important for the individual to be everywhere, not miss out on anything, and adorn themselves with "friends"—especially those who are in vogue at the moment. With the fading of their hipness, they are then dropped in favor of a new star that is rising on the social horizon.

The majority of the people with an emphasis in the eleventh field become exhausted the incessant need to see and be seen at the relevant events. However, small talk can also turn into a real art and be applied strategically for social-political purposes: for example, when it is used by diplomats.

The eleventh area of life is dominated by the idea of the intimate intellectual friendship with all of its advantages and disadvantages. The clique system functions according to sympathy and antipathy—like-minded people "belong" and others are excluded. But if egoistic interests predominate, these become purely utilitarian relationships in which "friends" just serve a function—which can take the form of nepotism and result in corruption.

The Eleventh House is ultimately about actively living our shared interests within the relaxed community of worldly peers, with its countless facets and great diversity of human beings. This can have very different benefits for the world. In comparison to the party animal who wants to see others and be seen, as mentioned a moment ago, diplomats—for whom a strong emphasis on the Eleventh House is advantageous—may accomplish much in terms of establishing positive relations of their country with other nations. But what everyone with one or more planets such as the Sun, the Moon, Jupiter, Saturn, Venus, or Mars in the Eleventh House has in common—despite all of their differences—is the theme of having a communicative connection with a smaller or larger collective.

12th House: Anonymity[183]

The last house in the circle of the horoscope is connected with the water sign of Pisces. In one very essential point, it differs from the two preceding fields of ten and eleven, both of which are also related to the public: In the twelfth field, everything takes place in secret and actions are based on anonymity.

As described earlier, this can involve anonymous powers such as the "grey eminences" of the times—those who pull the strings in the background of the economy and politics. Often the individual is sacrificed in the wake of major societal shifts.[184] Even dark power politics—exemplified by Mafia organizations in increasingly more parts of the world, which operate by extorting protection money, as well as threatening and murdering individuals—have an affinity with the Twelfth House.

On the other hand, self-sacrificing anonymous heroes and heroines in civilian life and wartime are associated with the Twelfth House, the field of ego dissolution. This also includes people who have gone to rack and ruin, become marginal social figures, or have fallen completely out of the social systems, like missing and displaced persons, refugees, or the homeless.

The mentally ill, as well as impoverished people, are often shuffled off to corresponding institutions. Depending on the legal, ethical, and moral level of a state, they are either given good care or tortured and murdered.[185] Deprivation is also possible.

In addition to psychiatric clinics, hospitals, rehabilitation centers, and health resorts, the world's concealed and secluded areas also include children's institutions, boarding schools, homes for children with behavioral problems, refugee camps, prisons, and concentration camps.[186]

Also included here, are places for retreat and religious devotion like a monastery. Secluded from the public world, the monks and nuns of certain orders pray for the good of humanity, write books[187], and teach, in addition to making foods or art, and providing other cultural services. Mystics who purify their ego through prayer and meditation are also among the people shaped by the Twelfth House. In addition to religious and private aid organizations, there are always many unknown helpers in mass catastrophes such as earthquakes, floods, and hurricanes.

The Twelfth House can be genuinely associated with everything that is secret, the invisible, and the unknown. Many mysterious things also happen here in the lives of individuals—who are often not just a mystery to themselves, but also for other people. Solitude can be used well for a retreat into one's inner being—whether through meditative techniques, writing a journal, or silence. This can allow space for what is unconscious and unspeakable, perhaps even allowing it to come to light.

4
Interacting Dispositions and the Influences of the Surrounding World: Aspect Structure and Complex Structure

The importance that astrological aspects have for a horoscope has already been discussed several times in the previous sections. But what does "aspect" actually mean? According to the origin of the word, aspect means "sight" (Latin: *aspectus*). Within our context, this means the view of the Earth from the changing angle of relationships between the planets in their orbit, the ecliptic.[188] Ring provides the vivid example of the Sun and the Moon, which we can observe with our own eyes: "Around every four weeks with the suitable visual conditions, we can experience that while the Sun is setting on the Western horizon, the Moon is just rising above the horizon in the eastern sky opposite from it. What powerfully presents itself to our eyes in this way is an aspect of the Sun and Moon, their opposition or the angle of 180°."[189] In addition to this example of an opposition between the two heavenly bodies, there are further aspects that will be presented in the following section.

Aspect Structure in the Horoscope

There are two groups of aspects, the *synthetic* and the *analytical*. Since the value judgments of popular astrology still lurk around in the background of many minds, it is important to dispel the notion that there are "good" and "bad" aspects—an erroneous valuation also attached to zodiac signs and planets. There are both constructive and destructive possibilities in synthetic and analytical aspects. And every aspect has the potential for development.[190]

Within this context, it is important to note that the person's level of consciousness and general state of development can*not* be determined solely on the basis of an aspect picture—which is the picture of the planets in relationship to each other at the time of birth—in the same way that it is not possible to do this based on the zodiac signs involved. People's level of differentiation, as well as their ethical character, can only be intuited or determined through living contact with them.

When astrology speaks of a *synthetic* aspect, it means the effortless, smooth interaction of two essential forces; there is a type of obviousness and ease to this, so it often does not become conscious at all. If it does, the interaction is felt to be harmonious. These essential forces help to balance psychological tension and promote the success of plans, projects, and enterprises—since everything is easier, allowing us to reap and enjoy much fruit.

In subjective experience, the synthetic aspects usually feel very pleasant because they support relaxation and the sense of well-being. However, this harmony-oriented cooperation between two essential forces also has its shadow side, that can lead to sluggishness and self-satisfaction. This can give individuals the sense that they are something special, even if they only have average talents and—in the worst case—they can just take each day as it comes in a state of inertia without any regret. The tendency toward self-reflection and self-criticism is usually diminished in such individuals, much to the chagrin of the outside world.

Many people maintain the view, based on popular astrology, that harmonious aspects (synthetic aspects) are "good" and tension generating aspects (analytical aspects) are "bad." Perhaps a drastic image will show the possible harmfulness of synthetic aspects. Two criminals—which have excellent chemistry with each other—plan a robbery murder.

The murderer and the robber work together so perfectly that they can successfully murder another human being and enrich themselves at the same time. Even though such a team may feel attuned subjectively, the two of them are harmful for the greater whole: society.

The same applies to an individual's overall personality, which can be sabotaged in its development through well-attuned mechanisms of inertia, self-satisfaction, and thoughtlessness. However, if the synthetic aspects can be constructively integrated into the overall system and have a supporting function within the individual's development, they are extraordinarily useful.

On the other hand, *analytical* aspects express the tension between essential forces. Such structurally based conflicts demand much attention from the affected individuals, since they disturb necessary processes with ambivalence, obstruction, and misunderstanding, which can lead to setbacks and failures.

Such conflicts can occur within an individual person and express themselves in self-doubts, fears, energetic blockages, anger, and frustration. These tensions and conflicts usually also lead to corresponding problems in relationships. This is what frequently prompts self-reflection, which allows the individual to become aware of what is disturbing their inner balance. If the affected person tackles the problem and grabs the bull by the horns, they can experience far-reaching development and generate a great deal of new energy. This leads to a different way of treating oneself and the outside world. Accordingly, analytical aspects are the actual motor of development in a birth chart, but this requires constant work on oneself. In addition, the influences of surrounding planets in a field play an important role. There is a big difference between whether they just fuel the conflicts or also create relaxation and helpfully support the affected individuals when they struggle with themselves and the world. In the latter case, these persons can establish new levels of balance and continue to grow.

Within this context, it is interesting to note the observation made by Ring—who conducted in-depth studies of many extraordinary personalities[191]—that many, if not all, geniuses and great public figures had a large number of high-tension aspects in their horoscopes. The accompanying conflicts and inner dangers associated with them had driven these individuals to their continuous self-development. In contrast, synthetic aspects are frequently found in the horoscopes of average citizens.[192]

The following tables outline important information on aspects, after which the most significant aspects that play a role in astrological birth charts will be discussed. Concrete examples are provided in Chapter 5.

Table 1 gives an overview of the number of aspects resulting from geometric divisions of the zodiac (360°), which generate certain degrees of angles between the planets:[193]

Symbol	Name	Degrees	Part of circle
☌	Conjunction	0°	0/1
☍	Opposition	180°	1/2
△	Trine	120°	1/3
□	Square	90°	1/4
Q	Quintile	72°	1/5
bQ	Biquintile	144°	2/5
✳	Sextile	60°	1/6
∠	Semi-square	45°	1/8
⛝	Sesquiquadrate	135°	3/8
⊻	Semi-sextile	30°	1/12
⊼	Quincunx	150°	5/12

Table 1: Overview of the aspects

Strong effect	Medium effect	Weak effect
Conjunction*	Sextile (blue)	Quintile (blue)*
Opposition (red)	Quincunx[194] (green)	Biquintile (blue)*
Trine (blue)	Semi-sextile[195] (blue)	Semi-square (red)
Square (red)		Sesquiquadrate (red)

* Is not drawn in the aspect picture but taken into consideration in the interpretation.

Table 2: Ranking of the aspect according to their degree of strength as strong – medium – weak (the colors correspond with the aspect quality; see Table 3)

Synthetic (blue)	In between*	Analytical (red)
Trine	Conjunction	Opposition
Sextile	Quincunx (green)	Square
Quintile		Semi-square
Biquintile		Sesquiquadrate
Semi-sextile		

* The conjunction is "colorless"; only the Quincunx is green.

Table 3: Aspect quality with respect to synthetic and analytical and "in between"

The Orb Table

Orbis is Latin for circle. The planets are related to other planets by the specific formation of angles (aspects). Each aspect can still be effective, even if the planets deviate from these angles to a certain extent. The stronger the planet—starting with the Sun as the strongest—the larger the deviations are allowed to be. The weaker the planet, the smaller the orb value (deviation from the exact angle formation) must be. The Orb Table provides information on which aspect is still possible for which deviation. So the Sun can still form an aspect with a 15° deviation from an exact angle in conjunctions (0°), oppositions (180°), squares (90°), and trines (120°). The aspects obviously get weaker when the deviation is larger. This is expressed in the horoscope drawing through the line thickness: The more exact the aspect, the thicker the line. However, the thickness of the line depends not only on the strength of the involved planets and exactness of the angle formation (aspects), but also on the strength of the aspects (see Table 2). This point is explained below.

In the Orb Table, it also becomes apparent that the strong aspects of conjunction (0°), opposition (180°), square (90°), and trine (120°) are followed by the medium aspect of the sextile (60°), which when formed with the Sun is only allowed to deviate by 10°. Only a 5° deviation is valid for the Sun in the half-sextile (30°), the quincunx (150°), the semi-square (45°), and the sesquiquadrate (135°). So the thickness of the line—which makes the effectiveness of an aspect clear—includes both the strength of the planets and their aspects. The thicker the line, the more influential it is in a horoscope.

Degree Orb Table:	0°	180°	90°	120°	60°	30°	150°	45°	135°	
to the Sun	15.00	15.00	15.00	15.00	10.00	5.00	5.00	5.00	5.00	d + r
to the Moon	12.00	12.00	12.00	12.00	8.00	4.00	4.00	4.00	4.00	d + r
to Mercury	7.00	7.00	7.00	7.00	5.00	3.00	3.00	3.00	3.00	d + r
to Venus	7.00	7.00	7.00	7.00	5.00	3.00	3.00	3.00	3.00	d + r
to Mars	7.00	7.00	7.00	7.00	5.00	3.00	3.00	3.00	3.00	d + r
to Jupiter	9.00	9.00	9.00	9.00	6.00	3.30	3.30	3.30	3.30	d + r
to Saturn	9.00	9.00	9.00	9.00	6.00	3.30	3.30	3.30	3.30	d + r
to Uranus	5.00	5.00	5.00	5.00	5.00	3.00	3.00	3.00	3.00	d + r
to Neptune	5.00	5.00	5.00	5.00	5.00	3.00	3.00	3.00	3.00	d + r
to Pluto	5.00	5.00	5.00	5.00	5.00	3.00	3.00	3.00	3.00	d + r
to the Moon's Node[196]	0.00	0.00	0.00	0.00	0.00	0.00	0.00	0.00	0.00	only r
to AC	0.00	0.00	0.00	0.00	0.00	0.00	0.00	0.00	0.00	only r
to MC	0.00	0.00	0.00	0.00	0.00	0.00	0.00	0.00	0.00	only r

Table 4: Orb Table: The possible scope for the astrological aspects depends on the strength of the planets.

Abbreviations in the table: d = direct and r = retrograde.

Conjunction 0° ♂ (aspects in between / ambivalence aspects)

Within the context of this aspect, ambivalence means that a conjunction may be experienced as harmonious under certain conditions (blue/synthetic aspects) but is experienced as tense under other conditions (red/analytical aspects). If two or more planets are located next to each other in a conjunction and even form a planet agglomeration, the essential forces of several planets may even manifest simultaneously on a certain field and can therefore either concentrate and amplify, or block each other. The resulting dynamic must then be worked on by individuals in order to develop, so they do not stay stuck in blockages or eternal ambivalences. Here are two examples:

Sun-Venus Conjunction ☉☌ ♀

In this case, there is a harmonious interaction between the two "gods" of the Sun and Venus. The effect on the person is that they are attuned to harmony and balance in their basic attitude, as well as being interested in everything that is beautiful—which often includes art and culture. So the tendency is to enjoy life and love pleasure, erotic and otherwise.

Sun-Saturn Conjunction ☉☌ ♄

The Sun and Saturn are two major antagonists that work against each other and can block each other. The Sun's yes to life encounters Saturn's no, and the will for self-development (the Sun) meets reality (Saturn), whereby boundaries are set to the joy of expansion. However, some obstacles and limitations also contribute to the protection of the personality by sparing it from hubris and inflation.

☍ Oppositions 180° and Squares 90° □ (analytical aspects)

The Opposition ☍

If two planets have a polar opposition to each other, this results in the greatest possible tension. An opposition aspect is an actual tensile test. The major challenge for individuals is to do justice to both of these essential forces, which as a rule are located in polar opposite signs of the zodiac and represent opposing areas of interest. These would like to develop according to completely different biotopes. This requires deliberate, conscientious work so that both essential forces can succeed in developing within their respective field.

If the conflict remains unconscious, it will control the individual and remain stuck in a state of ambivalence and tension. Or it one of the archetypal powers and split off and repressed, and sinks into the unconscious as a result. Here in its concealed state, it begins to make trouble and does everything it can to be taken into consideration in the person's life.

For a certain amount of time, people affected by this may be able to live with such an inner division. But a crisis usually occurs at some point, because the denied side finally wants to come into its own. Then the affected person may change from one pole to another, for example, and virtually turn his or her life upside down. This jumping back and forth from one pole to the other while simultaneously splitting off the respective other pole prevents holistic development and also causes a great deal of restlessness and stress in the social environment. The person is also very susceptible to conflicts in the surrounding world, which are experienced with great intensity. In this way, more inner tension arises due to the outer effects and this comes at the price of personal balance. If such a disposition that is sensitive to conflict remains unconscious, the result can also be neurotic developments and psychosomatic illnesses.

But things do not have to go this far. Here is an example to illustrate this description and how it may be resolved:

The Sun-Moon Opposition ☉ ☍ ☽

In the case of a Sun-Moon opposition, the affected person's feeling (the Moon) and intellect (the Sun) drift apart. This leads to a weakening of the self-image and self-confidence. In turn, the ambivalent signals to the outside world lead to correspondingly contradictory responses that additionally unsettle the affected person.

With the Sun and the Moon, the archetypes of father and mother are constellated in an incompatible way. A person in this state often has experienced a conflict-filled relationship between the actual parents, followed by separation and divorce. The individual's own relationships are also subject to the same tension. The conflict between professional development and the desire for children and a family life is also constellated here. Becoming aware of the Sun-Moon opposition generally leads to an increase in tolerance toward the partner; on the other hand, it leads to the knowledge that the inner conflict can only be satisfied by creative solutions that help enliven both the intellect and feelings, as well as professional ambitions and the desire for a family. This awareness of the contradictory dispositions can bring great enrichment to a person's life.

The Square □

Much of what was said about oppositions also applies to the square. In the example of the Sun-Moon square, there is also a tension between feeling and reason; all of the other kinds of conflicts that have been addressed under opposition are also virulent in the square aspect.

But while the tendency toward division and splitting off must be kept in mind for oppositions, the experience with the tension of ninety degrees—in which case there are also two different elements and areas of interest that want to assert themselves against each other—is more a matter of incessant friction between the involved essential forces. The two "gods," so to speak, are in a permanent conflict with each other. Such constant friction can produce a great deal of energy and can shake the individual awake so that he or she grows as a result, provided that there is the will to develop consciousness.

Sun Square Moon ☉ □ ☾

In the Sun-Moon example, the archetypal parental couple is fixated on each other in a conflicting way in the individual's psyche. The mother and father archetype or the mother and father complexes based on them are caught in an eternal dispute with each other; the self-image and partner image also contradict each other, which has a correspondingly unfavorable effect on concrete partnerships and can rarely be resolved by switching partners. We can easily imagine how much of the involved energy is released either in the tension and aggression or simply blocked, which is not exactly conducive to the creative shaping of a life.

However, there are possibilities for taking an entirely different, constructive approach in dealing with such a structural disposition, which is also called the "Sisyphus aspect."[197] But the precondition for this is that individuals have a growing understanding of themselves. Again, becoming aware is one of the magic formulas; the other is having a positive attitude toward the necessary struggle. After all, the essential forces involved do not work together voluntarily, but seek independence and want to move in different directions. Only when this never-ending demand for balance is confronted, is it possible to use this high-intensity engine of the square for personal development. If a person succeeds in using this energetic power plant correctly and finds a fruitful way of dealing with it, the energies generated in a square can be converted into creative accomplishment[198]—instead of repeatedly just throwing hot sparks and ultimately burning out.

Trine 120° △ and Sextile 60° ✳ (synthetic aspects)

The Trine △

The trine symbolizes a conversation of the gods that takes place in harmony and agreement. Things are easy and smooth, demanding no conscious exertion on the part of the individual. The communication between the involved essential forces takes places automatically and freely. Like all synthetic connections between the planets, trigonal aspects favor a reduction of tensions, such as those generated by squares. As a result, they contribute to harmonizing mental states.

If several trines interact—for example, by forming a large blue (synthetic) triangle in a birth chart—they mutually optimize each other. The flow of energy is smooth. Such a large blue triangle is also casually called a "talent triangle" because people who are blessed with it can more easily bring their creative gifts to light than someone without trines. But rarely do trines lead to the development of real genius like that found in Michelangelo.

With trines, individuals unconsciously attract situations in which they are "in the right place at the right time" and things play into their hands. Perhaps because the sense of satiety that tends to exist in trines, along with the diminishment of self-questioning, the resulting sluggishness often means that people who have many trines only allow their talents to blossom to some extent. Yet, they believe that their own significance is invaluable to the world. However, when someone has tension aspects in their horoscope, they could use the calm, flowing energy source of the trine, which has a balancing effect on centers of conflict in both the inner psychological household and in interpersonal relationships.

Sun Trine Moon ☉ △ ☾

If the Sun and Moon form a trine, feeling and reason work together harmoniously in individuals and promote an adequate evaluation of situations and people. The parental complexes are experienced as well-matched, and the actual parents are often idealized as a couple. The conflicts between them are experienced as less intense than they actually are. Personal relationships the choice of a partner are generally—unless other constellations bring strong dissonances into the overall disposition—under a favorable star. In the professional environment, much succeeds without a lot of effort or when effort is given it is usually rewarded with success. However, this can lead to an overestimation of one's own abilities.

The Sextile ✶

The sextile has a relaxing effect on the analytical aspects when it is connected with them, and generally has harmonizing and supportive qualities.

Sun Sextile Moon ☉ ✶ ☾

Quite similar to a trine—but less intense in its effect—the Sun sextile Moon supports a harmonious connection between the inner father and the inner mother, which is reflected in the undisturbed interaction of the mind and feelings. This in turn leads to a positive effect: on the one hand, this can be shown in a correspondingly positive self-perception and self-assurance; on the other hand, this is seen in the positive perception of others. As a result, this supports cooperative relationships in both private and professional life.

Quincunx 150° ⚼ (intermediate aspects / "aspects of longing")

The Quincunx ⚼

The quincunx appears as a subtle energy that can be compared to Neptunian's ethereal quality; it has an effect that is rather hidden but very lasting. These two essential forces, which stand in an aspect of 150° to each other, long to enter into a relationship with each other. But as is typical for longing, the desired object usually remains unattainable in the end. This restless striving toward each other, which is unable to achieve its goal, or only partially achieves it, can best be worked through in creative work that continually seeks to express itself in new ways.

Sun Quincunx Moon ☉ ⚻ ☾

If the Sun and Moon stand in a quincunx to each other, the relationship of intellect and feeling is determined by a reciprocal longing. The same applies to the relationship between the parental images, as well as to relationships with others. This can give the affected individuals the feeling that they are never really comfortable in the current partnership. The longing for a fulfilling contact often keeps driving them in their search for the ideal partner—but these seekers will not reach their goal and find peace on this level. Becoming conscious of the nature of the longing is essential in order to find a creative way of dealing with it.

Semi-Sextile 30° ⚺ and Other Fine Aspects

For the sake of completeness, the weaker aspects of the quintile Q, biquintile bQ, semi-square, and sesquiquadrate are included in the above table. However, they will not be discussed more extensively regarding their possible effects in an astrological birth chart within the scope of this book. It will suffice to include their effects in the concrete interpretations of the various horoscope examples in Chapter 5.

The aspect picture—which results from the interaction between the individual planetary positions within the zodiac—can be imagined as a conference among the gods. As already mentioned in Chapter 1, these gods are the equivalent of the most common archetypes, around which the corresponding complexes develop through experiences in the world. There is an archetype behind every complex; for example, there is a mother archetype behind a mother complex. There will be more about this in the following section, which is intended to provide more detailed information on the topic of "complexes"—since these are of primary interest when interpreting a horoscope.

C. G. Jung's Complex Theory

The word "complex" is actually a psychological term coined by Jung, but has long become a part of everyday language. As early as 1934, in his inaugural lecture at the ETH Zurich, titled *A General Review of Complex Theory*, Jung said: "Everyone knows nowadays that people 'have complexes.'"[199] Somewhat sardonically, he added: "What is not so well known, though far more important theoretically, is that complexes can have us."[200] With this formulation, Jung wanted to make it clear that human freedom can be temporarily restricted by the existence of complexes in the psyche; namely, when a complex becomes activated or constellated.

Everyone has probably had the experience more than once of being in the grip of a complex and controlled by it in terms of its corresponding emotional state and behavior. However, it is easier to recognize such complex reactions in others than in ourselves. We clearly see how someone else literally loses control and cannot be calmed down by any rational argument—until the complex-based emotional reaction has subsided. Then they once again become themselves, so to speak, and we can talk to them. However, identifying with a complex often means that we lack the necessary distance to recognize it as such and free ourselves from embrace of this overwhelming emotion. In such a situation, it becomes clear that the unity of consciousness can easily be broken and disturbed by an emotion—if it is stronger than the conscious will to be calm, confident, and controlled.[201]

Because of the strong emotional dimension of a complex, Jung often referred to them as *feeling-toned complexes*. In the words of Jung, this is "the image of a certain psychic situation which is strongly accentuated emotionally."[202] After the complex-related emotional surge subsides, we often feel ashamed, because we realize that our habitual attitude and its accompanying behavior have been temporarily possessed and we have involuntarily shown a side of ourselves that we would have preferred to hide from the surrounding world. When such a strong and uncontrollable emotional reaction overrides the normal conscious attitude, it is so massively surprising because it flashes into consciousness like a foreign object.

The feeling-oriented complex owes its penetrating power to its strong inner unity. It behaves quite autonomously within the space of an individual's consciousness, just like a foreign object with a life of its own. For example, it can also be encountered in mistakes[203], of which Jung gives some vivid examples:

> Complexes . . . seem to delight in playing impish tricks. They slip just the wrong word into one's mouth . . . they cause a tickle in the throat just when the softest passage is being played on the piano at the concert, they make the tiptoeing latecomer trip over a chair with a resounding crash . . . they bid us congratulate the mourners at a burial instead of condoling with them.[204]

Especially because feeling-toned complexes are energy centers (which lead an autonomous existence in the unconscious due to being split off from consciousness), when they are triggered, they not only can be experienced during the day in vehement emotional reactions or mistakes—but also at night when we dream. The persons or animals acting in our dreams are emotions depicted as images that are intensive enough to emerge from the darkness of the unconscious and play a role in the dream events.

Jung also understands the complexes as "splinter psyches" that often have their origin in a trauma or an emotional shock.[205] However, not just traumatic shocks are involved in the creation of complexes in our psyche. Many individual experiences with the surrounding world that repeatedly trigger emotional reactions in human beings, accumulate, and increasingly condense those experiences into a certain emotion. At the same time, these repeated emotional experiences that condense into a feeling-toned complex are not invariably negative. On the contrary, complexes can also be characterized by very positive emotions.

The Meaning of the Mother and Father Complexes and their Archetypal Core

The best way to illustrate the nature of a complex is to use the example of the mother and father complex, since everyone has a mother and father—even if they were never present, or especially so—and therefore also has a mother complex and a father complex. These parental complexes can be more positively or more negatively constellated, which correspondingly influences our attitude toward life, as well as our attitude toward ourselves and the surrounding world. However, not just experiences with the surrounding world lead to a more positive or negative mother and father complex, since the newborn's natural disposition must also be taken into consideration in order to understand the development of the corresponding mother and father complex. Astrology provides some very useful points of reference on this topic. Depending on the structural disposition with which the individual person is born, the interaction between the child and the mother or father is thematized. In Jung's Analytical Psychology it is assumed that,

> Every individual is essentially influenced in his development through the positively or negatively tinted family atmosphere, the family strains and conflicts, the family constellations and interactions, and their disturbances, the personalities of the parents and other reference persons, and that each individual in turn also influences his environment and the people around him.[206]

So on the one hand, mother and father complexes are therefore emotional structures that are formed from positive and negative experiences with the biological or social mother and the biological or social father. But on the other hand, the child's psychological disposition toward the mother and father, or those in those roles, is also important. This can be observed very clearly in siblings who respond differently to the same parents, just as the parents also react in different ways to their children.[207] The result is mother and father complexes of various shades in the individual children of the same parents. Such structural dispositions of the mother and father complexes can be recognized with special clarity in the birth chart on the basis of the Moon and Sun constellations. This will be illustrated by the examples in Chapter 5.

However, a further discussion of the influences of the surrounding world that play such an immense role—in addition to a child's personal disposition—is important here. Almost one hundred years ago, Jung was drawing attention to the fact that embryos and newborns, as well as growing babies and children are dependent on the parents' *psychological* state.

The child has a special psychology. Just as its body during the embryonic period is part of the mother's body, so is its mind part of the parents' mental atmosphere for many years. That explains why so many neuroses of children are more symptoms of the mental condition of the parents than a genuine disease of the child. Only a very little of the child's psychic life is its own; for the most part it is still dependent on that of the parents. Such dependence is normal, and to disturb it is injurious to the natural growth of the child's mind.[208]

The latest neurobiological findings demonstrate the astuteness of Jung's observation. The physician, neurobiologist, and psychotherapist Joachim Bauer demonstrates using many current studies that the caring mother has a positive effect on the brain's development and therefore on the development of the child's personality and intelligence—in contrast to the corresponding impairments found in those who are deprived of such experiences, and who experience trauma during early childhood.[209]

The English psychoanalyst and pediatrician Donald Winnicott formulated the notion of the "good enough mother"—whose presence leads to the development of the true self, which results in a self-confident and creative person.[210] He describes the qualities of a good environment for undisturbed development and points out that the true self already appears at a very early time in the infant: "As soon as there is any mental organization of the individual at all, and it means little more than the summation of sensori-motor aliveness."[211]

The precondition for this is found in the mother's attitude or emotional approach, which Winnicott calls the *primary maternal preoccupation* and makes it possible for the mother to have a "high degree of adaptation to the individual infant needs."[212] However, this complete adaptation to the child's emotions is only correct in the earliest years of life and should become less and less complete as the infant and toddler becomes increasingly mature. This is how the child learns to cope with reasonable frustrations and acquires an increasing degree of self-reliance, which can also be called ego strength.

Yet, C. G. Jung was not only focused on the complexes at work in the personal unconscious, he wanted to understand their archetypal background. His concept of the archetype entails that there are *a priori* psychic structures—archetypes—innate to and present with the child, which allow the child to seek out, recognize, and integrate experiences that meet certain needs, like the archetypal need for mothering and fathering. The mother and father archetypes provide the basis for the development of the mother and father complexes. In astrological terms, the archetypes of mother and father are symbolized by the Moon and Sun.

This should be looked at more closely. As long as the child's consciousness is still weakly developed, the parents of the child are often experienced less as unique human individuals and more as archetypal powers. The interaction between the archetype and the actual parents forms the parental image. Although these parent images are related to the actual parents, they also contain traits that come from the archetypal layer of the unconscious and so form into inner autonomous imaginal complexes infused with archetypal energy. The original archetypes of the father and mother stay present and active, even as relatively realistic inner psychological representations of the parents develop, called object representations.[213]

So, behind the personal mother is the mother archetype, which either has more of a life-promoting or life-denying effect—depending on the individual's own life experiences and their disposition, about which astrology can provide information. If the child experiences positive mothering, the positive pole of the mother archetype is constellated. If the positive mother archetype is constellated, which shows up in the image of the good mother, the child perceives the supportive qualities of the actual mother. The mother and child are well-attuned to each other, and this successful reciprocity develops into a positive primal relationship—because the child feels safe and secure in the relationship and can trust that it is supported. In turn, the primal relationship has a far-reaching significance for the development of the ego-self, which is important for individuation in the sense of self-realization.

However, if the mother does not appropriately perceive the needs of the child, the primal relationship is characterized by mistrust and fear. Since safety is lacking, the image of the devouring mother is constellated, and with it the life-inhibiting aspects of the mother archetype. The child must endure profoundly unpleasant tensions and fears, finding no sense of security. The functions of the ego such as thinking, feeling, or even affect control are inadequately integrated.[214]

The primal relationship has the two poles of mother and child; it is an archetypal constellation that the mother and child mutually constitute. There is initially no differentiation between them, just an overlapping identity between the mother and child: called *participation mystique*. Through this relatedness, it is possible that the child can read the mother's unconscious and vice versa. This can obviously have both good and bad consequences. With the development of individuality, the unconscious connection is dissolved—though this may not occur completely. Normally, a partial unconscious connection remains in effect between the child and the parents, and this is especially true between the child and the mother—at least until puberty. When differentiation from the parents is not adequately achieved in adolescence, the unconscious connection may extend indefinitely.

In the child's soul, all of the archetypes already exist as inborn structural elements. The actual mother and father archetypes are inaccessible to consciousness, since they are only form-giving psychological force that can only become conscious as symbols or images when they are filled in by culture or personal experience. So only the archetypal images of the father and mother—as symbolic expressions of these archetypes—can be perceived. These archetypal images are brought to life by interacting with real people. The parental images are shaped by these symbols on the one hand and by concrete experiences with mother and father on the other. The child can actually experience a parent in a completely distorted way, superimposing these archetypal pictures onto them. In this case, it makes little sense to simply attempt to change the child's relationship to the real person; instead, the archetypal structures of those involved must be taken into consideration when searching for ways to improve the relationship.

Synopsis: Our Inner Imprints

Jung's theory of archetypes and complexes can be easily combined with astrology because both the archetypes and the birth chart are primarily structural dispositions that contribute to the way the child experiences the world. This structural disposition, which can be recognized in astrology through the birth chart, is already expressed in the small child. In the interaction between disposition and experience, a very specific complex structure is developed within human beings. This contains not only the parents (the Moon and Sun) but also how the child approaches reality (Saturn), courage and activity (Mars), love and enjoyment (Venus), and so forth. Since the signs of the zodiac and the houses are also archetypal in nature and provide information about the different psychological functions (thinking, feeling, intuition, and sensation) and the attitude types (introversion and extraversion), the connection between Jungian Depth Psychology and astrology is obvious and fruitful.

5
Depth Psychological Astrology and Self-Knowledge: Eight Horoscope Examples

The effects of the various astrological constellations on the main themes of human life and how individuals deal with them will be illustrated by a few concrete selected birth charts in this chapter. With respect to the father and mother complex, the focus is on the Sun (creative center of life) and the Moon (feeling and relationship) in combination with the various zodiac signs, quadrants or houses, and their aspects among each other.

Depending on their importance, the aspects of Saturn (reality and setting limits), Mercury (thinking and communication), Venus (love and aesthetics), Mars (aggression and vigor), Jupiter (growth and meaning), as well as of the three trans-Saturnian planets of Uranus (ideas and changes), Neptune (imagination and the transcendence of limitation), and Pluto (power, helplessness, and transformation) will also be included in the discussion on the respective birth chart.

It is not inevitable that people will succeed in optimally developing their dispositions in life, since there are always many types of internal and external factors involved that favor or hinder this. In as far as it is possible, the following section uses examples to show how a respective core disposition is lived or obstructed. This includes various degrees of detail in examining the individual horoscopes. In addition to more differentiated descriptions, brief and succinct sketches are also provided.

What Constitutes a Birth Chart

To create a birth chart, it is necessary to know the individual's day, month, year, time, and place of birth. All of these factors are included to calculate the precise planet positions at the time of birth on a given day in the month of a given year—in relationship to a particular place. The same applies to the calculation of the Ascendant, where the circle of houses begins with the First House, since the Ascendant line that runs through a certain sign of the zodiac is simultaneously the house cusp—i.e. the start of the First House. In *Horoscope Example 1: Johannes*, which is discussed in greater detail below, both the Sun and the Ascendant are in Aquarius since Johannes was born in the early morning around 6 a.m. (cf. the section on "The Circle with Its Semi-Circles, Quadrants, and Houses in Astrology" in Chapter 3, which introduces the Ascendant).

As already mentioned in Chapter 3, the twelve houses or areas of interest have different sizes. This is due to certain complex astronomical factors that cannot be discussed in detail here. Consequently, it is rare for the quadrants (which always have three houses) to be precisely 90° as suggested by the word "quadrant" and schematically shown in illustrations 7 to 9 of the section, "The Circle with Its Semi-Circles, Quadrants, and Houses in Astrology," in Chapter 3. Instead, the quadrants can be quite unequal in their size. But as with the houses, the quadrants that are respectively opposite each other have the same size: so the First and Third, as well as the Second and Fourth, have the same number of degrees. The total number of degrees resulting from the houses or quadrants is always 360°.

In contrast to the twelve houses with their varying sizes, the zodiac—which also adds up to 360°—consists of a sequence of twelve signs of the zodiac that are 30° each: Aries (0°–30°), Taurus (30°–60°), Gemini (60°–90°), Cancer (90°–120°), Leo (120°–150°), Virgo (150°–180°), Libra (180°–210°), Scorpio (210°–240°), Sagittarius (240°–270°), Capricorn (270°–300°), Aquarius (300°–330°), and Pisces (330°–360°). From a geocentric perspective, the Sun travels through all twelve signs of the zodiac within one year. The zodiac sign in which the Sun was located at the time of birth is also known as the "Sun sign" or commonly called the "zodiac sign." The calendrical time frame, which is given in this book (in Chapter 2) for the twelve Sun signs is a general approximation. This is because the change from one Sun sign to the next can vary slightly from year to year, so there is no exact general data. It is necessary to consult the ephemeris (star tables) for a given year to get the precise dates for the segment of days connected to a specific sign that year.

Depending on the Ascendant, the circle of houses starts with a specific sign of the zodiac; its twelve fields can be occupied by one or several planets—and some may also be empty. If the Ascendant is not in Aries (the first sign in the zodiac), the circle of houses and the zodiac are shifted against each other (which was already described in the section, "The Circle with Its Semi-Circles, Quadrants, and Houses in Astrology," in Chapter 3). This requires a bit more interpretive work, as can be seen in the following eight horoscope examples. Since none of them have an Aries Ascendant, they each have new combinations of houses and zodiac signs as a result.

Horoscope Example 1: Johannes clearly shows what such a shift of the circle of houses and the zodiac means: The Ascendant and therefore also the First House are in Aquarius, which actually belongs to the Eleventh House, while the First House is basically associated with Aries. Due to this shift, the quality of self-assertion—which is actually the theme of the First House and a pronounced Aries talent—now occurs in an Aquarian way. This means that Johannes is not impulsive and spontaneous like an Aries, but thoughtful with a planned approach for becoming involved in the world and securing his place in it.

Like the Ascendant, the position of the planets in the various zodiac signs at the time of birth is precisely calculated on the basis of the exact astronomical circumstances. These precise positions that are calculated to the exact degrees, minutes, and seconds result in their relationship with each other—which then appear in the aspect structure or formation of angles with each other. Some planets can have a great many, few, or no aspects at all with other planets. The Orb Table, which was described in the section on "The Aspect Structure in the Horoscope" in Chapter 4, shows which deviations from an exact angle formation are possible for which aspects, depending both on the strength of the planets and the strength of the aspect. The more aspects that a planet has in a birth chart, the more influential it is and the better its specific qualities can be lived out. Consequently, an unaspected planet is difficult to experience; it usually takes much longer to discover and incorporate the qualities that it symbolizes into the individual's life.

Now to the practical horoscope examples: The example horoscopes are all from people whom I have either become acquainted with as clients in my practice and have accompanied for a time or from people whom I know well in my private life. I obviously have used aliases and otherwise also avoid possible identification by changing personal details (without affecting the coherence of the chart's interpretation as a result).

When I have a horoscope in front of me, I first look at the Sun (the father, the mind, and the will) and the Moon (the mother, the emotions, and the soul). In which zodiac signs and which houses are they located? I also consider the Ascendant (the unconscious nature) to get an idea about the parent complexes and their relationship with each other, as well as recognizing their relationship with the Ascendant—which can be harmonious or discordant. Saturn (boundaries and reality) in its relationships with the Sun, the Moon, and the Ascendant is also very important.

Then I focus my attention on all of the planet positions. Which quadrants and houses are especially animated by the planets and which are empty? This gives us an overview of the person's main motivations in life and whether they tend to have a more introverted or extraverted disposition.

Self-Reference and Self-Interest: Focus on the Ascendant and Position of the Self

Johannes—Taking responsibility in shaping his own personality

Johannes is our first example. He was rejected by his father but loved by his mother, and consequently developed a rather negative and weak father complex and a more positive and dominant mother complex.

On the basis of his horoscope, we can see how the structural disposition of the parent complexes may appear; this is apparent in how the Sun and the Moon are embedded in the aspect picture and also have a relationship with each other. The aim is to illustrate the perspectives and approaches the man—who is now over seventy years old—has used in dealing with his structural disposition and the concrete experience with his personal parents. It will be interesting to see how the disposition and experience with the parents have influenced his professional and private development. The themes of self-worth, identity formation, and self-development, as well as anima development and choice of partner, all play a role here.

As in every birth chart, the focus of interest is also taken into consideration. This can be seen in the quadrant and house emphasis, as well as in the specific aptitudes and difficulties for translating them into real life. The interaction and opposition of the essential forces involved—symbolized by the synthetic (blue) and analytical (red) aspects—is made visible in combination with their characteristic way of expression, which is colored by the respective zodiac sign and the houses to which they belong. These were and partially still are the main life tasks for Johannes. How Johannes dealt with them in the past and still deals with them will be taken into account while examining his horoscope.

Quite generally speaking, it can be noted that this is a man who is still very vibrant. He has lived a full and diverse life that has been successful and fulfilled in many ways. He has also faced critical moments that have arisen on his path and is still active in life, with age-appropriate shifts in emphasis as to the way he is now active—which also includes being a devoted and reliable grandfather to his large flock of grandchildren.

Johannes' birth chart shows two accents. The Sun (consciousness, main motive for living, and fatherly principle) is in his First Quadrant, which involves establishing an independent personality (cf. Chapter 3), as well as in the First House and in close proximity to the Ascendant. This puts the spotlight on the themes of self-reference and self-interest, as well as on finding and representing an entirely personal standpoint based on his own subjectivity. The emphasis on the self becomes a main purpose of life (the Sun) for Johannes as a result; this is about defining the personal center of life and the goal in life (the Sun in the

First House: self-definition and self-assertion). But also present are the requirements that Johannes' pronounced disposition as a family man (2nd Quadrant) brings with it. Finding a balance between these two poles has been a topic for him throughout his entire life.

Johannes' birth chart (see Illustration 1 in the color table section at the end of the book)

With the Sun (consciousness, main motive for living, and fatherly principle) located in the First House, as already mentioned, the themes of self-reference and self-interest, as well as subjectivity, stand in the foreground. The Moon (the unconscious, motherly principle, and the anima) in conjunction with Jupiter (expansive principle) in the family quadrant in the Fifth House shifts the focus to the themes of mother and child, creative self-expression, intimate love, and friendship. Saturn (reality and the boundary-setting principle) in conjunction with Uranus (striving for freedom) near the house cusp of the Fourth House just before the Imum Coeli (IC, Lower heaven) emphasizes the family theme and his own roots (cf. Chapter 3).

So the emphasis in this birth chart is on the Ascendant (AC)/ First House (self-reference/First Quadrant), and on the Fourth and Fifth House (family and children, friendship/Second Quadrant). This shows that Johannes has a structural disposition both as an independent personality and a pronounced family man.

Planet Positions and the Ascendant[215]

The Sun in Aquarius	26° 42'	– First House
The Moon in Cancer	13° 11'	– Fifth/Sixth House
Mercury in Aquarius	0° 25'	– Twelfth House
Venus in Pisces	18° 32'	– First House
Mars in Capricorn	14° 58'	– Twelfth House
Jupiter r retro[216] in Cancer	16° 6'	– Sixth House
Saturn in Gemini	5° 41'	– Third/Fourth House
Uranus in Gemini	0° 36'	– Third/Fourth House
Neptune r in Libra	1° 34'	– Seventh House
Pluto r in Leo	5° 39'	– Sixth House
Moon's Nodes in Leo	25° 4'	– Seventh House

AC Aquarius	13° 53'
MC in Sagittarius	7° 16'
2nd House: Aries	8° 40'
3rd House: Taurus	14° 1'
5th House: Gemini	26° 22'
6th House: Cancer	16° 10'
DC Leo	13° 53'
IC Gemini	7° 16'
8th House: Libra	8° 40'
9th House: Scorpio	14°1'
11th House: Sagittarius	26° 22'
12th House: Capricorn	16° 10'

Extraversion or introversion?

Before we turn to the individual life themes in detail, here is an initial overview on the distribution of the planets and their essential forces in the current horoscope to clarify the question of the attitude type of extraversion or introversion.

All four quadrants—if not all of the houses as well—are "occupied" in Johannes' horoscope by certain planets. This makes it possible for them to cultivate wide-ranging relationships with each other. So the spaces in the circle is also used in a diversity of ways, but with clearly different emphases: Both the Sun (center of life) and the two emotional planets of the Moon and Venus are located below the horizon, together with four other planets; so they are beneath the Ascendant-Descendent line. This means that the majority of the essential forces develop their energies in the First and Second Quadrants, which is accompanied by an emphasis on the personal and private sphere (cf. "The Circle with Its Semi-Circles, Quadrants, and Houses in Astrology" in Chapter 3).

The First Quadrant accents the subjective personality, the ego person, through the Sun (Aquarius) in the First House. This is followed by Venus (Pisces), which is also in the First House. The core attitude with the Sun in the First House is egocentric and therefore concerns the issue of values and goals, which—from Johannes' entirely personal viewpoint—have major significance for how he shapes his life and

169

should determine his actions. The feeling for harmony (Venus) is also discernible, so his own male standpoint (the Sun) becomes "softer" through feminine influence. Uranus (Gemini) is also located in the First Quadrant, namely in the Third House (personal development), but its effect is in conjunction with Saturn; the latter is located almost at the boundary of the Fourth House and its influence extends into the family field. When a planet is located close to the line of the following field of interest, it brings a lot of energy into this next house and develops its power there as well. In this case, Saturn—and with a bit more distance, also Uranus—is located at the very end of the third field, but is more strongly associated with the Fourth House.

In the Second Quadrant, accents are also found in the Fourth House—the field of the family that includes physical, emotional, and mental roots; Saturn is constellated (the theme of reality and boundary-setting) with Uranus (the unpredictable, ideas, and sudden changes).[217]

The Fifth House is strongly accentuated by the Moon (Cancer) with the themes of the mother-child relationship, feelings, and relationship issues in general; however, this is simultaneously the field of creativity, play, sports, personal friends, intimacy, and sexuality. But since the Moon is located at the end of the fifth field of interest, it also has an effect into the sixth field. The themes here are work as service in both private and professional life, maintaining good health, and caring for the body in a holistic sense—but also fatigue and diseases.

Retrograde Jupiter (expansion) on the cusp of the Sixth House—as the transition from the Fifth to the Sixth House—is enthroned in Cancer and focuses on all themes of the Sixth House. These will be explained in detail below. The themes of the Sixth House play a large role in Johannes' life, and there will be more information on this in correlation with the themes of "mother" and "anima" or "partner" and "profession."

In addition to the emphasis on the two personally and privately oriented Quadrants One and Two, Johannes has Mercury (intellect and communication principle) and Mars (aggression and activity principle) in the Fourth Quadrant, but in the Twelfth House (into which Mars enters with energy); although the latter is above the horizon, it is associated with anonymity, solitude, and what is concealed. In fact, Johannes often gets feedback that people do not know what he is thinking or that he does not communicate enough—however, these critical statements have been limited to his private environment. In terms of his profession and therefore on the collective level, Johannes actually is very successful at communicating. But in keeping with the Twelfth House, his far-reaching work in leadership positions within internationally relevant institutions occurred less in the public spotlight than in the background.[218]

The question about extraversion or introversion is relatively simple to answer in this case, especially if we also include the three retrograde planets with their libido turning away from the outer world and therefore towards the inside. Jupiter, Pluto, and Neptune are all retrograde and located next to the Descendent, the point where interest shifts away from private matters to familiar people, strangers, and the others in general. The explanations based on the astrological structure shows that the subjective and private components predominate.

But does this conclusion also correspond with the reality of Johannes' personality? Long years of experience and many discussions with Johannes confirm that the introverted attitude actually dominates in his case. This can be easily recognized in his slower and sometimes absent reaction to the stimuli of the outside world, especially when they are of an emotional nature. In contrast to an extraverted person, an introverted individual does not directly respond to outer stimuli or "objects" but absorbs the impressions, processes them, attains a personal (subjective) attitude about them, and answers them accordingly.

For Johannes, the introversion of his attitude toward to the outer world is found in him taking the greatest possible personal responsibility. This is especially emphasized by the Sun in the First House and the associated sense of being the "center of the world" in his personal and/or subjective attitude, which he considers to be correct. His Sun in Aquarius also allows him to act and react in a moderate and well-balanced way on the basis of his personal overview regarding any concrete situation. In the process, he always keeps an eye on the bigger picture.

In summary, the question about introversion or extraversion can be answered as follows: With the existing strong emphasis on the first two quadrants, introversion is more strongly emphasized than extraversion since the focus in Johannes' dispositions is on the private individual who—based on subjective and personal concerns—shapes his life with a high degree of autonomy.

The dynamic structure: Insights into the aspect picture

The following section takes a closer look at the "conversation styles" that various "gods" as archetypal forces use to communicate with each other. This includes the aspects and therefore the angles at which the planets in Johannes' birth chart are related to each other.

Trine (120° angle between two planets): In this birth chart, the large blue triangle formed by the planets at 120° to each other is immediately noticeable. This is also called the "talent triangle" or the "success triangle" and is even doubled here. Due to the easily flowing communication between the essential forces, such a talent triangle is accompanied by successes that are achieved relatively effortlessly (cf. "Aspect Structure in the Horoscope" in Chapter 4). This is relative in comparison with the quadratic aspects (90°) that only lead to success through consistent work and struggle against all types of resistance.

However, such large trines in horoscopes often manifest in individuals as feelings of satiety, sluggishness, and the delusion that they are a gift to humanity. There are many dilettantes who have been given certain aptitudes at birth, but believe that they are already entitled to a special place among their contemporaries—although they have not achieved the corresponding outstanding accomplishments. From what has been said so far about Johannes' personality, it is already clear that this man has not gone through life in a sluggish and complacent way, but has used his talents and untiringly worked for his success.

However, the success of his untiring efforts has been favored by various "divine" forces. In figurative terms, this occurs through the harmonious interaction of his intuitive Aquarius Mercury with Uranus, and the useful ideas that it produces in Gemini; the atmospherically open Libra Neptune connects with the demands of reality in Saturn (also in Gemini), which brings the idea-sparking nature of Mercury (Aquarius) in the trine to Uranus in Gemini (with which Saturn is in conjunction) back down to earth in terms of what is feasible. The harmonious trigonal connection of Mercury (intellectual abilities) with

Saturn (concentration and memory) probably supports Johannes with his extremely good memory—above all, this applies to knowledge and facts in specialized fields, as well as to psychological-interpersonal topics.

The positive role of Saturn as a boundary-setting reality principle cannot be emphasized enough here. In similar constellations that do not integrate Saturn as well, there is the danger that good ideas (Uranus and Mercury in the Aquarius)—which includes staying true to set goals and persevering despite the resistance of reality—fail in their implementation, resulting in even the greatest of aptitudes simply fizzling out.

Squares (90° angle between two planets): The quadratic creates potential tension between the "gods" of Uranus—the untiring producer of ideas, which could lead to an actual tendency toward fragmentation in Gemini—and the Aquarius Sun in the First House. This First House Sun specifically provokes the question: What is of central importance to me personally, what do I want to concentrate on as a result, and what do I want to achieve with my life? The Sun principle, which is set on a systematic approach instead of noncommittally in Aquarius (in contrast to the sign of Gemini), also rubs against Uranus—the inexhaustible source of creativity—in Gemini. This aspect is promoted by the synthetic aspects of Neptune to Uranus through wishful thinking and a lively imagination. The friction leads to a never-ending struggle between the Sun principle, which represents the main values, and the carefree orientation of Uranus. The lifelong work on becoming conscious must be kept in motion. This has been mastered in the current case, and occurs despite the original father problem that will be discussed in detail below.

Oppositions (180° angle between two planets): In a tension of 180° and therefore in a perpetual tensile test, Mars in Capricorn is located at the end of the Eleventh and start of the Twelfth House. It is joined by the Moon-Jupiter conjunction in the Fifth/Sixth House. Individuals with this type of Mars apply all of their energy to fulfill their obligations—in this case, there is an international context in keeping with the Twelfth House and he has often spent time abroad—and masters these tasks in an extremely reliable way with a tendency toward perfectionism. The

Moon in the opposite sign of Cancer emphasizes the main topics of family, wife, and children, and intimate friendships in the fifth field of interest with Jupiter's support. With reference to the Sixth House, this is also about the emotional relationship with work and the relationship components in the professional environment.

During his working life, this conflict became acute for Johannes time and again since parents with growing children focus on different life themes and daily challenges than a man who is in the middle of his professional life. However, coping with an opposition requires that both areas of life come into their own. Jupiter's optimizing effect is beneficial for the process of integrating the two diametrically opposed areas of interest by making both inseparably meaningful for Johannes life as a whole. The influence of Venus in Pisces is also helpful (and will be described in more detail below).

Sextile (60° angle between two planets) and other trines (120° angle between two planets): Another major help for Johannes can be found in the Pisces Venus with its synthetic aspects in the First House. With its fine instinct and pronounced capacity for empathy, it knows how to cushion the sharpness of the opposition. In the case of Johannes, this is expressed by a high level of sensitivity and capacity for love toward his relatives—for whom he has been as active as possible, even in the practical management of everyday life, throughout his entire life and even in the busiest years of his career.

In the past and even today, Johannes' concrete actions in reducing tensions have been brought about by Mars in the sextile (60° angle) to Venus. We could say that this actively supports Venus in its promotion of empathy and harmony. This Pisces Venus in the First House with its trigonal aspects to the Moon and Jupiter in Cancer has good flowing communication with them and gives Johannes a deep ability to empathize. This disposition also allows him to perceive the unspoken needs of his family members, as well as those of his close friends. He shows his sympathy through energetic support for everyone who is close to his heart.

In addition, Johannes has cultivated some friendships since his schooldays and become acquainted with many other people during the course of his life. He remains in personal contact on a regular basis with a large number of them—even though this is an aspect of the fifth life field that has a tendency toward short-lived friendships. However, if this is linked by synthetic aspects with Venus in the First House that specifically selects friends who match the personality due to its position in this field, there can be a greater constancy with regard to cultivating friendships—as seen in this case. With the help of Mars in Capricorn (activity principle) in the Twelfth House, Johannes' care in relationships is expressed in an organized and concrete way.

Above all, Johannes' Sun in the First House plays a principal role in everything that he does. On the basis of this, he wants to arrange his life according to the ideas that have a central value for him—and friendships are a central value for a person with an Aquarius Sun.

The Aquarius coloration also brings cultural values to the same extent. Johannes' far-reaching interest in art and culture has therefore allowed him to become the patron of museums, and he is also successfully involved in their development. His emphasis on the twelfth field with Mercury in Aquarius and Mars in Capricorn lets Johannes be open to those who are marginalized and need help. This means that he also actively supports international aid organizations that help others in need to improve the quality of their life.

But despite all of the activity and dedication, the essential forces in the Twelfth House should be taken into consideration. In order to revitalize and restore himself, retreat from the social environment is necessary.

Father and mother complex, self-image, and anima

Father complex: Some allusions have already been made about the parent complexes, which should be examined more closely. As a child, Johannes grew up in a middle-class house in a beautiful city that had been spared the ravages of the war. However, the war still had an indirect effect on his life because all men—including Johannes' father—had to go into military service at that time and were often absent as a result. The Sun in the First House shows Johannes' wish for closeness with his father, but the predominantly analytical aspects to the father image (the Sun) simultaneously indicate the disappointment of this wish in the structural terms his horoscope. Since the Third and Fourth Houses symbolize everyday life and home, and we can see here that there were repeatedly sudden separations (Uranus—unpredictability, Saturn—reality principle, which also requires separation) from the father that were very painful.

During his childhood, Johannes did not see his father very often. On the rare occasions he was at home, the boy experienced the contact as even more of a disappointment, since there was no warmhearted connection between them. The father actually quite openly preferred Johannes' younger and more extraverted brother. This preference by the father, which was clear and visible to the entire world, led in turn to alienation between the brothers.

This may be partly due to the father's own structural dispositions, who perhaps experienced a better match with his second son; however, it can also be recognized in the structural disposition at work in Johannes' father image, which obviously also influences their concrete relationship. A person with an Aquarius Sun—who embodies an intellectual-mental principle since it belongs to the air element—is seen as being "cool" instead of "warm," and the child might unwittingly project this onto the father; this applies in any case when the child has such a highly sensitive emotional disposition as Johannes (Venus in Pisces in the trine to the Moon-Jupiter conjunction in Cancer). This may have had the effect that the boy approached the father in a rather reserved way—in contrast to his extraverted brother, who was much less complicated in his contact with the father.

In connection with the two "house planets" of the family field (Fourth House)—Uranus and Saturn—breaks, impatience, and unpredictability (Uranus) come into play, as well as objectivity, pragmatism, strictness, commandments and prohibitions, and rules and restrictions (Saturn). These two essential forces—together with Mars, whose activist and spontaneous side is tamed by its Capricorn imprint—have an irritated conversation with the Sun when seen in metaphorical terms. This results in a strict, austere father image, which can contribute much to the development of a strong ethic of duty and/or a demanding super-ego. So, Johannes can live with few material things and nourishes himself in a healthy, conscious, and rather simple way in everyday life.

Mother complex: The question arises as to how Johannes managed to develop enough security in his male identity despite the massive rejection by his father in order to still be able to follow his own path. As a boy, he had the ability and good fortune to be positively reflected in the predominantly favorable encounters with male teachers and schoolmates; as a result, he was strengthened in the development of his self. Some of the friends from his school days are still important for Johannes and he is also important to them.

He grew up in a big house in the city with his mother as the main figure, together with a domestic helper and one grandmother. So, the father's frequent absence led to the boy growing up in a household that was dominated by women. The husband's rejection of the first son apparently caused the mother to suffer as much as Johannes, since she felt very sorry for him. His father's devaluation of Johannes—who was more sensitive and complex in his character—and his preference for the more robust and uncomplicated younger son prompted the mother to give Johannes as much positive affection as possible. In turn, this promoted a deepened relationship between mother and son, which still made it possible for Johannes to develop in a good way despite the insufficient fatherly affection and support.

The barely visible and analytically (red) aspected Sun shows that the father relationship can be problematic. The way in which this occurred has already been described. It is very interesting that Johannes—in contrast to his father and brother, who both had a very materialistic orientation—has spent his entire life mentally and culturally educating himself, in addition to acquiring professional competences in the organizational field. This occurred under the influence of the culturally and artistically interested and talented mother (Moon in Cancer, Fifth House in conjunction with the promoting principle of Jupiter, the two of which form a trine with the aesthetic principle of Venus in Pisces in the First House). This is also where the sign of Aquarius shows up, which arouses a great many interests as the "window to the world."

In the combination of the Aquarius sign with the First House, Johannes does not allow himself to be limited in his thirst for knowledge about all cultural achievements; as a result, he still cultivates his great interest especially in fine arts from every part of the world and in music. So, he is an impressive example of a person with the Sun in the First

House in Aquarius, since he has responsibly shaped his own personality in the sense of the openness of the Aquarius principle for all relevant cultural achievements. This also allows his disposition for imagination to adequately develop its creative potential through the feminine planets of the Moon and Venus.

In view of Saturn, which has an effect into the Fourth House (family field),[219] the question arises as to whether there were further restrictions in Johannes' life than those related to the above-mentioned biological father. Unfortunately, the answer to this question is yes, because these restrictions are also related to the topic of illness—which has played a significant role in Johannes' life as well. The Sun sign of Gemini (located in Saturn) is associated with the respiratory passages in the body. In the trigonal aspect with retrograde Neptune in Libra at the end of the Seventh and start of the Eighth House, it points to the theme of permeability for the outside world and therefore also the susceptibility to infections, and every possible disease that is difficult to diagnose and treat.

Johannes did not actually experience this in his own body, but in his mother through projection. When his mother was sixty years old, she was diagnosed with a rare lung disease. Within the context of Johannes' choice of life partner, it is very interesting to note that she was a healthy woman in her younger years—but at the age of sixty also began to suffer from a very similar inexplicable disease that massively weakened her lungs.

The retrograde Jupiter[220] in conjunction with the Moon and certain "disruptive signals" by Uranus in the Third/Fourth House in a semi-square with the Moon and Jupiter can point to certain limitations in the experience of motherly affection, as well as in interpersonal connection with the wife and children—which are structurally indicated to be loving and warm with the Moon in the Fifth House. The high expectations that come with Jupiter and refer to the motherly symbol of the Moon in this case cannot be experienced according to the individual's wishes.

These disturbances to unrestricted motherly affection can be understood as being based on the outer living conditions, which demanded from the mother that she also had to be a businesswoman—and she apparently fulfilled this job quite well—in addition to her role as mother. The gliding of the Moon into the Sixth House (occupational field) fits in well with this. The Moon is closely connected with Jupiter on the cusp of the Sixth House, which is the transition from the Fifth to the Sixth House. This means that the mother has a structural disposition of not just being a housewife and mother, but also finds her optimal state in the double role of "mother and businesswoman" (the Moon as a mother symbol in conjunction with Jupiter as the symbol of the optimum). The thin aspects—semi-squares of Uranus with a Moon-Jupiter conjunction—indicate a weak tension between Uranus and the motherly disposition, which has already been indicated in this particular case.

The deep connection with the ill, but still living elderly mother, can be traced back to Johannes' experiences of the way she supported and strengthened him to the best of her ability—so that he could survive the daily struggle for his place in the family. Her efforts had an extraordinarily positive effect on the shaping of his later life as a whole. Johannes is a good example of a man with a dominant and mostly positive imprinting of a mother complex, which is also expressed very well in his appreciation of women.

Self-image and anima: Anima development is strongly based on the mother complex, which in turn comes about through the interaction of the constellated mother archetype and experience with the actual mother. In the young years, the anima is still strongly linked with the unconscious image of the mother and this is why men usually choose their partner in keeping with this type. The unconscious elements of falling in love are very powerful. However, a young man may believe that he is entirely conscious in his choice of a partner—who he superficially experiences as very different from his mother. So, he rarely knows that his choice is controlled by an unconscious schema, which is built upon the mother complex with an archetypal core at work behind it.

This was also true in this case, because Johannes' vibrant young wife became ill with a severe, mysterious allergy after the birth of their first child and required much medical support to adequately master her everyday life. Even though this allergy also disappeared just as mysteriously as it had come, the theme of "illness" in connection with female relatives continued to exist in Johannes' life—but will not be discussed in detail.[221]

The theme of insufficient boundaries and defense against influences from the outside world definitely exists in Neptune with its dissolution of boundaries in the more sociable Libra principle. This is found at the end of the Seventh and start of the Eighth House, in which the topic is openness toward familiar people, strangers, and the unknown. In its various facets, the theme of dissolving boundaries has always been and is still present for Johannes.

One of the obvious correlations for this, is the choice of a partner. This theme belongs to the familiar area of intimate relationships in which this Neptune disposition can be characterized by insufficient setting of boundaries toward the outside world, seducibility, susceptibility to infection, and lack of structure. In turn, this may be projected onto a possible partner, who then also embodies these projections to a certain extent. A woman who seems to be strong at first may turn out to be structurally weak in the course of her life.

How things will continue for Johannes

This unequal weight in the parent complexes—a weaker, more ambivalent father complex and a dominant, more positive mother complex—has led Johannes to assuming a great deal of responsibility throughout his lifetime. This not only includes responsibility for himself, but also in his professional and relational life. In recent years, he has increasingly learned to give up some burdensome obligations and create sufficient freedom for himself to be independent and move in his own rhythm. His lifetime goal will probably remain to achieve a stronger balance between his sense of responsibility and duty toward everything and everyone in the family environment and allowing himself the freedom for ease and playful serenity.

Theodor—Architect of the ivory tower

Theodor is an example of a partially successful individuation, despite his birth chart's "talent triangle" that is composed of three trines (180° angle between two planets). As it was for Johannes, the core attitude (the Sun) is egocentric, but in contrast to the former's case—it is embedded in the synthetic triangle. So we could also assume that he had to fight less than Johannes to realize one of his two main personal concerns: namely, either developing professionally as an artist or as a historian. He actually has had to struggle much less than Johannes, but also has achieved much less. Like Johannes, Theodor has a dominant mother complex that tends to be more ambivalent; in contrast to Johannes, he has a somewhat weaker positive father complex. How this affects his life will be shown below.

Theodor's birth chart (see Illustration 2 in the color table section at the end of the book)

With the Sun (consciousness, main area of life, and the fatherly principle) in the First House, almost exactly on the Ascendant line, the Ascendant of Scorpio and the Self Point is strongly emphasized. As in *Horoscope Example 1: Johannes*, self-reference and self-interest dominate here; the Moon (the unconscious, maternal principle, and anima) in the Ninth House indicates a great interest in travel, philosophy, politics, and world-historical connections. Through the square (90° angle) between the Sun in Scorpio (water; doubt) in the First House and the Moon in Leo (fire; unbroken self-confidence) in the Ninth House, there is a struggle between his core attitude based on depth and seriousness of his core attitude and his anima, which is focused on the enjoyment of life and pleasure.

Planet Positions and the Ascendant

Sun in Scorpio	21°	54'	–	First House
Moon in Leo	10°	42'	–	Ninth House
Mercury r in Scorpio	11°	6'	–	Twelfth House
Venus in Libra	5°	20'	–	Tenth House
Mars in Scorpio	13°	49'	–	Twelfth House
Jupiter r in Pisces	23°	39'	–	Fourth House
Saturn in Sagittarius	8°	3'	–	First House
Uranus r in Gemini	29°	45'	–	Fourth House
Neptune in Leo	29°	6'	–	Ninth House
Pluto r in Cancer	17°	1'	–	Eighth House
Moon's Nodes in Gemini	20°	7'	–	Seventh House

AC in Scorpio	20° 59'
MC in Virgo	7° 28'
2nd House: Sagittarius	21° 30'
3rd House: Capricorn	29° 7'
5th House: Aries	8° 38'
6th House: Taurus	2° 16'
DC in Taurus	20° 59'
IC in Pisces	7° 28'
8th House: Gemini	21° 30'
9th House: Cancer	29° 7'
11th House: Libra	8° 38'
12th House: Scorpio	2° 16'

Extraversion or introversion?

Among other factors, this only partially successful individuation is probably related to the rather one-sided distribution of the elements. Theodor has the majority of the planets, namely six, and also the Ascendant, in water signs—which are also associated with Jung's feeling type.[222] The fire element is the second strongest with three planets, and the air element is represented with one planet, as well as the Moon's Nodes.[223] However, the earth element is almost lacking completely.[224] Theodor can also easily be seen as an introverted feeling type who drifts and indulges in his rich world of imagination, but never really gets his feet on the ground.

On the one hand, this introversion is favored by the emphasis on the First Quadrant with the Sun (life center) in Scorpio and Saturn (boundary-setting principle and reality) in Sagittarius in the First House (self-reference and self-interest); on the other hand, it is also facilitated by the accentuation of the Second Quadrant with retrograde Jupiter (introversion tendency of the expansion principle) and also retrograde Uranus (ideas and sudden changes), both of which are in Pisces and the Fourth House (family and roots). In addition, the occupation of the Twelfth House (tendency to retreat and anonymity) by two planets is in keeping with the tendency toward introversion.

Extraverted tendencies can be found in the two emotional planets of the Moon (imagination, motherly principle, and anima) in Leo in the Ninth House and Venus (aesthetic principle, harmony and balance, and anima); this addresses the Third and Fourth Quadrant. However, Theodor has not really lived these extraverted tendencies himself, but projected his extraverted anima on corresponding women.

He is actually an extremely talented man, now in his late eighties. Yet, he has not been successful in professionally implementing his pronounced musicality (Neptune in Leo, Ninth House) nor his great talent for architecture with Venus (sense of aesthetics) in Libra in the Tenth/Eleventh House and in sextile with Saturn (talent for forms and structures) in Sagittarius in the First House—nor his pronounced interest for world-historical and world-political topics (emphasis in the Eighth, Ninth, Eleventh, and Twelfth House). In order to understand this, we should take a more precise look at his anima that is found in the Moon and Venus constellation.

Anima and mother complex

From his perspective, the main obstacle in Theodor's life has been the extreme dominance of his wife; but this was only possible due to his pronounced mother complex and weaker father complex. However, we should first explore Theodor's image of women. It is based on the following constellations: his Moon is in the Ninth House, which brings with it a strong appreciation of the maternal woman; this strong appreciation is further intensified by its position in the sign of Leo. With the Moon in Leo, the woman is seen as powerful and independent—a "mother lion" with diva airs and graces.

In addition, she must be beautiful and cultivated since Venus also plays a very dominant role. The Moon is in a harmonious aspect with Venus, whose significance as the Goddess of Beauty and Love is further amplified by her position in the associated sign of Libra, as well as by her very accented position in the Tenth/Eleventh House. Moreover, Venus is located on the cusp of a smaller blue triangle that consists of one sextile from Venus with the Moon and one with Saturn. In turn, these two communicate smoothly with each other through a trine. With Venus in this constellation, the need for harmony, a sense of aesthetics, love of pleasure, and cultivated forms of sociability are especially emphasized.

This characterizes Theodor's own feminine side, which has remained largely unconscious; however, as can easily happen when a man encounters an appropriate woman, he projects this onto her. A woman is "appropriate" for projection when she appears to embody important aspects of his anima image. Theodor also experienced this as a young man when he met a woman who was as youthful as she was strikingly beautiful, so he soon married her.

In terms of the female principle, Theodor shows not only a very lofty, idealizing, and admiring disposition—which can be read in the above-mentioned Moon and Venus constellation—it has been concretely manifested in his life. This is reflected in his general behavior toward women, since he has always encountered them with respect.

However, a first glance at this birth chart reveals that the Moon (the emotional realm, motherly principle, and anima) in the sign of Leo (self-confidence and an unbroken yes to life) actually has three squares (90° angle) of tension with the three planets in Scorpio (doubt and an ambivalent relationship to life): the Sun (will, main concerns, fatherly principle, and male identity); Mars (drive, energy, fighting power, assertiveness, and male libido); and Mercury (communicative principle).

On the intrapsychic level, this means that Theodor experiences a constant tension between his emotional disposition—the Moon as the female principle symbolizes the unconscious, dreams, and fantasizing—and his core attitude (the Sun), which is colored by doubt (Scorpio) towards self through the position of the Sun in the First House (self-reference and self-interest). This signifies that Theodor is actually in a constant tension between feeling (Moon) and intellect (the Sun), as well as between trust and affirmation (Leo) and mistrust and a critical attitude (Scorpio). These inner tensions manifest not only on the inside, but also in projections on his wife, which led to much friction between the couple in younger years. Arguments or at least flaring tensions were part of their everyday life![225]

In order to understand which type of frictions these were, we must ask what it means when the reality principle (Saturn) is harmoniously connected with the Moon and Venus, but has no aspects with the person's own core attitude (the Sun). In Theodor's case, the answer is quite simple. Throughout his life (and for the most part, up to today) his relationship to reality has been based on his pragmatic and organizationally talented wife. She is actually very capable of coping with life and has also always taken care of all financial matters.

Theodor's self-image

Theodor identified with his male images of the gods. On the astrological level, this means he identified with the Sun and Mars in their aspects with additional planets. The special element of this is that his entire male disposition is very emotional, since it lies in the water signs of Scorpio, Pisces, and Cancer. Neptune in the Ninth House, just before the Medium Coeli—just like the water signs—also symbolizes sensitivity and impressionability. As a result, his relationship with reality is underdeveloped.

In fact, Theodor has always lived in his imagination, in literature, art, and culture. He has practically lived in an ivory tower, but very much enjoys debating and discussing when he has the appropriate dialog partner. He does this with passion and forgets time—a typical theme when the water elements are involved along with the boundary expanding principles of Pisces and Neptune.

Theodor has lived strongly from a sense of abundance, to which been primarily by Jupiter in Pisces (Fourth House) standing in a harmonious trine with the Sun (First House). Pluto in Cancer (Eighth House), which lets its excessive energy flow to both the Sun and Jupiter in Pisces, has an additional exorbitant effect. This feeling of fullness has been accompanied by the fact that Theodor has always been very generous in his hospitality and ability to enjoy—which he shared with his wide circle of friends in endless social events—sometimes to the chagrin of his wife, who has had to make sure that there was enough money for everyday life with all of its obligations.

When Theodor receives too little attention from his surrounding world, he quickly runs into problems with his self-esteem. Throughout his life, it has been a matter of course for him to demand much more affection and prestige than the outside world—above all, his family— has been able to give him. This is because his self-image has primarily been based on his extraordinary talents, but he has only lived them as a hobby and not professionally. Accordingly, Theodor was frustrated for a certain time. Although he is one of the fortunate people with the "talent triangle," he belongs to the majority of those who feel that just having talent is enough—and cannot adequately recognize that this is a potential treasure that they can only unearth with much effort.

The distribution of roles in the marriage of Theodor and his wife has allowed Theodor to live a type of enchanted private existence, which means immersing himself in music, cultural, social, political, and historical topics and leading the life of a "bookman"—which has been difficult to reconcile with the demands that real life has on him as a husband and family father.

Although he willingly left this Saturnal side of coping with reality to his wife, this simultaneously resulted in him feeling patronized by her. In turn, this evokes his wife's personality structure, which is actually very much oriented toward dominance.[226]

The three red aspects—squares between the Leo Moon in the Ninth House and the Scorpio side around the Ascendant[227]—are indications of endless tension and friction between these two halves of Theodor's personality. On the one hand, this means that he is very vulnerable and sensitive from his water side (feeling); on the other hand, he likes to show off due to the imprinting by the Moon in Leo (fire and impulsiveness) and draw other people into discussions on topics that personally drive him. He practically forces these on them without making sure that the other person is also interested in them.[228] These imperial gestures in his life quite obviously have led to tension—above all, with his partner, who is not interested in his spiritual and intellectual topics but prefers to stay at the more concrete levels of life.

In the projection of the Leo Moon—which has harmonious contact with Venus and Saturn—on his pragmatic and more superficial-cheerful, but strong wife, Theodor experiences her as a person who "chokes off" his important ideas and discussions and restricts him. The almost exact squares between the Leo Moon and Scorpio Mercury in conjunction with Mars (aggression principle) allow us to imagine the fierceness of the discussions between Theodor and his wife. We can assume that they sometimes really made the sparks fly—at least when the tensions could no longer be held under adequate control. However, these tensions also show very positive effects since the couple has never turned indifferent toward each other and are still together. But Theodor has become much more relaxed, both within himself and in his contact with his surrounding world.

Parent complexes

The question about the parent complexes shows Theodor's mother wearing a true halo. According to Theodor, she was not only loved, but also revered by his father and his siblings. Theodor's father was a successful contractor, but died when Theodor was just entering puberty. As the youngest child, he lived alone with his mother for a number of years after the loss of his father; this brought the two of them even closer. The Leo Moon in the Ninth House came to bear in the projection onto Theodor's mother in all of its idealizing characteristics, to which the connection with Venus in Libra also contributed.

As we know, the sign of Scorpio is associated with death and rebirth; Theodor has his Sun—the father principle—in Scorpio. The harmonious connection through two trines (120° angle between the Sun and the Jupiter-Uranus conjunction in the Fourth House) with both the retrograde Jupiter and Uranus (unpredictable events and sudden changes) in Pisces in the Fourth House can indicate unexpected and unpredictable changes. For example, this can show up as a sudden loss—be expressed in the figurative sense of a sudden change of the core attitude or quite generally the creative development.

Intensified by the trine aspects (120° angle) between Jupiter (question of meaning and what is optimum) and the Sun (father) with Pluto—which belongs to the sign of Scorpio and is also located in the Scorpio-affine Eighth House (so there is an emphasis on the theme of changing shape and transformation)—this constellation is manifested in such a way that his father died too early and could no longer support and accompany his son in the important phases of building the male identity. At the same time, all of Theodor's older brothers had long moved out and some of them were abroad for educational and professional reasons. Due to these circumstances, Theodor's assertiveness—which is already not very pronounced as a disposition and would have needed continual encouragement from his surrounding world—was correspondingly weakened.

Due to a lack of fatherly and brotherly role models and under the influence of his beloved and revered mother—who knew how to keep binding Theodor to her by pampering him—he did not adequately learn to lastingly activate his driving energy for the purpose of professionally developing any of his true talents; instead, he has been mostly content with living in his dream world.

Theodor today

The purpose of these anamnestic comments is to show how much a person's destiny can be influenced by the interplay of a disposition and the lack of male and structuring support. This would have been important for such a pronounced emotional personality such as Theodor.

In his encounters with women in general, and his spouse in particular, this weakened masculine core attitude was constellated with a simultaneous tendency to revere women. On the one hand, this was an advantage since it helped Theodor cope with his everyday life by compensating for one of his weak points. On the other hand, he has quickly felt patronized and controlled by his wife. He has tried to elude her influence by hiding behind newspapers and burying himself in books that she had no interest in.

He seemingly rescued himself from her control by escaping into his private and personal world of the mind and fantasies. Here he is free and can practically turn into a nomad, despite his middle-class existence. Throughout his life, Theodor has remained in this state and therefore prevented himself from bringing his talents to fruition. Now that he is older, he has become aware that his tendency to live in his fantasies and intellect has come at the cost of reality; he has also recognized that he has delegated coping with reality to his partner. These insights have made it possible for him to take back certain projections and personally live some of the practical everyday life skills that he had delegated to his wife for several decades. He is finally taking the problems of everyday life into his own hands.

Rootedness in the Family and in the Self: Focus on the Lower Heaven

Anton—In the prison of facts

Anton, a top-notch scientist still in the first half of his life, found his way to my practice when he was trapped in a moderate depression that had serious effects on both his professional and private life. This inclination to depression is widespread on both sides of his family. Anton's father was directly affected by it and his depression worsened in phases as he got older. Several relatives on his mother's side also suffer from very severe depressive episodes, which has also resulted in suicide (Moon-Saturn contact, see below). So, there is a hereditary factor that facilitates depression in Anton.

Anton experienced the relationship with his mother as very positive and close, while he saw his father less and less during his adolescence, as the latter became increasingly successful at work. For Anton, the mother complex is dominant and positive in contrast to the father complex, which is somewhat weaker and fluctuates between positive and negative.

Anton's birth chart (see Illustration 3 in the color table section at the end of the book)

Anton's horoscope has a distinct focus on the lower semi-circle with four planets in the First Quadrant and three in the Second Quadrant.

As a result, the Sun (main concerns, consciousness, and father principle) and the Moon (unconscious, imagination, mother principle, and anima) are both located in the earthy zodiac sign of Taurus; the Sun is in the Third House (personal development) and the Moon in the Second House (profession as a means of securing the existence). The Ascendant Aquarius (freedom, systematic thinking, and intuitive thinking) adds the third element of air to the earthy sign of Taurus with its core attitude (the Sun) and the emotionally functioning water sign (the Moon). At the end of the First House, there is also Venus (love, harmony, aesthetics, and anima) in the sign of Aries (emphasis on will;

fire sign). Jupiter (expansion, optimum, and question of meaning) is found in the First House in the sign of Pisces. So the First Quadrant focuses on personal assertion (First House), self-preservation (Second House), and personal development (Third House), while the Second Quadrant with Mercury at the start of the Fourth House (family, origin, and rootedness), as well as Saturn (boundary-setting principle) and Mars (activity and male libido) are both in the emotional water sign of Cancer in the Fifth House (intimate love, friendship, children, games, and sports) and point to a personality that is oriented toward privacy.

Planet Positions and the Ascendant

Sun in Taurus	28° 36'	–	Third House
Moon in Taurus	4° 48'	–	Second House
Mercury in Gemini	15° 25'	–	Third/Fourth House
Venus in Aries	17° 4'	–	First House
Mars in Cancer	17° 50'	–	Fifth House
Jupiter in Pisces	14° 18'	–	First House
Saturn in Cancer	3° 8'	–	Fourth/Fifth House
Uranus r in Libra	24° 25'	–	Eighth House
Neptune r in Sagittarius	8° 31'	–	Ninth House
Pluto r in Libra	4° 14'	–	Seventh House
Moon's Nodes in Sagittarius	20°34'	–	Tenth House
AC Aquarius	29° 34'		
MC in Sagittarius	15° 49'		
2nd House: Aries	22° 49'		
3rd House: Taurus	24° 13'		
5th House: Cancer	4° 50'		
6th House: Cancer	26° 14'		
DC Leo	29° 34'		
IC Gemini	15° 49'		
8th House: Libra	22° 49'		
9th House: Scorpio	24° 13'		
11th House: Capricorn	4° 50'		
12th House: Capricorn	26° 14'		

Introversion or extraversion?

Anton's horoscope shows at a glance that he is an introverted man, because all of the personal planets are located in the First and Second Quadrants. This means that the focus of Anton's life is on personal and family themes, as already mentioned above. In comparison, the upper semi-circle—which reveals the relationship with the surrounding world (Third Quadrant), as well as society and public life (Fourth Quadrant)— only the trans-Saturnal planets of Pluto (dying-and-becoming principle and metamorphosis), Uranus (unpredictable changes and need for freedom), and Neptune (sensitivity, desirability, and dissolution of boundaries) are found.

The relationship between the introverted and extraverted tendencies is clear in Anton's case. Without a doubt, we can see that Anton is an introverted personality. This is all the more so since even the three collective planets (Pluto, Uranus, and Neptune), which are located in the Third Quadrant, which is associated with the surrounding world (extraverted attitude), are retrograde and therefore show an introversive tendency. This means that they develop toward the inside instead of the outside.

Consequently, the real goal in Anton's life is to get to know himself better on the personal level and increasingly allow himself to blossom.

The mother and other female relatives; the father

Anton is married and has two daughters of school age and one son of kindergarten age. He comes from a family of natural scientists that emphasizes reason, achievement, and perfection; the emotional world with its fantasies and dreams is given less attention.

With their material orientation, the Sun and Moon in Taurus indicate Anton's sense of reality but also his parental images. His father and mother are also natural scientists. In addition, Saturn—the reality principle—is connected with the Moon in a harmonious aspect (sextile), which reflects Anton's experience with a rational mother who was nevertheless able to offer him emotional support and protection in some respects.

However, as implied by the description of Saturn in Chapter 1, it can also play an important role in the topic of depression (see the section on "The Ten Planets in Astrology"). This has been the case for Anton. When Saturn (the boundary-setting principle and reservoir of all experiences) is positioned at the end of the Fourth House and start of the Fifth House (family and children)—and moreover in the family-related sign of Cancer—there may be a family disposition toward depression. The harmonious connection between the Moon (in Taurus) and Saturn (in Cancer) through the sextile (60° angle) can be an indication that there is a predisposition for a depressive disorder.

In this case, this harmonious aspect led to Anton not noticing for a long time that he was in a depressive episode and that something was wrong—since the topic of depression had quite obviously been part of the family history ever since he was a young child. As is the case for all dispositions, this can be either lived out by the respective person or also experienced externally in projections on other people or situations. In Anton's case, it was actually true that even a number of female relatives had in the past suffered from depressive episodes with every degree of severity.[229]

Profession and depression

Anton was looking for psychotherapeutic support because he felt emotionally blocked, which resulted in all types of private and professional problems involving communication. At the beginning of the analysis, Anton actually suffered intensively from the conflicts between his wishes and reality. This is structurally reflected by the retrograde Neptune (wishes and dissolution of boundaries) in Sagittarius (freedom, travel, and distant countries) in the Ninth House (affinity to Sagittarius), in opposition to the earthy Sun (core attitude) in the earth sign of Taurus (sense of reality and materialism) in the Third House (personal background and further development). In addition to this conflict between wanderlust (Neptune in Sagittarius in the Ninth House) and groundedness (the Sun and Moon in Taurus), the topic of depression as a family burden is what led him to the analysis.

The Moon principle in Taurus with its aspects with Saturn in Cancer in the two first fields of the family quadrant (Fourth and Fifth Houses) structurally indicates a limitation (Saturn) of the motherly principle (Moon). This may be expressed in examples such as Anton's demand of perfection (Saturn) in the care of children. The Moon disposition corresponds with his own emotional disposition (the Moon); but this is also the disposition for experiencing his personal mother (also the Moon). His mother—who had given up her profession in favor of the children and did her best to give them a happy childhood—suffered from a depressive episode when Anton was still an infant. She was correspondingly limited in her emotional accessibility during this time. This and further depressive episodes suffered by the mother may have encouraged Anton's later depressive development.

This ultimately led him into analytical therapy, in which he initially described the difficulties that he had with his previous flawless ability to concentrate. He felt completely overwhelmed by the daily flood of emails, which overwhelmed him from the outside like an enormous natural disaster; he tried to deal with it in a compulsive and perfectionist way, but this no longer left him enough time to work on his scientific projects. He had a major problem with the structuring of his everyday working life and believed that everything was slipping away from him. In turn, this triggered his fears of no longer being adequate and losing control over his demanding areas of responsibility.

This can be understood in the astrological constellation of Pluto and Saturn. Pluto as a generally reinforcing principle, located in Libra in the Seventh House, has the effect of an unconscious compulsion for perfection in the square with Saturn. Pluto is the principle of high guiding ideals, and this is why Pluto constellations are very powerful. In subjective terms, this is experienced as a strong demand for perfection and is accompanied by "pressure." Because it has aspects with the two main essential forces of the Sun and the Moon here, as well as standing in a strong square tension with Saturn—which already has a great deal of perfection pressure on its own—Anton's experience of feeling pressured to be perfect had become extreme and simultaneously triggered intense fears of failure.

This means that Anton was on the verge of breaking down emotionally and intellectually under the pressure of the compulsion to be perfect, and under what he felt to be an enormous burden of professional obligations that were increasingly growing like an avalanche and threatened to crush and bury him. The question as to whether he was in the right profession began to torment him.

Partnership and sexuality; children

Anton's tendency to objectify and restrict his emotional side, as well as suppress and cut off feelings, is related to the position of Saturn in emotional Cancer at the end of the Fourth House (emotional and mental rootedness; family) and start of the Fifth House (intimate love, children, games, and sports).

This is intensified by his Moon in Taurus standing in a sextile with Saturn and therefore reinforcing his earthy heaviness—crushed by the Saturnal lead weights of fear of failure and existential dread (Saturn). For example, this was also shown in the fact that Anton and his wife—even though there were no medical reasons at all—had to wait a long time to conceive children in comparison to other couples of the same age. This is not unusual when Saturn is in the Fifth House. Wherever Saturn, the boundary-setting reality principle is located, we can reckon with restrictions; a couple may even remain childless in this case. Although Anton had to wait years for desired offspring, he is now the happy and loving father of three healthy children.

Constricting life situation

As already mentioned, in the early stages of his depth psychological work, Anton was suffering from compulsions to be perfect and the irrational guilt feelings of not achieving enough professionally; in turn, this was promoted by energy blockages and concentration disorders, and ultimately became his reality. What does a person do when things suddenly become worse and they have no explanation for it? They look for reasons. The most obvious explanations are usually found in the current life situation, in both the professional and private realm.

Not only at work, but also in his life as a husband and father, Anton began to feel imprisoned and inadequate. Was this all he could expect from life? Saturn—here as the correspondence to depression (lived through perfectionism and compulsions)—in the water sign of Cancer had produced Anton's deep, unconscious fears and guilt feelings toward his daughters and his son. Anton loves his children devotedly, but often felt overwhelmed by their liveliness and vitality during those depressive phases, especially in how they took great pleasure in throwing themselves at their father when he returned from work and wanted to play with him immediately. Anton felt exhausted from his working day, so he sometimes treated his children quite harshly and sometimes even raised his voice. In turn, this behavior brought guilt feelings with it since he could emotionally harm his beloved children as a result.

Anton's ability to have relationships or the anima problem and transformation of the anima

In Anton's life, there was also an anima problem and therefore relationship problems at the beginning of the analysis. Although he had a very good and stable relationship with his wife—which was also reflected very positively in his dreams—something seemed to be missing. In addition to his wife, a very different type of woman suddenly entered his life with an emphasis on erotic and sexual attractiveness. These women behaved like huntresses who made Anton into the target of their desire. This was also reflected in his dreams, which were dominated at the start by these concrete "huntresses,"[230] and by quite undifferentiated anima figures with an affinity for the red light district.

As analysis progressed, these female dream figures—who had at first only specialized in seduction—began to change into supportive and helping women. His female dream figures became stimulating conversation partners, educated and mentally active women who were generally interesting, and they sometimes also had something mysterious about them.

But where is this strong, active, and independent anima type found in Anton's horoscope? At the end of the First House and start of the Second House, we see his Venus in the fire sign of Aries—a true Amazon! This anima is attuned to conquest, very active, and entirely different from the sedentary Moon principle in Taurus that harmonizes with the synchronicity of things in its earthiness.

In addition, Venus is in a quadratic tension to its own libido planet and activity principle of Mars (which increases the tension of the sex drive) as well as in a harmonious aspect to Mercury in Gemini, which is the communication principle. A semi-sextile to fiery Venus with the expansion orientation of Jupiter in the romantic and boundless Pisces principle brings a further component into play. This is all the more true, since this emotional Pisces-Jupiter in a trigonal connection spurs on the equally emotional Cancer-Mars. We therefore find an anima that is very lively, with an intense sex drive, that is freedom-loving, and has a strong focus on activity for romantic togetherness, education, mental flexibility, and communication.

Up to the birth of the first daughter, Anton's wife could apparently cover these components quite well; they had travelled the world with each other and experienced adventures together. With the shift of his lover (Venus) into the mother role (the Moon), and his own accompanying transformation of lover (Mars) into the role of father and husband (the Sun), the crisis was triggered. Together with the issues of family, the Saturn theme also unfolded through the constellation of depression, and in the preoccupation with his own emotional depths and his rootedness in it. The entire anima theme ultimately played a very important role in awakening Anton, who can now relate more deeply and vividly to himself and also to his children and his wife. The intensive analytic work brought Anton in contact with his own feminine side in a variety of ways, which has now made him into a mature, relating, and reliable partner for his wife.

Anton's tendency to flee

At the beginning of the therapy, Anton developed various tendencies to flee from the daily professional demands that overwhelmed him as they increasingly accumulated, not to mention the never-ending private demands as a father of several small children and as a husband.

Seen in astrological terms, Neptune moves into focus to show how each of these archetypal forces can be lived on various levels. In this critical phase of Anton's life, Neptune showed up as a continual longing for foreign lands. In principle, this corresponds with his position in Sagittarius and especially so in the Ninth House (which is simultaneously the Sagittarius House). As a result, Anton was caught in the ambivalence of wanting to stay at home and devote himself to his family, but at the same time wanting to go abroad and work there. But this desire remained a dream, since Anton did not do enough to actually realize this desire that he had always cherished. This is not surprising since his Neptune is retrograde and therefore less oriented toward the outside world than the inside. So this longing for foreign worlds is less about exploring the concrete Earth than the adventures that can be experienced on the journey into the cosmos of our own unconscious.

Anton also looked for a way to escape by drinking excessive alcohol at times. But as we know from the description of the water signs, they tend to be more receptive than active. So Anton had a problem with his drive, symbolized by Mars in Cancer, during his depressive phase. The fire of Mars was figuratively extinguished by the water—or in other words, Mars sank into the water element of Cancer, which means that this principle became unconscious. It has the trigonal connection with Jupiter (striving for independence) in Pisces in the First House, which offers many types of options. However, since Jupiter never became concrete in the tension to Neptune, there was no energetic implementation (Mars)—for example, in relation to the wish to go abroad. The harmonious connection of Jupiter with Mars, both of which are located in water signs, was manifested by Anton occasionally drowning their fiery energy in alcohol.

After such a fall into alcohol, Anton's bursts of anger occurred more frequently. He was not considerate of his partner and his children, and this was followed directly by feeling guilty, which was reinforced in turn by the loss of control in the affective outbreak. It was a true vicious circle, but it became possible for his growing awareness to ultimately transform it into a positive upward spiral.

Anton today

Anton learned to recognize that he has different sides that all want to be lived. He has also learned to better bring these various parts of his personality into harmony with each other—instead of playing them against each other, or just living one at the cost of the others. He has become aware that both the earthy side (which brings him existential safety) and the freedom-loving water and fire sides want to and must be lived.

Anton does much to animate his water or emotional side. He dreams a lot and likes to draw, which he does very well. In therapy sessions, he is also open to sand play.[231] In his development process, this preoccupation with his unconscious also ultimately had the effect of centering his personality. The very positive result of this is a newly won joy in his profession and his family. Anton's psychological equilibrium has very much improved on the whole, and today he can calmly reflect on his tendency to flee, but is no longer at its mercy. He finds himself on a productive path in dealing with himself and his fellow human beings.

Eva—The path to freedom

Eva is a middle-aged, attractive, and well-kempt woman who is very successful in her profession. However, her motive for going to a therapist was not fed by this well-functioning part of her life, but by issues related to her relationship life that had caused her much suffering. She was in the process of separating from her husband, to whom she had been married for more than two decades. She wondered why she had allowed herself to spend so many years in an unsatisfactory relationship. A look at her horoscope shows that Eva has a very strong disposition to adapting. The astrological details of this analysis will be presented below.

The topic of adaptation versus freedom has always been central in Eva's life, but she had not been aware of it enough to be able to change something until quite recently. So the years of extreme adaptation in her private life—which came at the expense of important aspects of her personal freedom and development—had led her into a dead end, from which she wanted to find her way out again. This extreme adaptation was accompanied by a lack of inner strength that would have allowed her to set boundaries and make demands in her marriage.

Eva's main concern is now to regain her autonomy, advance her own individuation, find and strengthen her roots within the scope of intimate relationships, and rediscover her vital emotions. Her horoscope structure shows this in the strong emphasis of the Second Quadrant, which means an accentuation on the private or deep person. With the exception of Saturn—which is located in Aries in the Eleventh/Twelfth Houses—this is where all of the planets are distributed, between the three houses of the Second Quadrant. Eva has been working steadily on this goal of gaining autonomy and individuation. She is firmly resolved to only get involved in a relationship that makes it possible to have a fair giving and taking—equally satisfying for both partners.

Eva's birth chart (see Illustration 4 in the color table section at the end pf the book)

A look at her birth chart shows that almost every planet is located in the Second Quadrant, the family quadrant that starts with the Lower Heaven (Imum Coeli, IC) and ends at the Descendent (DC); the exception to this is Saturn, which is located at the end of the Eleventh and start of the Twelfth House. With such a strong emphasis on the Second Quadrant, Eva is rooted in personal and instinctive spheres, and has the disposition of an introverted personality.[232] We can also immediately see that the Fifth House is strongly emphasized with the planet agglomeration of Jupiter, Pluto, and Uranus in Virgo, as well as the Sun in Libra. This shows that friends, love, and children have a central importance in Eva's life.

The Sixth House, which is also heavily occupied, shows that her profession plays an emotionally significant role for her. The two emotional planets of Venus and the Moon are connected there with the communication principle of Mercury. Eva's talent for relationships makes her professionally so successful in a service branch of the private sector, where she reliably cultivates a large network of relationships.

Planet Positions and the Ascendant

Sun in Libra	1° 50'	–	Fifth House
Moon in Scorpio	3° 25'	–	Sixth House
Mercury in Libra	27° 30'	–	Sixth House
Venus in Libra	27° 39'	–	Sixth House
Mars in Virgo	1° 56'	–	Fourth House
Jupiter in Virgo	19° 48'	–	Fifth House
Saturn r in Aries	23° 39'	–	Eleventh/Twelfth House
Uranus in Virgo	29° 46'	–	Fifth House
Neptune in Scorpio	24° 26'	–	Sixth House
Pluto in Virgo	23° 1'	–	Fifth House
Moon's Nodes in Aries	9° 49'	–	Eleventh House

AC Gemini	15° 29'
MC Aquarius	14° 47'
2nd House: Cancer	5° 25'
3rd House: Cancer	23° 46'
5th House: Virgo	13° 37'
6th House: Libra	26° 49'
DC Sagittarius	15° 29'
IC Leo	14° 47'
8th House: Capricorn	5° 25'
9th House: Capricorn	23° 46'
11th House: Pisces	13° 37'
12th House: Aries	26° 49'

Introversion or extraversion?

Eva's main themes relate to family (Fourth House), love and children (Fifth House), and her profession in the service sector (Sixth House). These are private issues that require an entirely personal and subjective solution. Eva can therefore be recognized as an introverted personality. However, due to the "airy" style of the core attitude in the sign of Libra and the Ascendant in Gemini, she makes a lighter impression than Anton, the previously discussed introvert.[233]

Eva has obviously developed good extraverted abilities, since hardly anyone is entirely introverted or extraverted, but has something of both attitudes. Not remaining trapped in one of the two extremes is an advantage in coping with life. So Eva is mainly an introverted personality in her core attitude, which is rooted in privacy, but has gained the necessary extraverted abilities within the course of her professional development.

Separation as liberation and problem: Animus and self-image

As mentioned, Eva did not come to therapy due to professional problems, but because she was in the process of separating from her husband. So we should look at her masculine side, the animus, which is always involved in choosing a partner. The Sun (fatherly principle and animus) in Libra and Mars (activity, aggression principle, and animus) in Virgo. Libra personalities are known for their love of harmony, which is often practiced as an aversion to conflict. This applies in this case. Eva had long idealized her husband and glossed over his problematic behavior—although her circle of friends had been asking her for years why she was taking the trouble to stay with this man.

However, this question did not come from her parents since they considered it important for married couples to stay together even under strained conditions. Since Eva cultivates a close relationship with her parents, her own need for harmony that tries to avoid difficult conflicts as much as possible was also reinforced by the parent's harmony-loving attitude.

The Virgo and Scorpio principle, as well as Saturn—but without a connection to the Sun in this case—provide competence in facing critical questions. The Sun principle as the main portion of the masculine image is therefore unaffected by reality, but is even idealized here in three ways. Through the sextile to Neptune in Scorpio, the Sun principle in Libra is enriched by empathy and depth with an orientation toward the beautiful side of the visible world (which her former partner clearly did not show in how he treated Eva); the half-sextile between the Sun and the Mercury-Venus conjunction in Libra also brings into play an equally well-intended and sugarcoating side that tends toward repression. This is why the man in question—who is many years older than Eva and already has two daughters and a son from his first marriage—could afford to break off the very good sexual relationship with Eva after ten years of what had been a happy marriage, because she had taken the risk of expressing her desire for children. He apparently could not comprehend that having children of her own was a legitimate and very natural wish for his still young wife.

Only the essential forces of Mars and Uranus in Virgo, in connection with the Sun, provide a good analytical view of what the situation actually is; however, they were not able to exercise enough influence for years. Eva stayed with her husband for another ten years, who acted completely stony and cold toward her ever since she expressed her desire to have children. By the time she actually started to face the facts, many comments had been made to her by the couples who were her friends. Even her stepdaughter and stepson thought that their father's behavior toward their stepmother was unbearable and asked her why she—as a beautiful, intelligent, and professionally successful woman in the best years of her life—would allow herself to be treated like a Cinderella by her unloving and aging husband. This is a good question. What is at work in Eva's self-image as a woman?

Parent complexes, experience of the mother, and self-image

Eva, who always only spoke very positively about both of her parents and has a good relationship with them, describes her mother as an overprotective parent who did everything for her children. She describes her father a bit less clearly, since he always seemed to be somewhat in the background—perhaps because he is apparently a quiet man with no problems. But he is also supportive of her. At the start of the therapy, her parent complexes seemed positive—at least in Eva's conscious perception of them. However, her unconscious with its pictorial language allowed itself to reveal a different truth, which will be discussed in more detail below. We could perhaps say Eva has an overly positive father complex; in any case, her stories cast no shadows of any kind on her father.

The majority of her mother complex is also positive, but a problem has become visible as she has been engaging with her unconscious, and is already hinted at in the term "overprotective parent." The mother's perpetual fear that something bad could happen to her daughter is a strain on Eva since it expresses a lack of trust. This excessive concern on the mother's part may be based on the loss of her own mother at an early age, which had given her a difficult and sad childhood. She grew up in a loveless situation with a stepmother who treated her like a maid; as a result, she swore to give her own children only the best and make it possible for them to have a harmonious family life. She was completely successful in fulfilling this wish. But she could not let go of her children and was constantly worried about them. Furthermore, harmony was her supreme principle and conflicts had to be avoided at all cost.

In Eva's case, where does this mother show up in astrological terms? The mother-child theme always involves the Moon and its aspects. Eva has a Scorpio Moon in a further conjunction with Neptune (boundary expanding and idealizing principle) in Scorpio (emotional depths) and

202

in a closer conjunction with Venus in Libra. This is a double disposition for the tendency towards sugarcoating reality, which points to a mother image that is full of tension in the sense that emotional depths and human suffering—as well as overcoming it—are important themes. In addition, the Scorpio element in which the Moon (mother image and mother-child relationship) is located and is attuned to symbiosis. Since the motherly principle (the Moon) is colored by Scorpio, it is no surprise that there is a symbiotic connection between mother and daughter in Eva's case. Moreover, the Neptune disposition (Neptune in Scorpio) brings with it additional boundary problems with the surrounding world since Neptune is specialized in the dissolution of boundaries (cf. the section on "The Ten Planets in Astrology" in Chapter 1). This can also be expressed in the desire for merging and fears of possible dangers.

Through the additional conjunction of Mercury (thinking) in Libra to Venus in the conflict-avoiding Libra principle, her thinking and not just her feeling has placed harmony above the truth, ultimately leading to the standstill of her development in this case. However, the Mercury-Venus conjunction in Libra (attuned to perpetual harmony and therefore the status quo) stands in opposition to and therefore in a tensile test with Saturn (reality principle) in Aries, the sign of courageous new beginnings. Unfortunately, the reality principle of Saturn especially curbs this fiery energy of awakening in Eva's case. The experience with her mother is marked by her exaggerated fear and concern, primarily in relation to what is new and unknown. In Eva's horoscope, Saturn (the master in drawing boundaries) is also in retrograde, which means it behaves introverted and oriented toward the inside, to the unconscious—which makes it even more difficult to draw boundaries to the outside world.

Of all the important people in her environment, it was Eva's mother who did not want to lose her son-in-law—since he had belonged to the family for more than twenty years—even though her daughter was emotionally withering next to this man. The mother—who only looked at the successful, respected couple with a certain superficial perspective—could apparently not adequately perceive the prevailing coldness between the two and was therefore unable to truly support her daughter in this important matter.

At the start of the analysis, Eva's self-image as a woman was secretly weak. In the depths of her unconscious, she was defined by this fearful mother image that nipped any development in the bud. This was impressively shown in Eva's dreams, in which her emotions were frozen in ice. For example, high waves in a river were frozen into sculptures in an evocative dream image. In the course of the analytical process, these frozen waves turned fluid and Eva's previously hidden tears were able to flow once again. Her emotional life has started to stir again.

Her soul had become frozen after the shock of her ex-husband's total withdrawal of his love. As a young, barely thirty-year-old woman at that time, she functioned quite unconsciously in her identification with her mother, according to the latter's pattern of "you must sacrifice much to keep the harmony." As a result, she sacrificed a great deal after this shocking turning point of her ex-husband's total withdrawal of love for more than ten years of her life—which would have been a good time to have her own children in a natural way. This topic of childlessness is associated with much pain for her.

But thanks to the Scorpio Moon, she also possesses the distinct gift of recovering from a crisis, finding a new attitude toward life, and transforming the situation—in addition to her capacity for devotion and symbiosis. Like no other zodiac sign, the Scorpio principle as the dying-and-becoming principle teaches people the ability to endure crises with perseverance and to regenerate time and again like the phoenix, which burns away when old and rises as a newborn from the ashes. Today Eva is a happy and active godmother for a number of children, as well as a beloved and highly esteemed step-grandmother.

Eva today: What about love?

Eva is taking her time in finding an appropriate partner because she wants to first sufficiently work through the old relationship. The accompanying inner images that shape her can be further changed in this way and will contribute toward her opening up to an affectionate, appreciative partner who will support and respect her newly won freedom—because love is a part of Eva's life.

Heidi—Trapped in Saturn's tower of performing duties

Heidi is a youthful looking, very slender, and elegant older woman who still exudes a lot of nervousness and trembles all over her body. It is not possible for her to just sit calm and relaxed. She always has to move, which is not a surprise after looking at her distinctly tension-filled horoscope and hearing her talk about how she has lived up to now. She is agitated because this is the first time that she has gone to someone to talk about the personal problems that trouble her. Heidi has worked hard all her life in a successful family business. Bent by the never-ending burdens that she has taken upon herself throughout her lifetime, Heidi is somewhat insecure as she sits there because she is only allowing herself to have a conversation about herself at an advanced age. She is not at all accustomed to being the center of attention, and it is therefore also difficult for her to openly speak about what is bothering her. It is also difficult for her to recognize where the main problem in her life has been. She thinks she has a good husband, but otherwise, she feels very lonely since she never had one single female friend. She would like to know about the possibilities for changing this and also how to make contact with other people—above all, with other women. This is her declared goal.

Heidi's birth chart (see Illustration 5 in the color table section at the end of the book)

Heidi's birth chart shows two accents, which can be summarized as follows:

Heidi's spectacular-looking birth chart shows a quadratic square formed by four square aspects (90° angle) between two respective planets, whereby two planets—the Sun (main attitude in life, fatherly principle, and animus) and Mercury (thinking and communication)—are in a close conjunction in the Imum Coeli (IC). Each of them respectively even forms two angles with one of the three other essential forces.

With the Sun in the Lower Heaven (Imum Coeli, IC) in the zodiac sign of Capricorn—which is simultaneously the Sun sign since the Sun together with Mercury are located in Capricorn—the focus in Heidi's horoscope is on the family quadrant, namely in the Fourth House (family and own roots). With the Sun in Capricorn in the Fourth House, the father principle has a dominant position at the root of this horoscope picture; in view of this main position of the Sun, the question immediately arises as to how this has manifested in Heidi's life. The image of a house tyrant spontaneously appears, and this theme will be discussed in detail below.

In this birth chart, it is conspicuous that the red aspects clearly prevail. First, the Sun in conjunction with Mercury is in a quadratic tension (90°) with Jupiter (desire for expansion and question of meaning) in Libra (love of harmony) in the First House, where the issue is self-formation and self-development. Second, the Sun and Mercury also have a tension aspect with Uranus (freedom, the unforeseen, and new ideas) in Aries in the Seventh House (90°). And third, they have an opposition (180°) with Pluto (power, helplessness, and principle of dying-and-becoming) in Cancer in the Tenth House (public life, society, and representative functions). This shows that there is much friction, inhibition, and tension in Heidi's horoscope.

Outside of this red, tense structure, there is a large concentration of planets (several conjunctions) in the sign of Aquarius and the Fifth House (intimate love and friendships, children, games, sports, and creative self-expression) led by Saturn (boundaries, reality, and blockages) in a very close conjunction with Mars (drive, active energy, and animus), as well as Venus (Goddess of Love, aesthetics, and balance) and the Moon (soul, dream world, and motherly principle). Throughout her long life, Heidi has not been able to access this great potential for ease, a sense of freedom (Aquarius), and creativity (Fifth House). There are tensions that are so overpowering due to the analytical aspect figure in the form of a square spanned in two oppositions, which Heidi cannot control; these are expressed in the constant trembling movements.

Planet Positions and the Ascendant

| Sun in Capricorn | 27° 09' | – | Fourth House |
| Moon in Aquarius | 29° 59' | – | Fifth House |

Mercury in Capricorn	25° 44'	– Fourth House
Venus r in Aquarius	23° 31'	– Fifth House
Mars in Aquarius	16° 22'	– Fifth House
Jupiter in Libra	22° 33'	– First House
Saturn in Aquarius	16° 16'	– Fifth House
Uranus in Aries	23° 34'	– Seventh House
Neptune r in Virgo	12° 4'	– Eleventh/Twelfth House
Pluto r in Leo	23° 35'	– Tenth House
Moon's Nodes in Aquarius	20° 41'	– Fifth House

AC Libra	7° 7'
MC Cancer	9° 32'
2nd House: Scorpio	1° 24'
3rd House: Sagittarius	2° 15'
5th House: Aquarius	15° 37'
6th House: Pisces	14° 39'

DC Aries	7° 7'
IC Capricorn	9° 32'
8th House: Taurus	1° 24'
9th House: Gemini	2° 15'
11th House: Leo	15° 37'
12th House: Virgo	14° 39'

Extraversion or introversion?

Heidi has most of her planet positioned below the horizon, in the
First Quadrant (personal needs, subjectivity, and egocentrism) with
an emphasis on the First House (self-formation and self-assertion), the
Second Quadrant (family and private life), the Fourth house (family
and own roots), and the Fifth House (creativity, children, and intimate
relationships). Heidi's personality is clearly introverted. This is further
reinforced by retrograde Mercury, the communication principle, which
is turned inward as a result and has difficulty in coming out of its
shell and communicating. Moreover, Mercury is virtually imprisoned
in the red tense aspect structure and is also under the control of the

207

pragmatically oriented Sun in Capricorn, due to its place next to it. With such a "tense" Mercury function, these individuals find it difficult to express themselves; this becomes even more acute when talking about their own feelings. With her strongly introverted attitude, Heidi— at least at an advanced age—has dared to take the step out of herself toward a familiar other person (object reference), which has awakened a very tiny bit of extraversion within her.

Harsh father figures

With a look at the structural disposition of a Capricorn Sun (father image) in the Fourth House (family field) and its complex aspects, the question arises about Heidi's relationship with her biological father and other men. Heidi reports that her own father, who she barely remembers, died in an accident before she started school, and that she had to grow up with a strict stepfather. Her mother had apparently been "difficult" and was unable to protect her from the harshness of the stepfather, who had been quite a house tyrant.

Seen in astrological terms, the experience of the unexpected and sudden death of Heidi's father can be associated with the constellation of Uranus (sudden changes) in fiery Aries in a square with the Sun; this can also be linked with Pluto, which is associated among other things with violence, power, and helplessness—and also death and rebirth. Pluto is also in a square with Uranus, as well as in an opposition (conflict and tensile test) with the Sun. The Capricorn Sun is also under a great deal of pressure and tension. Since it is located in the family field as the center of personality, this means that the dramas around the father principle play out in the private sphere.[234]

The same negative role as the stepfather was assumed by Heidi's father-in-law, and she was not able to please him. Fortunately, she always received support from her husband. According to her own description, she has been living with him in a long and good relationship. He set strong boundaries against his own father, whom he called a "dominant house tyrant." But why can the father-in-law even play such an important and oppressive role in Heidi's life? In reality, this was because he served as the head of a traditional family business and wanted to control it up to the time of his death—even though his son and his wife Heidi had been successfully running the company in the meantime.

Astrologically, the Capricorn Sun in the fourth field (family field and own roots) corresponds with the structurally given father archetype and also indicates Heidi's dominant father complex. Together with Mars in Aquarius, which in turn stands under the influence of Saturn due to a close conjunction, the Sun forms the basis for Heidi's animus.

But Saturn is also extremely influential: on the one hand, due to the Sun in Capricorn (Saturnal zodiac sign since it is associated with the planet Saturn); on the other hand, due to the very close conjunction of Saturn with Mars in Aquarius, the playful possibilities of which are very restricted through its connection with "old man" Saturn. The latter only gets somewhat more optimistic support through Jupiter (trine and harmonious aspect) in Libra. With such a dominant Saturn, relaxation is a foreign word for Heidi. Work and accomplishment, being even better, and doing even more are her norms. Throughout her life, these have been dictated to her by the perfectionist animus that can hardly be satisfied. She responded to the constant excessive demands with psychosomatic complaints, which are classically chronic and sometimes severe back tension.

Her constant acquiescence to meeting demands has led not only to back problems but also knee problems; as a result of her nightly bruxism—"sinking her teeth" into the obligations that need to be met even during sleep—she has ultimately also developed dental problems due to the tension in her jaw.

Heidi also suffers from a further problem, which she already mentioned above. She trembles all over her body. According to her story, her nervous system has always been very "weak" and the slightest agitation has always caused her to start trembling even at a young age. When she was stressed—like when her father-in-law treated her tyrannically or she did not know how to defend herself—it turned into a severe tremor.

This trembling also intensified whenever she said yes to some sort of obligation that she was asked to do. Heidi could also not set boundaries when an acquaintance wanted something from her. This automatism of saying yes is related to the unintegrated spontaneity of the Uranus principle in the activist Aries on the Descendant. Since

Heidi's mother had not taught her daughter how to protect herself, she overexerted herself not only in her professional, but also her private acts of helpfulness. People could always count on Heidi's absolute reliability and constantly functioning perfectionism.

The path ahead: What must Heidi still learn?

The issue for Heidi is having the guts to say no. She must learn to pause and consider whether she really wants to take on a certain obligation or not. The better she succeeds at this, the more she can loosen and ultimately get rid of all the constraints. In the best case, she can transform the spontaneity of Uranus—with which she has automatically maneuvered herself into the "yes trap" throughout her life—into the possibility of opposing the outside world's wishes and requirements by saying no. In this way, she can gain the space to bring her two feminine planetary principles of Venus and the Moon in Aquarius to fuller development.

This means that Heidi must concretely reserve the time for everything that she would like to do, but had always sacrificed for the sake of fulfilling her obligations. In her case, these are pleasures such as dancing or necessary, well-deserved, and enjoyable relaxation-bringing baths and massages. In a very general way, it would be quite important for her to spend more time with women friends without having to accomplish anything—just in leisure.

Relationship with the Surrounding World and Interest in Other People: Focus on the Descendant and Position of the Familiar Other Person

Paul—The artist and Don Juan

Paul is a great charmer who hardly anyone—and above all, almost no woman—can resist. Based on his core attitude, his energies are intensely directed toward the surrounding world with his Sun and Saturn in Scorpio, as well as with Neptune and Venus in Libra in the Seventh House; together with the Moon in Leo in the Fifth/Sixth House, this gives him a strong charisma radiating to his fellow human beings and especially women.

So Paul's social life always showed the following pattern: a young woman would move in with Paul and would sometimes get replaced by the next muse within a few weeks. Those around him often wondered how the usually average, but sometimes attractive women—often with just a moderate amount of education and no special artistic abilities—suddenly began to paint, sculpt, and play music in the brief time that they spent at Paul's side and under his instruction.

But as soon as the honeymoon period was over, and Paul was together with a new Venus, the blossoming creative tendencies of his ex-lovers dried up and they generally returned to their quite prosaic everyday lives. This rarely happened without tears, since Paul's obsessive joy of conquest always quickly focused on a new female being.

Paul's birth chart (see Illustration 6 in the color table section at the end of the book)

Paul's birth chart shows the following accents:

With the Sun (consciousness, will, core of the personality, main interests, and fatherly principle) in Scorpio in the last third of the Seventh House (partnerships), and therefore in the Third Quadrant, Paul's main interest is found in his contacts with other people. Ascendant Aries (spontaneity, courage, and drive) allows Paul to approach his environment with spontaneity. This interest in the other person is supported by further planets in the Seventh House, which starts in the sociable sign of Libra. Venus (eros, love, aesthetics, art, and culture), which can develop quite well in its associated sign of Libra, shows up in the importance of his encounters with women.

Venus also has a further conjunction with Neptune (boundary-eliminating and idealizing principle), which is also located in Libra. The theme of illusion (Neptune) and disillusionment plays a large role in Paul's life since the illusion is followed by the dis-illusionment of reality, which is symbolized by Saturn. It is located at the start of the sign of Scorpio and forms a conjunction with the Sun in Scorpio.

In addition to his main interest in other people (Seventh House), erotic-sexual contact is also a pronounced need (Uranus in Cancer at the end of the Fourth/start of the Fifth House and the Moon in Leo in the Fifth/Sixth House). Moreover, work and profession are significant with three planets in the Sixth House (Moon-Pluto conjunction in Leo and Mars in Virgo), and furthermore, self-improvement has been an important topic (Jupiter in Gemini in third house) through his entire lifetime. The Eighth House (dying-and-becoming themes) with Mercury (thinking) in Scorpio is also oriented toward the surrounding world, but more existentially in terms of ultimate things and the deeper background of life than superficial pleasures—as is the case for his Venus-Neptune side in the sign of Libra.

Planet Positions and the Ascendant

Sun in Scorpio	6° 53'	–	Seventh House
Moon in Leo	3° 25'	–	Fifth House
Mercury in Scorpio	29° 31'	–	Seventh House
Venus in Libra	14° 50'	–	Seventh House
Mars in Virgo	28° 46'	–	Sixth House
Jupiter r in Gemini	26° 05'	–	Third House
Saturn in Scorpio	0° 58'	–	Seventh House
Uranus r in Cancer	23° 6'	–	Fourth/Fifth House
Neptune in Libra	24° 7'	–	Seventh House
Pluto in Leo	24° 50'	–	Fifth House
Moon's Nodes in Capricorn	28° 3'	–	Eleventh House
AC Aries	10° 41'		
MC Capricorn	4° 46'		
2nd House: Taurus	21° 37'		
3rd House: Gemini	15° 28'		
5th House: Cancer	24° 56'		
6th House: Leo	22° 13'		
DC Libra	10° 41'		
IC Cancer	4° 46'		
8th House: Scorpio	21° 37'		
9th House: Sagittarius	15° 28'		
11th House: Capricorn	24° 56'		
12th House: Aquarius	22° 13'		

Extraversion or introversion?

In terms of how the quadrants and houses are occupied, the following picture emerges:

With the core attitude and three further planets (Venus, Saturn, and Neptune) in the Seventh House (sociability and partnerships), as well as in the Eighth House (Mercury), there is a great interest in other people, even though the Seventh House with Saturn in Scorpio simultaneously always allows a certain quiet restraint to be felt. The quadrants below the horizon are both occupied by planets; the Second Quadrant with four planets (the Moon, Mars, Uranus, and Pluto) is much more strongly emphasized than the First Quadrant with Jupiter (Third House). This total of five planets below the horizon has an introverted tendency, which is amplified by retrograde Jupiter (Third House) and Uranus (Fourth/Fifth House), both of which face inward.

A clear answer to the question of whether Paul is mostly introverted or extraverted cannot be found so easily since both tendencies are strongly present. However, it appears that his extraverted tendency slightly predominates because—in addition to the core attitude (the Sun) in the Third Quadrant facing the outside world—the Aries Ascendant constantly attunes Paul to new beginnings. This is reflected in his high level of activity in both his professional and private life.

Paul and the women: The anima or "The eternal feminine draws us ever onward and upward"[235]

We should first look at the theme of "women" and "love." As already mentioned, Paul is a great seducer who interacts with women with much charm and interest. They immediately sense that he appreciates and idealizes them—which the women usually perceive as flattering. So it is no wonder that they flock to him.

His anima is constellated by the Moon in Leo in conjunction with Pluto, the reinforcing principle. In this case, women are elevated and almost become a compulsion. Venus in Libra has a further conjunction with Neptune (also in Libra), which likes to paint everything that it directs its energy at in more beautiful colors than are present in reality. This supports the dispositional tendency to project eros, beauty, and artistic talent onto the familiar female other. In addition, the Libra

213

Venus has a harmonious aspect (sextile) with the Moon in Leo, which is associated with a high degree of radiance and is oriented toward the two topics of play and sexual intimacy, as well as work, through its position in the Fifth/Sixth House in this case.

The dominant mother complex and image of women

Paul revers his mother above everything else, as tends to be the case with the Moon in Leo. Reinforced by Pluto, the Moon qualities in Paul's case are elevated into an untouchable ideal—and this happens entirely unconsciously. Based on his description of his mother, it is difficult to actually imagine what she is like because she seems to float above other human beings like a goddess. This exaggerated mother image is always activated in his encounters with women and must be transformed if Paul does not want to remain the eternal seeker, the seduced man, and the seducer who cannot actually commit—but wanders from one beautiful vision to the next. This requires the help of Saturn, the reality principle (more details below).

Father complex and self-image

This primarily involves the Sun, which is located in Scorpio, the energetic water sign that usually has a direct connection with the depths of the human psyche.

Paul speaks less idealistically about his father, who he describes as rather strict, a very responsible and faithful husband, and a successful businessman. This enterprising side is provided by Jupiter, the expansive principle in Gemini with its talent for business matters (utilitarian principle). It has a harmonious trigonal connection (120°) with the Sun, Saturn, and Neptune. This business talent not only largely applies in the projection on his father, but also to Paul himself. The latter actually shows much seriousness in the development of his artistic power and an extraordinary ability to market himself. When it comes to his core concern for art, he is helped by his charm and a realistic eye for facts and circumstances.

Despite his Don Juanism, Paul is first and foremost an artist who is both versatile and successful. The careful and patient implementation of his creativity is promoted by Mars (assertiveness and drive) in Virgo (principle of self-preservation and being active), whereby Mars in its connection with Saturn (reality principle) wants to bring ideas down to the earth. This is also assisted by the Scorpio-Mercury (exchange, intelligence, and manual dexterity), which forms a sextile with Mars and a semi-sextile with Saturn, as well as Jupiter in Gemini. In addition to its high standards (Jupiter), it also lends a pronounced and versatile manual dexterity (Gemini); in turn, this is in a square tension with Mars (principle of concrete trade), and this increases the energy level. So Paul's preference for stone and metal in his artistic works also matches the hardness of the Saturn principle.

Art and love: Paul today

Paul had to deal with his tendency to idealize, which he had done with women. In time, he met a woman who was willing to stay with him despite his Don Juanism, who supports him in his creative energy, and started a family with him. The new role as a husband and father allowed him to mature and assume more responsibility. Above all, this involved the Saturn conjunction with the Sun in the Seventh House, the house of living together in which the focus shifts to the familiar other person.

The increasing integration of his Saturn side was shown in Paul being able to perceive himself in a more realistic way, especially in his superficial Don Juan side. He also became more aware of his tendency for self-deception regarding women. This allowed him to increasingly reduce his respective short-term erotic-sexual addiction.

The more conscious Paul became of the Don Juan pattern—which he described like a hamster running in the wheel—the better he succeeded at sublimating the pull of the anima and making it fruitful in the dimension of his artistic creation. This also increasingly produced delicate, dream-like, and meditative pictures in addition to his work with the previous hard materials such as stone and metals. Paul is now the father of a large group of children (the Moon and Pluto in Leo) and is still together with the mother of his children.

Charlotte—The idealist

Charlotte is a generous, idealistic, and attractive woman who has dedicated her entire life to her family, relatives, and friends; as a result, she is embedded quite well socially.

Charlotte is a natural scientist; she is very intelligent and creative in her thinking. She also is also highly educated and musically quite talented: She plays a number of instruments and sings solo. But even though all of this is on a very high level, she only does it as a hobby. This will be the topic below.

Charlotte's birth chart (see Illustration 7 in color table section at the end of the book)

With the Sun in Aries, she is spontaneous, impulsive, and direct in her core attitude. Fire is very much the dominant element in this horoscope, because the Sun is closely accompanied by Mercury in Aries; the Ascendant with Uranus and Pluto is located in Leo, and Saturn and the Moon in Sagittarius. With such a temperamental personality, we should not expect much patience. Instead, her impatience can break out unchecked with Uranus in Leo, strengthened by Mars in Gemini, and Mercury and the Sun in Aries. This applies because these masculine-oriented archetypes are harmoniously connected with each other by a sextile or trine, which means that they reinforce each other. With Mercury in this alliance, this Uranus-Sun-Mars constellation also supports a wealth of ideas related to topics that are very important to Charlotte; with the help of Mars in Gemini, they are also inventively put into practice.

Planet Positions and the Ascendant

Sun in Aries	1° 39'	–	Ninth House
Moon in Sagittarius	24° 12'	–	Fifth House
Mercury in Aries	3° 27'	–	Seventh House
Venus in Pisces	25° 47'	–	Eighth/Ninth House
Mars in Gemini	2° 55'	–	Tenth/Eleventh House
Jupiter r in Virgo	26° 16'	–	Second/Third house
Saturn in Sagittarius	14° 18'	–	Fifth House

Uranus r in Leo	3° 1'	–	Twelfth House
Neptune r in Scorpio	2° 1'	–	Fourth House
Pluto r in Leo	28° 27'	–	First House
Moon's Nodes in Scorpio	22° 27'	–	Fourth House
AC Leo	14° 34'		
MC Taurus	0° 25'		
2nd House: Virgo	3° 51'		
3rd House: Virgo	28° 25'		
5th House: Sagittarius	8° 36'		
6th House: Capricorn	14° 58'		
DC Aquarius	14° 34'		
IC Scorpio	0° 25'		
8th House: Pisces	3° 51'		
9th House: Pisces	28° 25'		
11th House: Gemini	8° 36'		
12th House: Aquarius	14° 58'		

Extraversion or Introversion?

When people meet Charlotte, they are simultaneously captivated by her sparkling spirit and highly sensitive nature. Her lively presence has a direct effect on those close to her. With the Sun in fiery Aries in the Third Quadrant, the orientation of which is on familiar people, the environment, and the surrounding world, Charlotte's core attitude is extraverted. This is reinforced by the location of both the Sun and Mercury (the clear principle of thought) in Aries and flanked by the sensitivity-attuning Venus in Pisces. Individuals with this disposition can be in danger of losing themselves in relationships with familiar people, since boundaries are dissolved in the Pisces principle. So, Charlotte can lose herself in the surrounding world with its needs and demands of her. Some aspects of the horoscope that are related to this theme will be examined in closer detail below.

Dissolution of boundaries and threatening loss of self

With her Venus (aesthetic principle) in the sign of Pisces at the end of the Eighth House—which creates a symbiotic tendency—and the start of the Ninth House, that is accompanied by an interest in religion, philosophy, and other cultures, Charlotte is open to the surrounding world. She is flowing, and boundless since the Pisces principle is oriented toward the dissolution of boundaries. Quite similar to Venus in Pisces, the Neptune principle in the Lower Heaven (IC) in Scorpio (the passionate water sign) has boundary-eliminating, highly sensitive, and transfiguring tendencies. For Charlotte, the theme of boundary dissolution and idealization is constellated not only in her Venus function but also with Neptune at her roots (IC/Fourth House: family and inner roots).

This is why the ability to make decisions for herself Venus in Pisces has been hampered for Charlotte—at least in the first half of her life— since she did not know how to say no, especially when her father or some other male whom she idealizes asks for her support. With her action-oriented Aries disposition, she is always in the mood for new beginnings and therefore open to the world. Then saying yes happens completely on its own. Venus is weakened not only due to its position in boundary-dissolving Pisces—and with it the ability to give a firm no—but also through the longing aspect of Pluto in Leo, which creates the feeling of being able to live for others out of inexhaustible energy reserves.

The retrograde Jupiter in Virgo (the principle of self-preservation) contrasts with the opposition to the self-sacrificing tendency of the Pisces-Venus, which is under the spell and in the wake of the activist Aries-Sun with a Mercury conjunction. However, it did not have any effect against the Venus disposition that pours itself into familiar other people during the first half of Charlotte's life. In concrete terms, this means that Charlotte not only has difficulty in setting boundaries and taking care of herself but that she has found it to be normal, in her projection on her father and other important men, to allow herself to be exploited by them in her intellectual and artistic abilities—as well as in her talent of mastering everyday life in a successful way.

Pisces-Venus, which makes people very receptive, also has a square tension with the Moon (emotional life and mother-and-child symbol). The Moon in Sagittarius produces a magnanimous, generous, believing-idealistic attitude toward life that is based on fairness and justice. It also awakens the desire to open up to different kinds of people—but in a fiery, energetic, and enthusiastic way; as a result, it amplifies the movement away from the self to the familiar others, as is the case for the Pisces-Venus.

In contrast to people defined by the flowing and resonating eros principle (Venus) that is shaped by Pisces, those imprinted by the Sagittarius Moon always require meaningful goals—since they would otherwise become somewhat depressive. We see that the Moon has an analytical-quadratic tension and its only trine is with Pluto in Leo (First House). This raises the question about the realization of Charlotte's meaningful life goals, as well as her mother image and concrete mother experience (which will be discussed in detail below).

When it comes to the dissolution of boundaries in everyday experience, we must always consider the corresponding archetype in its astrological constellation—which is Neptune in this case. This principle of dissolution of boundaries (at the start of the Second Quadrant and on the cusp of the Fourth House) is at the root of Charlotte's horoscope. In its characteristic of transcending everyday life that evokes the longing for the divine, Neptune attains an especially deep and intensive quality of experience through Scorpio.

Moreover, Neptune is located in the quincunx (150°)—the "longing aspect" with the animus-influenced planets: the Sun and Mars, as well as the thinking principle of Mercury. This leads to a religious exaggeration of the father image and the animus that is built upon it. However, the deep longing for religious rootedness could not be lived out with either the father or her later husband—both of whom were successful and very pragmatic businessmen—which was not surprising since this disposition demands a reconnection to the self and ultimately cannot be found in the outside world. But as long as this Neptune disposition was still very unconscious, it could not be expressed adequately through creativity.

Mother image and self-image

In the Fifth House, there is much creative potential in the Sagittarius Moon with its attunement to self-expression and expansion. But the reality principle of Saturn stands in front of this like a wall; in this case, it came to bear in such a way that Charlotte repeated her mother's fate to a certain degree. Charlotte's mother came from an artistically significant dynasty and was herself very musical; however, her fate prevented her from developing in this direction. In the end, she was content with her role as a housewife and mother of three children. Certain creative hobbies only opened up to her when she was older.

Charlotte also encountered difficulties similar to those of her mother. Born into a merchant family, her father did not respect her wish to become a professional musician or actress, because he wanted to see her have a "solid" education as a natural scientist. Charlotte obeyed and only lived her artistic talents as a hobby from that time on with a heavy heart.

This shows in an exemplary way how Saturn in connection with the Moon can be accompanied by an inhibition of emotional development. In the case of Charlotte and her mother, this meant that that the artistic disposition could not be lived out and resulted in corresponding depressive episodes for the mother.

With a trine between Pluto (First House) and the Moon (Fifth House), the topics of mother, child, and family are given an exaggerated significance. In keeping with this, Charlotte gave birth to four sons and one daughter, becoming compulsively fixated on everything domestic and family-related. This occurred at the expense of a genuine creative life; with Saturn accompanying the Moon, a fateful component was added—in this case, her father saying no. This destiny of not being able to develop a major artistic talent affects Charlotte just as much as her maternal ancestors.

Father image and animus

But how could it happen that Charlotte gave up her artistic ambitions with so little resistance? This is related to the idealized father image, which will be examined in more detail below.

Pluto in aspects of longing (quincunx) with the Sun and Venus, exorbitantly increases the Pisces-Venus' dissolution tendencies. This is reinforced by its harmony aspect (sextile) with Neptune, which in turn stands in the quincunx with the Sun and Mars. The result is that the inner male image is immersed in an exaggerated light of illusion, which applies even more since it also affects Mercury as the principle of thought.

The exaggeration of the animus—which is expressed in the projection on actual men in the form of idealization, which makes them appear like gods—receives even more nourishment through the Jupiter opposition to the Aries-Sun with Mercury and Pisces-Venus; moreover, Pluto reinforces Jupiter (idealization) in its aspects with the father archetype (the Sun) within its overall constellation. This means an increase of the attitude that demands giving one's all (Jupiter)—which is already exaggerated in itself—to an exorbitant extent. Charlotte's pronounced trait of making her energies available to others is also reinforced by Virgo (the principle of services and care for others), where Jupiter in its tendency toward generous exuberance is located.

While the father image already idealized through its Neptune, Jupiter, and Pluto aspects, a further elevation occurs in this respect through the position of the Sun in the Ninth House and Mars in the Tenth/Eleventh House. While the father image is related to the wider world (Ninth House, as well as Tenth/Eleventh House) and also with the cosmos through the Neptune contacts, Charlotte's mother image tends to be associated with limitations, restrictions, and coping with everyday life. In any case, this corresponds with the position of the Moon in the family quadrant. But this Moon in the sign of Sagittarius—for which freedom, independence, travel, philosophy, and religion are main themes—but is partially restricted there in its development due to the connection with Saturn (the boundary-setting principle of reality).

In Charlotte's psyche, femininity does not receive the same high valuation as masculinity; as the typical daddy's girl, she automatically elevates and idealizes the male world. For years, she had allowed herself to be exploited by various bosses in underpaid part-time jobs while advancing the men with her abundant abilities. Charlotte had no idea how to use her abilities for her own benefit until well after she reached middle age. She made them available to male beneficiaries almost for free. How could this happen?

In addition to the already-mentioned factors such as Jupiter in Virgo, the following constellations are important: The Sun and Mars play with Mercury and Uranus—all of them are harmoniously connected. Without friction, nothing disrupts and nothing stimulates reflection! Furthermore, Venus in the sextile harmonizes the father image and the longing aspects of Neptune in the family field and the Sun and Mars promote idealization of the father, while Pluto amplifies this mechanism. Only Jupiter is put to the test by the oppositional position: Charlotte's high expectations of her father are disappointed because of his work reality, which causes him to spend months at a time abroad. What is important within this context of frustrated idealizing projections is that Jupiter is retrograde. This means that its energy is turned inward, which is why the qualities of this archetype can be found less in the outside world than within a person.

Creativity

Especially when it comes to the frequently mentioned fact of creativity, it is worthwhile to focus on the many green aspects known as the "longing aspects." Charlotte has five, which is quite rare. Accordingly, she is ruled by a fine, driving restlessness that could best be translated into reality as creative energy.

Charlotte today: A creative development [235]

In recent months, Charlotte has begun to recognize her brilliant animus qualities as her own masculine abilities and to take back her idealizing projections on men. At the same time, she has started to develop a greater appreciation of her feminine qualities and has become increasingly aware of her weakness in setting boundaries. This has made it possible for her to better protect herself against an automatic dissolution into the outer world. Charlotte is in the process of strengthening her own boundaries and assuming her own standpoints, as well as setting and implementing her personal goals in both professional and private areas.

Relationship with the World and Roles in Public Life: Focus on the Midheaven

Maria—The lioness

When Maria enters the room, all heads turn toward her because she radiates something majestic together with a strong energetic presence.

She is a woman who has taken life into her own hands. In addition to a large family with her four children, she has been very successful in running various small- and medium-sized companies. She was married but has been a widow for many years. Her horoscope provides a illustrative example of a strong emphasis on the Medium Coeli (MC, Midheaven).

Maria's birth chart (see Illustration 8 in the color table section at the end of the book)

With the Sun (consciousness, main purpose in life, and fatherly principle) in Leo in the Tenth House accompanied by Venus (aesthetic principle, love of harmony, and eros), also in Leo in the Tenth House, the focus is on the themes of making an illustrious public appearance, assuming a public role, and the accompanying sense of responsibility. Due to her Leo disposition, Maria fulfills her tasks as a representative person with self-confidence, self-assurance, and a natural assertiveness; the shadow side shows up in her dominance over others. The Moon (the unconscious, motherly principle, and anima) is in Libra in the Twelfth House just before the Ascendant line. It therefore has an effect on the First House, emphasizing the sense for what is beautiful and the joy of refined pleasures, coupled with much charm (Libra); this is also accompanied by receptivity and adaptability (Moon in Libra).

Jupiter in Taurus in the Seventh House focuses on the theme of high expectations in the relationships. As a Venus-oriented sign, the Taurus element is attuned to enjoyment and harmony. This attitude of expectations of the familiar other receives additional weight through Mars, which is also in Taurus, but at the transition into the Eighth House. Saturn (reality and the boundary-setting principle) retrograde in Sagittarius in the Second House emphasizes Maria's will for personal responsibility and material independence. This urge for independence and will for autonomy—which is already expressed through the Sun in Leo in the Tenth House—is reinforced by the large fire trine with Uranus in Aries, Venus in Leo, and Saturn in Sagittarius. Mercury (thinking, speaking, and manual dexterity) in conjunction with Pluto in Cancer in the Ninth House indicate the desire to travel and interest in other cultures.

It becomes clear that the main emphasis in this birth chart is in the Seventh, Ninth, and Tenth Houses (living together, key goals, and public sphere), but also in the Third and Fourth Quadrants above the horizon, which represents an interest in the surrounding environment and in relationships with the world. Maria therefore has a disposition that is structured as an extraverted, charming leadership personality.

Planet Positions and the Ascendant

Sun in Leo	0° 20'	–	Tenth house
Moon in Libra	17° 47'	–	Twelfth house
Mercury in Cancer	10° 27'	–	Ninth House
Venus in Leo	6° 23'	–	Tenth house
Mars in Taurus	18° 59'	–	Seventh/Eighth House
Jupiter in Taurus	8° 9'	–	Seventh House
Saturn r in Sagittarius	12° 58'	–	Second House
Uranus r in Aries	7° 21'	–	Sixth House
Neptune in Leo	27° 51'	–	Tenth House
Pluto in Cancer	17° 3'	–	Ninth House
Moon's Nodes in Gemini	6° 49'	–	Eighth House

AC Libra	23° 38'
MC Cancer	29° 45'
2nd House: Scorpio	20° 43'
3rd House: Sagittarius	23° 18'
5th House: Pisces	3° 43'
6th House: Aries	1° 36'

DC Aries	23° 38'
IC Capricorn	29° 45'
8th House: Taurus	20° 43'
9th House: Gemini	23° 18'
11th House: Virgo	3° 43'
12th House: Libra	1° 36'

Extraversion or introversion?

The distribution of the planets in the quadrants and houses makes it immediately clear that Maria is not a woman who can find happiness in the role of a housewife and mother. The family quadrant is "empty," apart from Uranus in the Sixth House. There is neither an emphasis on the Fourth House with the theme of family nor the Fifth House, which involves intimate love and friendships, children, games, and sports. On the other hand, the two quadrants above the horizon have a strong emphasis, which provides a first indication of an extraverted personality.

Partnership and animus

In the Third Quadrant, which strongly relates to the surrounding world, the Seventh House (in which the familiar other person comes into focus) is emphasized with Jupiter in earthy Taurus. This implies high expectations of the partner, but also Maria's willingness to get intensively involved. Together with the Taurus principle, the concrete and material level of everyday life comes into play.

The Eighth House (which is connected with social symbiosis, as well as give and take) is also animated for Maria through the activity principle of Mars, which is also in Taurus. The Libra Ascendant with the Moon at the end of the Twelfth House radiates into the First House. This means that Maria is willing to actively invest a great deal in partnership-like relationships, but she also expects just as much. With her Libra disposition, she also brings a natural openness into play within her relationships.

We should initially focus on the perspective of the animus projection since it plays a major role in any choice of a partner.[236] The tension aspect (square) between Jupiter (which represents the optimum) in the Seventh House and Maria's Sun-Venus conjunction in the Tenth House

225

and the sign of Leo gives an indication of much potential friction with the partner since no male partner (symbolized by the Sun and Mars) can meet Maria's standards. As a result of the Jupiter-Mars conjunction in Taurus (Seventh House), an almost insatiable orality develops—an urge to veritably assimilate the partner as a "possession"—which must lead to disappointment, since no man would willingly allow this to happen. In any case, this has not happened in Maria's life.

Maria's deceased partner had an entirely different structure. In contrast to Maria, with her practical disposition, he was very introverted and lived in an artistic, intellectual, and spiritual world. He was happiest surrounded by his books. Unfortunately, his happiness was not Maria's happiness. Mars, which also symbolizes the potential center of conflict, showed its effect almost every day when they were living together.

A woman with Mars positioned in the Seventh House (socialness) in the transition to the Eighth House (deeper aspects of a relationship) wants a partner who she can encounter in an entirely natural way (earthy Taurus principle) and who actively (Mars as the principle of drive, activity, and action) approaches her—and not someone who tends to retreat into his own world. However, the longing aspect (quincunx) that connects Mars with the Moon indicates that she has a lifetime longing to find the way to harmony with another person. In addition, this wish for harmony is reinforced in that the two affected essential forces are located in a Venus sign, along with Mars in Taurus and the Moon in Libra. But longing aspects are defined by the fact that the by two "gods" communicating with each other like this never really find, but are always just on the path to each other.

Maria's other animus aspect can be found in the Sun. This is a Leo-Sun, which usually goes hand in hand with a life-affirming attitude that is full of self-confidence and coupled with the belief in one's own power and strength. So Leo qualities also come to bear in the projection on her partner. The Leo-Sun is found here in the Tenth House and therefore in the highest position and most highly rated zone. So the greatest demands are placed on success in professional life and society—both on herself and her partner. He should also have a strong persona, which means the outward side of the personality with which he can adequately move within the collective. The projected Leo side is actually only satisfied when this persona is so brilliant that everyone else is overshadowed. Her husband, who had to bear these projections during the entire marriage, did not adequately meet her expectations, for reasons that have already been suggested.

Father image

Maria's psyche is also ruled by a powerful, positive father complex. She was stuck in an idealization of her father, still describing her father's entire personality as if it were surrounded by a halo.[237] But no partner can be adequate when all of the positive masculine qualities are projected onto the father.

It is interesting to see that this idealization of the father image receives further support through Venus in Leo, which is also in the Tenth House. Venus as the companion of the Sun relates its eros to the Sun and therefore the father. So everything involved with him is colored in beautiful and harmonious shades. In any case, Maria has always characterized her father as the kindest, dearest, and most handsome man in the world. Since he died at a relatively young age when Maria was in puberty, she no longer had the chance to relativize this glorious image of the god who had merged with her father image through real encounters with her actual father.

Her husband, who had come into Maria's life soon thereafter, could never compete with the deceased father—since the former continued to live eternally as a god-like archetype in Maria's psyche. The connection of the Sun with Neptune—also still in Leo and the Tenth House—further reinforces the tendency for idealization through a half-sextile. But at the same time, this Neptune connection means a dead end. It does not help Maria in the development of her inner image of her father and all other relevant men if she remains trapped in illusions (Neptune) of powerful males (the Sun in Leo, Tenth House). Especially through contact with Neptune, the Sun (and with it the inner male image) is simultaneously more sensitive and also weakened as a result. The means that she unconsciously feels attracted to men who show these Neptune qualities. This applies even more since the reality principle of Saturn (Sagittarius, Second House) is not connected with the Sun and therefore cannot give it any grounding in reality.

Maria's Leo nature: Self-image and self-realization

Although Saturn does not offer a reality anchor for Maria's exaggerated male image, it is still harmoniously linked with the Moon and Venus. As we know, the Moon and Venus in their entire aspects and positions in the horoscope symbolize the woman's self-image. As long as she can remember, Maria has actually assumed responsibility not only for herself but also for others. As the oldest of a number of children, she already helped her mother in raising and caring for her many siblings—and received much praise for this from both her mother and father. To this day, she still enjoys a high level of respect from her siblings. In addition, her strong Venus disposition with the Libra Ascendant and also the Moon in Libra, as well as Venus in the Tenth House, are intensely shown in an aesthetic competence that is not only expressed in Maria's tasteful clothing style but in everything with which she surrounds herself.

Together with her deceased husband, she started a family and had four children. Maria assumed the main responsibility for raising the children, which she did gladly and in a balanced, reliable way. Her husband also supported her in this.

So, Maria projected the animus, but she has simultaneously also used her masculine qualities for her own development. It is typical with the Leo-Sun in the Tenth House that Maria would show a high level of personal responsibility and also likes to serve as a type of lighthouse and offer her fellow human beings orientation. It is no coincidence that many successful CEOs have a horoscope structure similar to Maria's. She has been able to realize these leadership qualities in part by holding certain management positions and successfully leading larger groups of subordinates.

These leadership qualities often also prevail in her private life; however, this isn't an entirely positive experience for affected family members, women friends, or male friends since they sometimes feel that she bosses them around. But with the Libra disposition and also the Moon as relationship components, Maria uses her charm and cheerfulness to compensate for the Leo-Sun that tends to be somewhat bossy. Her surrounding world responds positively to this.

All in all, we can say that Maria has made much of her disposition. More and more, she understands that even Leo ladies are allowed to do less at some point, since they too are not spared the aging process.

Conclusion

I have made an attempt in this book to connect C. G. Jung's Analytical Psychology with astrology—an ancient empirical teaching that Thomas Ring revised in the last century and made fruitful for the present. What both theories have in common is the archetypal dimension, upon which their most important components are based, and together provide a holistic understanding of the human psyche.

In order to illustrate this, Jung's concept of the archetype was first introduced in Chapter 1. This was followed by a description of the ten planets from the astrological perspective as archetypal forces that affect every human being—followed by a synopsis of the Jungian archetypes and the astrological "pantheon of the gods."

Chapter 2 developed a depth psychology-astrological typology showing parallels between the four elements of fire, earth, air, and water in the twelve zodiac signs and the four functions of the self according to C. G. Jung: thinking, feeling, sensation, and intuition.

Chapter 3 is an attempt to connect C. G. Jung's theory of the two attitude types of extraversion and introversion with the astrological quadrant and house system.

The topic of Chapter 4 is the interaction of disposition and environment from the perspectives of astrology and depth psychology. It shows how both the aspect structure in the horoscope and the depth psychological complex structure have formative effects on an individual's personality.

Finally, Chapter 5 discusses eight actual birth charts to offer insights into how the various astrological dispositions and archetypal dominants were translated into reality through in interaction with concrete circumstances over the course of these eight people's lives.

It should be emphasized that it was only possible for me to formulate these individualized written statements on horoscopes within the context of this book, because I know the people who live with these different horoscope structures very well. As a result, I have an insight into the very personal way in which they have filled their structural dispositions with life to this day.

They have read my written representations and have given their permission to have these descriptions appear in print. I am deeply indebted to them for their trust, because I could only have made general statements about certain horoscope dispositions without their generous willingness to provide living illustrative material for this introduction to depth psychological astrology. It would not have been possible to provide readers with such differentiating insights into the concrete implementation of various structural dispositions. But these eight horoscope examples have made it possible to sketch out how a structural disposition that becomes apparent in the birth chart influences how the outside world is experienced—especially the individual's own parents—and what this means for the complex structure, as well as how this impacts the development of the individual in turn.[238]

What is the point of all this, and what is the benefit of depth psychological astrology? My daily experience shows that this is extraordinarily useful for becoming aware of our own personality structure, our complex landscape, and our personal strengths and weaknesses. By studying our own horoscope, we generally have many epiphanies. Comparing the horoscopes of two people also proves especially fruitful in everyday life—whether it simply allow them to better understand each other, or helps them face and transform virulent and chronic couple conflicts. An explanatory approach based on depth psychological astrology can contribute not only to recognizing our own structural dispositions, but also those of our partner.

In an elegant way, this comparison can make the similarities and differences in the dispositions very clear. It can initiate fruitful conversations between partners, help minimize conflicts, and increase the tolerance and understanding that they have for each other in many cases. This method can also be applied successfully in the mother-child or father-child relationship. So it is just as enriching for educational guidance as it is for couples counseling.

Depth psychological astrology—in which an ancient, highly differentiated typology is brought together with Jungian concepts—can therefore be used for every type of conflict management. But above all, it can be consulted with major benefit when there is a desire for deeper self-knowledge. I wish the readers much success in both of these applications of the material discussed in this book.

Notes

1   Ring, 1985a, p. 3.
2   Riemann, 1986, p. 9.
3   Ring, 1985a, p. 23.
4   Jung, *Briefe II* (Letters II), p. 400.
5   Ibid., p. 401.
6   Goethe, 1961, p. 523.
7   Cf. Jung, *Briefe II* (Letters II), p. 402.
8   Jung, *CW 8*, § 392.
9   Cf. ibid., §§ 816–987, especially § 977 and id., *Briefe II* (Letters II), p. 400ff.; 230f.
10   Id., *CW 8*, § 866.
11   Id., *Briefe II* (Letters II), p. 402.
12   Cf. ibid., p. 400ff.
13   Ibid., p. 94.
14   Cf. ibid., p. 400ff.
15   Cited in: Jones, 1969, p. 477.
16   Cf. Jacobi, 2012; Kast, 2012; Dorst, 2015.
17   Cf. Jung's statements on topics such as archetypes and collective unconscious, planets as archetypes or "gods" in: *Briefe II* (Letters II), p. 400.
18   Noam Chomsky has dealt with such questions in connection with his "generative grammar." The current field research of the psycholinguist Sabine Stoll in a major international project is also investigating the ways in which children come to their native language. Cf. *Magazin der Universität Zürich* (Magazine of the University of Zurich), 2014, No. 3.
19   Cf. Jung, *CW 8*, § 270, § 417, and § 440; *CW 9/I*, § 99 and § 155.
20   Cf. ibid.
21   Id., *CW 9/I* § 151.
22   Cf. the above statements on the inherent disposition of a child.
23   Cf. Winnicott, 1994 and 1995.

24 A special chapter within this context are adopted children. It is usually a major challenge for adoptive parents to establish the necessary closeness and familiarity between themselves and their adopted child – especially when this does not occur soon after the birth. It takes a great deal of awareness and commitment on the part of the parents to build a good, trusting relationship with their adopted child. For example, if the child had to live for months or even years in depriving conditions, the emotional damage may already be so extensive that it becomes a very difficult undertaking for adoptive parents that often leads to great disappointments.

25 Stierlin, 1980.

26 Cf. Scharfetter, 1996.

27 Jung, *Briefe II* (Letters II), p. 400.

28 The period from one Full Moon to the next is called a synodic month = 29.6 days (New Moon 0.0 – first quarter 7.4 – Full Moon 14.8 – last quarter 22.2).

29 Howling dogs or wolves are also associated with the Full Moon; people like the Anthroposophists take the moon phases into consideration when planting and picking fruit, vegetables, and herbs; some people only allow their hair to be cut during the waxing Moon so that it grows faster and stronger; police and hospitals report more accidents, murders, and suicides, as well as births, during the Full Moon.

30 This also includes the Active Imagination, a special technique that Jung developed.

31 It corresponds with a lunar month of 29.6 days.

32 A normal pregnancy lasts ten lunar months.

33 Comment: The fit between mother and child was mentioned above. It makes it easier for the two to relate or more difficult when there is insufficient "chemistry."

34 The trickster side of Hermes already appeared shortly after his birth when he fooled his adult brother Apollo despite just being a newborn: According to the Greek mythology, Hermes/Mercury already jumped out of his cradle as a newborn and stole the herd of cattle from Apollo that belonged to King Admetos of Thessaly and that Apollo must guard. After his work is done, Hermes lies down like an innocent infant in his cradle and lets Apollo search for the thief without a clue for a long time. Hermes is so clever that he lays false tracks so that no one gets the idea that they lead away from and back to the cradle. Zeus is amused by his cunning son and finally orders Hermes to show Apollo where the herd of cattle is hidden. To appease the angry Apollo, the infant Hermes plays for him on the lyre – which he made himself from a turtle. Cf. Ranke-Graves, 1984, p. 52–55, and Fink, 2001, pp. 135–137.

35 In Greek mythology, he is called Ares; in the Roman, he is called Mars; in Homer's poem *The Iliad*, Ares is depicted as a courageous fighter.

36 Zeus, the supreme god in Greek mythology who the Romans called Jupiter, very nicely shows what is meant by broadening the existing horizon of experience; however, the mythological Father of the Gods – to the chagrin of his wife Hera – focused on catching the most beautiful mortal or even immortal female beings, with whom he conceived many extramarital children.

37 Ring, 1986, p. 83.

38 Ibid., p. 83.

39 The difference between synthetic and analytical aspects will be explained in the subchapter on "Aspect Structure in the Horoscope" in Chapter 4.

40 For the signs of the zodiac, see Chapter 2.

41 This refers to women with a heterosexual orientation. The relationship between male and female qualities is somewhat different for homosexual women – which also applies to homosexual men. Due to the enormous complexity of this topic, it will not be treated in greater detail within the scope of this book.

42 There are impressive examples of this in art and literature.

43 Cf. also Jung, *Psychology and Alchemy, CW 12*, Ill. 103 "Sponsus et Sponsa" and Ill. 218 "The bath of the philosophers."

44 See the subchapter on "The Twelve Zodiac Signs in Their Functional Sequence" in this chapter.

45 For example, Libra and Aries can be lived more fully if both are present in the horoscope disposition. When there are additional planets in the polar opposite sign, the person will feel both zodiac signs much more distinctly, especially in their oppositeness, than when they are "empty." This is because the tension between the antipodes is intensified, increasing the chance of becoming aware of both poles. Through the individual's increasing awareness of the opposite zodiac sign in the personality, one-sidedness can be corrected. For example, the Libra's difficulties in making decisions can be balanced by the Aries side that is quick to act decisively; conversely, the Libra side can temper the impulsiveness of Aries. Such work on inner psychological opposing dispositions creates a more balanced, whole personality.

   If a Libra and an Aries meet on the outer level of reality and enter into a partnership, each of them will project their own unconscious opposite side onto the counterpart. This may lead to fascination on the one hand, but can also trigger tension and conflicts. By working through these projections and taking them back, an individual becomes more conscious and therefore also richer and more mature as a personality.

46 Ring, 1985b, p. 167.

47 Ibid., p. 196.

48 Ibid., p. 226.

49 Ibid., p. 174.

50 Ibid., p. 203.

51 Ibid., p. 234.

52 Cf. ibid., p. 235.

53 Ibid., p. 181.

54 Ibid., p. 211.

55 Ibid., p. 241.

56 Cf. also ibid., p. 241.

57 Ring, 1985b, p. 188.

58 Cf. "The Moon" subchapter.

59 John the Evangelist, Jesus' favorite disciple, symbolizes the archetype of unconditional devotion to the ideas of truth and selfless love (Jesus as a symbol for the self).

60 Ring, 1985b, p. 249.

61 Cf. the statements on "Neptune" in the subchapter on "The Ten Planets in Astrology" in Chapter 1.

62 Cf. the statements on Jupiter in the "The Ten Planets in Astrology" subchapter in Chapter 1.

63 Important: This note applies to all 12 zodiac signs: The data fluctuate slightly from year to year since the Sun does not change from one zodiac sign to the next on a completely regular basis. So it is important to consult the Ephemeris from year to year since it contains the exact positions of the Sun and the planets that orbit around it. For this book, I used the data of the Sun positions in the twelve zodiac signs from 2019 and 2020, beginning with Aries in 2019 and ending with Pisces in 2020.

64 Goethe allows Faust to critically question the Bible verse in the Gospel of John that says, "In the beginning was the *Word*.": "Is it the *thought* that does all from time's first hour? It should say: "In the beginning was the *power*!" But Faust is still not content and only becomes so when he reaches this conviction: "In the beginning was the *deed*!" (*Faust*, verses 1224–1237).

65 Cf. Jung, *CW 6*, § 666ff. A description of the four functions in polarities may seem somewhat schematic. It may best apply to people who are either less developed in their personality differentiation or have a very one-sided disposition. Very differentiated personalities with versatile dispositions may feel like this does not apply as much to them, but it is useful as an auxiliary construction for our purposes here.

66 Jung, *CW 6*, § 667.

67 It should be taken into consideration that there are various degrees of "unconscious" or "inferior" and this classification should therefore be relativized.

68 Cf. Jung, *CW 6*, § 669.

69 The shadow contains not only the unconscious aspects of our self that we keep suppressed because of their incompatibility with our ego ideal but also because they have not been promoted enough through education and further factors of the surrounding world. Every human being probably has such underused resources that are found in the shadow of his or her conscious personality.

70 Unfortunately, Jung's typology is not yet fully developed; this can be seen primarily in the descriptions of the introverted attitude and especially clear in his description of the introverted feeling type. Since the Jungian typology can only take up a little space within the scope of this book, I must limit myself to a few critical remarks regarding its weak points.

71 At this point, I would like to point out the problem with the term "subjective factor" because it does not seem to me to be really adequate when the main accent in the characterization of people with an introverted attitude is on subjective experiencing. It is also possible to have experiences with the collective unconscious which, in contrast to the personal unconscious, has an objective character. Cf. note 11.

72 Cf. Jung, *CW 6*, § 666.

73 Ibid., § 584.

74 Cf. ibid., § 577.

75 However, I would like to critically note that the inner reality of the subject can also have collective and therefore generally valid aspects. After all, Jung defines the collective unconscious as a piece of nature that encounters the consciousness

as something that is an objective given and therefore oversteps the boundary of the personal unconscious.

76 Jung discusses the difference of philosophical thinking: Is it directed at ideas as abstractions from subjective experiences or at ideas borrowed from the history of philosophy? He only appears to see an extraverted attitude of thinking in the latter case.

77 Cf. Jung, *CW 6*, § 557. I would like to counter that introverted thinking can also be related to outer objects but processed in a subjective way.

78 Jung, *CW 6*, § 590.

79 In his novel *Henry of Ofterdingen*, Novalis describes the contrast between the dry intellect of the Scribe and the living wisdom of Sophia in a fairy tale, the figures of which are personified depictions (allegories) of human virtues and vices.

80 Cf. Jung, *CW 6*, § 628.

81 Ibid.

82 Ibid., § 630.

83 The contrast of "subjective" and "objective," which Jung untiringly celebrates in order to distinguish the introvert from the extravert, does not seem adequate to me since both refer to objects – one tends more to the inside and the other more toward the outside.

84 Cf. ibid., § 632.

85 Ibid., § 633.

86 Cf. ibid.

87 Ibid., § 635.

88 Cf. ibid., §§ 620–637.

89 Cf. ibid., § 595.

90 Ibid., § 603. I would like to anticipate Chapter 4 at this point and state that the orientation toward collective values and norms corresponds with the function of the 10th House.

91 Cf. Jung, *CW 6*, § 595.

92 Ibid.

93 Cf. ibid., § 596.

94 Cf. ibid., § 600.

95 Ibid., § 639.

96 Ibid., § 640.

97 In addition, Jung may be adding a pinch of psychopathology with his statement that they are often of "melancholy temperament." Freud equates melancholy with depression in his essay on "Mourning and Melancholia."

98 Ibid., § 640.

99 Ibid., § 641.

100 Ibid.

101 The original title is *À la recherche du temps perdu*. Proust's main work consists of seven volumes; he wrote it from 1908 to 1922 and it was published between 1913 and 1927.

102 Jung, *CW 6*, § 643.

103 Ibid.

104 Cf. Adam, 2011.

105 Cf. Jung, *CW 6*, § 714.

106 Ibid., § 605.
107 Cf. ibid., §§ 606f.
108 The extraverted sensation type in women can be found, for example, in the cult TV series *Sex and the City* in various forms and manifestations.
109 Ibid., § 608.
110 Ibid.
111 Ibid.
112 Morality does not play a role in sensation; this is "just" about the sensual and aesthetic world. Aesthetics and ethics are opposites since ethics involves mental principles and/or basic attitudes or morality – the proper actions. We can therefore speak here of a moral indifference or lack of restrain.
113 Jung, *CW 6*, § 649.
114 Ibid., § 651.
115 Ibid.
116 Ibid.
117 Ibid.
118 Cf. ibid., § 651.
119 Cf. ibid., § 713.
120 Ibid., § 754.
121 Ibid., § 611. Every intuitive person knows this certainty about the right action and also can sing a song about the consequences when making an exception and not following the intuition.
122 Jung, *CW 6*, § 611.
123 Ibid.
124 Ibid., § 612.
125 Ibid., § 613.
126 Cf. ibid.
127 Cf. ibid., § 614.
128 Ibid., § 615.
129 Cf. ibid.
130 Ibid.
131 Ibid.
132 Ibid.
133 Ibid., § 655.
134 Ibid., § 660.
135 Cf. ibid., § 661.
136 Ibid., § 662.
137 Ibid.
138 Klaus-Uwe Adam is mentioned here since he has contributed a great deal to the improved understanding of Jungian typology with his book *Therapeutisches Arbeiten mit dem Ich* (Therapeutic Work with the Self, 2011). However, he establishes no connection with astrological theory.
139 Jung, *CW 6*, § 669.
140 In the previous chapter, it became already clear that there is a problem with Jung's one-sided reservation of the term "object" – which he implicitly perceives as an outer object and associates solely with the extraverted type of attitude. Jung does not make it clear enough that there are just as many inner objects to which the

introvert relates. Such inner objects can be either introjects of outer objects, i.e. inner conceptions produced through experience with outer objects – and even inner images of them – or archetypal new creations. We also encounter both of these variations in the world of dreams.

141 The following, very condensed astronomical explanations about the Ascendant are orientated upon Thomas Ring's extensive clarifications of the horizon-meridian system (cf. Ring, 1985b, p. 257–268).

142 When comparing these descriptions with a birth chart or a radix illustration (as in the case of the following eight horoscope examples), it becomes conspicuous that the birth picture is quasi "standing on its head" when compared with the directions on the compass: East and west, north and south are inverted: While a compass shows north as "up," south as "down," west as "left," and east as "right," the situation is exactly the opposite in a birth chart: The MC/Midheaven in the south is above, the IC/Lower Heaven in the north is below, east is on the left, and west on the right. This is presumably due to the Eurocentric view of the world, which has shaped astrology: If we imagine standing as an observer on the northern hemisphere with our back to the North Pole and face to the Equator, the cardinal directions are precisely as in a horoscope.

143 Synonyms used for the astrological house are field, area of life, area of interest, or motivation area.

144 Cf. Ring, 1985b, p. 324.

145   According to ibid., p. 103ff., and id., p. 1986ff.

146 Imum Coeli (IC) means Lower Heaven and represents access to the unconscious in the horoscope. People who are born around midnight have their Sun at the IC, in the 4th House, in contrast to those born around noon. The latter have their Sun at the MC and in the 10th House – Goethe is an example of this. From an astronomical perspective, this point is created by the intersection of the ecliptic, i.e. the orbit of all astrologically relevant phenomena (zodiac signs and planets) with the northern meridian.

147 Ring, 1969, p. 116, Ill. 4.

148 Ibid.

149 Ring, 1985b, p. 116. When analyzing a horoscope, it is important to ask about the conditions of nutrition on the material and emotional-spiritual level beginning at birth since too little or also too much can have serious consequences for the later life. It is also important to ask about the opportunity for inner equilibrium, which may be very or just partly possible, depending on the signs and planets with all of their aspects; each of them has corresponding consequences for the regeneration of the organism.

150 When analyzing the horoscope, the focus is on the issue of family origin and the associated support and blockages; the self-established or lacking family; the desire for children; rootedness in one's own emotional depths; as well as the love life – which often depicts a problem when there is a strong emphasis on the Second Quadrant. In everyday life, one of the most common problems is dealing with the sexual urge, which can become independent – even for family fathers and mothers, which usually leads to conflicts in relationships and the family. The question about how to make one's own creativity fruitful also arises in most cases.

151 Ring, 1985b, p. 115.

152 Relationship issues are often at the forefront when examining a horoscope. This may involve a couple relationship, group constellations, or even relationships with other cultures. But this always involves relationship dynamics, in which power and helplessness also play a role. It is also important to look at possible exertion by the horoscope owner since the Third Quadrant – in contrast to the polar opposite of the First Quadrant, which is specialized in taking – is attuned to giving; as a result, there is a danger for the respective individuals of using their energies and resources too lavishly on behalf of the other person or causes.

153 Ring, 1985b, p. 116.

154 Cf. Ring, 1985b.

155 Just as in these examples of the Sun and Moon, every other planet has an effect in its typical essential force and entire aspects with other planets – with all of their resources and problems – which makes it correspondingly multi-faceted.

156 The inscription according to Ring, 1986, p. 119.

157 The titles for the twelve houses of Ring are so accurate that I have also used them in this book. See Ring, 1985b, p. 325–336.

158 Abbreviation of "AC", morning, 6 a.m., sunrise.

159 For detailed descriptions, please see Ring, 1985a and 1985b, p. 144ff.

160 Cf. Ring, 1985b, p. 325 and 326.

161 Whether egocentricity is shown and how pronounced it is depends very much on the type of zodiac sign, as well as the character of the involved planetary principles: While the sign of Leo and the planets of the Sun, Jupiter, and Pluto strengthen the force of personal appearance, the sign of Pisces and the planet Neptune tend to have more personality-dissolving effects.

162 Ibid., p. 326.

163 A funny example of an insatiable mentality of wanting to have everything is the stingy Scrooge McDuck, who swims in his giant swimming pool – which is filled with gold ducats instead of water – in front of his poor nephew Donald Duck.

164 Ring, 1985b, p. 327.

165 Ibid., p. 327.

166 Ibid., p. 328.

167 Abbreviation of "IC," Lower Heaven, 12 a.m., midnight.

168 How the connection with our own roots can ultimately be linked with the theme of religiosity and the personal image of god is expressed very distinctly in the life of reformer Martin Luther: He had the Sun, Venus, and Saturn in the socially critical sign of Scorpio, as well as Mercury, Neptune, and Uranus in the "religious" sign of Sagittarius in the fourth field.

169 Ring, 1985b, p. 329.

170 Ibid., p. 330.

171 Ibid., p. 331.

172 Abbreviation of "DC," sunset, about 6 p.m..

173 The 7th House was also seen as the marriage house in antiquity.

174 Ring, 1985b, p. 332.

175 Ibid., p. 333.

176 Ibid., p. 333.

177 Cf. Lessing's essay on the Age of Enlightenment: Lessing, 1997.

178 The latter is reminiscent of Jung's introverted intuitive type, without being congruent with the rest of the descriptions – in which the extraverted elements predominate. This example shows how difficult it usually is to make clear classifications between the Jungian typology and the astrological system.

179 Ring, 1985b, p. 334.

180 Abbreviation of "MC," Midheaven, 12 p.m., noon.

181 The polarity between the tenth and fourth field of interest reflects the conflict between private and professional life. This still affects women more intensely than men since mothers are sometimes faced with just an either-or situation when the care of family and children is difficult to reconcile with a demanding professional career: Either the children suffer or the job gets neglected – or the woman is steered into a situation of overload – while the father can still live a full professional commitment much more naturally. More part-time jobs even for demanding professional positions would therefore be appropriate for people who have to reconcile opposing tendencies and integrate both of them into their lives.

182 Ring, 1985b, p. 335.

183 Ibid., p. 336.

184 Cf. ibid., p. 337.

185 Unfortunately, such inhuman variations are still practiced today in certain states.

186 Likewise, in the seclusion of educational institutions such as orphanages or boarding school – which normally contribute a great deal to the healthy development of children and adolescents – events can sometimes occur that cause more suffering than support. For example, Musil describes this in his novel *The Confusions of Young Törless*. Schiller also describes his stay in the Karlsschule, the ducal military academy, as chastening; the pupils were deprived of any right to privacy. Also see Hermann Hesse's *Beneath the Wheel* or – something more current – the film *Dead Poets Society*, which plays in the USA at the beginning of the 1960s.

187 In addition to the grueling life that she had to cope with as the founder of several convents, Teresa of Avila wrote books such as the well-known *The Interior Castle*.

188 The ecliptic is the apparent orbit of the Sun around the Earth, as well as the general orbital plane of the planets. This serves as the ideal measuring circle for the respective positions of the planets in the changing angle degrees. Cf. Ring, 1985a, p. 245 and 292. Due to the rotation of the Earth around its own axis, the Sun seems to move by apparently rising in the east and setting in the west. From our perspective, it also seems as if the fixed stars and planets are moving around the Earth.

189 Ibid., p. 245.

190 I share the basic attitude of a non-judgmental astrology and with it the rejection of vulgar astrology misunderstandings with Ring. Cf. id., 1985a, p. 245–287.

191 In his extensive book *Genius und Dämon* (Genius and Demon).

192 Ring mentions Rilke and Baudelaire as examples. Cf. Ring, 1985a, p. 259.

193 This table is based on the one by Thomas Ring: 1985a, p. 250.

194 In contrast to Ring, who considers the quincunx to be one of the weakly effective aspects, I have often found that its effect on the personality structure is medium strong at the least.

195 In my experience, the semi-sextile also develops a medium-strong effect.

196 From an astronomical perspective, the Moon's Nodes are the intersections between two orbits: namely, between the Moon's orbit and the apparent Sun's orbit (ecliptic) around the Earth. There are two such intersections: the Ascending Moon's Nodes and the Descending Moon's Nodes. The Northern (Ascending) Moon's Node is the one at which the Moon changes from the southern to the northern side of the ecliptic; on the other hand, the Descending Moon's Node is where the Moon changes from the northern to the southern side in its orbit.

The two Moon's Nodes are 180° apart and therefore have a polar opposition with each other. In the birth chart, usually just the Northern (Ascending) Moon's Node is drawn; it has a solar quality and is associated with the free will. The Southern (Descending) Moon's Node usually does not appear in the horoscope picture. The latter symbolizes the instinctual reaction patterns and therefore the early conditioned behavior patterns that cause people to always react the same way in certain situations. On the other hand, the Northern Moon's Node shows new behavioral possibilities and therefore also our development potential in the sense of possibilities for us to make new decisions and act differently than accustomed.

For the sake of completeness, the Ascending Moon's Nodes are drawn in the eight horoscope illustration (see color table section) and listed in the related horoscope tables in Chapter 5. However, it is not possible to go into greater detail about the significance of the Moon's Nodes in this book for reasons of space. At this point, it must be enough to say that both the house and also the zodiac sign in which the Ascending Moon's Node stands means a development potential.

197 According to the myth of Sisyphus, who as punishment had to ceaselessly roll a stone up the mountain that – when it had finally just reached the top – rolled back down again so that he constantly had to start all over again. Cf. Ring's seminar on "Revised Astrology" in 1974 in Copenhagen, Ring, 1974.

198 Rilke is an outstanding example of a birth chart with many squares; he even had a "tower," which means four squares that each form a square and therefore lead to a tower-like structure. He even had a total of seven squares and three oppositions but only a few synthetic aspects that could balance the tensions to some extent and help to bring the energies bound within them into a flow. The creative uncovering of his extraordinary talent was not just handed to Rilke.

199 Jung, *CW 8*, § 200.

200 Ibid.

201 Cf. ibid.

202 Ibid., § 201.

203 Jung's complex reactions are also known by the term of parapraxis, which Freud used for such incidents (now known as the "Freudian slip.")

204 Jung, *CW 8*, § 202.

205 Cf. ibid., § 204.

206 Jung, *CW 17*, § 107.

207 See the Introduction and Chapter 1, subchapter on "The Ten Planets in Astrology," where the interactive dimension between mother and child have already been discussed under the descriptions of the Moon.

208 Ibid., § 143.

209 So, neurobiological research has confirmed the importance of the dyadic aspects and therefore the reliable nurture and care of the infant and young child through his or her environment. The adequate mothering in the earliest phase of a child's life is therefore so decisive for his or her entire life because the baby is almost completely dependent on her from the start. The phase of primary motherliness according to Winnicott corresponds with that of Balint's "primary love" and Neumann's "dual union." The environment in the earliest period of a person's life is usually represented by the personal mother. This function can also be assumed to a certain degree by the father or some other person. But for practical reasons, these early mothering figures will be called "mother."

210 Cf. subchapter on "The Archetype Concept of C.G. Jung" in Chapter 1, as well as Winnicott, 1994 and 1995.

211 Winnicott, 1993, p. 194.

212 Cf. Winnicott, 1994, p. 159.

213 Cf. Müller, 2003, p. 118.

214 Cf. also ibid., 7/8, P. 286-294.

215 The seconds were rounded up or down to the minutes. This also applies to the data on the following seven other birth charts.

216 A retrograde planet (astronomical background: It moves from east to west) usually has a more restrained effect than one in direct motion (astronomy: Its movement is from west to east); this can lead to a certain shyness or reclusiveness. Seen psychologically-astrologically, a retrograde planet proves to have a tendency toward introversion, which is often accompanied by emotional-spiritual depth. The vitality of the retrograde planets is turned inward, to one's own unconscious, while the planets in direct motion express their qualities and energies in the outer world. If we succeed in becoming more familiar with our own unconscious due to the retrograde quality of a planet, this can lead to increased autonomy.

217 Although it is actually located at the end of the Third House, it still develops its effect at least as strongly in the Fourth House due to its proximity to it and its conjunction with Saturn (which is attributed to the Fourth House because of its position directly before the Fourth House line)

218 His emotional sensitivity due to the Moon in Cancer in connection with the inwardly-oriented Jupiter (retrograde) and the two planets in connection with Venus in Pisces brings a high degree of sensitivity and also shyness with it. This promotes his reserve in the personal expression of feelings. In business life, no one is interested in feeling so there was also no criticism from that direction.

219 Cf. the subchapter on "The Twelve Houses as Archetypal Life Fields" (Chapter 4) in the section on "Strength of a planet and field cusp."

220 Retrograde moving/retrograde planets only develop under certain conditions in the outer world; they turn even more to the inside, which is why they are also called "introverted" in the above section.

221 There is still much to be said about the mysteriously appearing parallels in terms of the age and nature of the mother's and the wife's illnesses. However, this is not possible here due to reasons of anonymity and to protect the personality of individuals discussed here.

222 Cf. the subchapter on "The Four Functions of the Self According to C.G. Jung" in Chapter 2.

223 The Moon's Node is not a planet but an intersection between the Moon's and Sun's orbit. Cf. the extensive explanation in note 196.

224 Only the splinter planet Chiron that has the function of uniting the two contradictory tendencies of Saturn (conservative, preserving, and boundary setting), Uranus (desire for freedom and opposition against all traditional things) – which is not included within the scope of the interpretations in this book – and the Medium Coeli (Midheaven) are earthy.

225 This is what the two of them told me when they came to a horoscope analysis so that they could find a better way of treating each other in old age.

226 His wife has a "manager horoscope" with the Sun in the Tenth House and other dispositions that point in this direction.

227 Theodor is a "double" Scorpio since both his Ascendant and the Sun are in the sign of Scorpio.

228 This lack of an eye for the reality of the other (the object) is a typical problem of people with an introverted attitude since they act from their subjective perspective.

229 There was also a disposition for depressive disorders on the father's side, but no detailed information in this regard.

230 After various failed relationships, they were themselves in a life crisis; perhaps they also had eleventh hour panic or simply needed a lover. That Anton was a married father did not influence them.

231 Sand play is practiced throughout the world as a very effective therapeutic method that is capable of stimulating the psyche's forces of self-healing. It was developed by Dora Kalff in the mid-20th century.

232 See the subchapter on "The Circle with Its Semi-Circles, Quadrants, and Houses in Astrology" in Chapter 3. This is where the Quadrants I and II are related to introversion and Quadrants III and IV to extraversion.

233 However, Anton's core attitude and emotional character are mainly earthy and quite "watery"; earth and water are slower and tend to be "heavier" than the lively air element.

234 This obviously does not mean that every woman with a similarly tense aspected Sun will lose her father. But it shows that the approach to the father image and external men is not simple but requires work.

235 Goethe, 2003, Verse 12110–12111.

236 Just as the man in his encounter and choice of the wife is constellated in the anima, his inner "search image" of the woman.

237 She belongs to the same age group as Felix, so she was in her late eighties in 2015.

238 The necessary methods of anonymization have obviously been applied with great care in the publication of personal material. Not only the respectively date of birth was omitted, but also other personal details were changed without affecting the coherence of the astrological description.

Bibliography

Adam, Klaus-Uwe (2011): *Therapeutisches Arbeiten mit dem Ich. Denken, Fühlen, Empfinden, Intuieren – Die vier Ich-Funktionen.* (Therapeutic Work with the Self: Thinking, Feeling, Sensing, and Intuiting – The Four Functions of the Self) 2nd revised and expanded edition. Stuttgart: Opus Magnum.

Balint, Michael (1992): *Thrills and Regressions.* 4th Edition. Abingdon-on-Thames: Routledge.

Balint, Michael (1992): *The Basic Fault: Therapeutic Aspects of Regression.* Reprint. New York: Brunner/Mazel, Publishers.

Bauer, Joachim (2015): *Selbststeuerung. Die Wiederentdeckung des freien Willens* (Self-Control: The Rediscovery of the Free Will). Munich: Blessing.

Bishop-Köhler, Doris (1994): *Motivationale Entwicklung* (Motivational Development). Zurich: Zentralstelle der Studentenschaft der Universität Zürich.

Bischof-Köhler, Doris (1997): *Die Entwicklung der sozialen Kognition* (The Development of Social Cognition). Lecture on General Psychology, held in the Summer Semester of 1997 at the University of Zurich.

Bischof-Köhler, Doris (1997): *Geschlechtstypisches Verhalten. Evolutions-biologische Grundlagen und entwicklungsbiologische Fakten* (Gender-Specific Behavior: Evolutionary Biological Fundamentals and Developmental Biological Facts). Lecture on General Psychology, held in the Winter Semester of 1997/98 at the University of Zurich.

Bischof, Norbert (1989): *Das Rätsel Ödipus. Die biologischen Wurzeln des Urkonflikts von Intimität und Autonomie* (The Mystery of Oedipus: The Biological Roots of the Original Conflict of Intimacy and Autonomy). 2nd Edition. Munich: Piper.

Bischof, Norbert (1996): *Das Kraftfeld der Mythen. Signale aus der Zeit, in der wir die Welt erschaffen haben.* (The Power Field of Myths: Signals from the Time in Which We Created the World). Munich/Zurich: Piper.

The Blue Angel Film adaptation of the novel *The Small Town Tyrant*, 1929–1930 with Marlene Dietrich according to the screenplay by Karl Gustav Vollmoeller and Carl Zuckmayer.

Dorst, Brigitte (2015): *Therapeutisches Arbeiten mit Symbolen* (Therapeutic Work with Symbols). 2nd expanded and updated edition Stuttgart: Kohlhammer.

Fink, Gerhard (2001): *Who's Who in der Antiken Mythologie* (Who's Who in Ancient Mythology). 9th Edition. Munich: dtv.

Flüe, Bruno von (1988): *Das ganze Gesicht meiner Jahre. Das Geburtsbild Rainer Maria Rilkes. Eine astrologische Deutung* (The Entire Face of My Years: The Birth Chart – Rainer Maria Rilke. An Astrological Interpretation). Stuttgart: Kreuz.

Freud, Sigmund (1975): "Mourning and Melancholia." In: *On Murder, Mourning and Melancholia.* Penguin Classics 2005 London: Penguin Books

Frey-Rohn, Liliane (1990): *From Freud to Jung: A Comparative Study of the Psychology of the Unconscious.* Boulder: Shambhala Publications.

Goethe, Johann Wolfgang (1961): *Urworte. Orphisch* (Orphic Sayings). In: *Gedenkausgabe der Werke, Briefe und Gespräche, Bd. 1: Sämtliche Gedichte.* (Commemorative issue of works, letters and discussions. All poems.) Einführung und Texüberwachung von Emil Staiger. (Introduction and text interpretation by Emil Staiger) 2nd Edition Zurich: Artemis.

Goethe, Johann Wolfgang (1986): *Faust: A Tragedy, Parts One and Two.* New Haven: Yale University Press.

Lessing, Gotthold Ephraim (1881): *The Education of the Human Race.* London: C.K. Paul & Co.

Jacobi, Jolande (1950): *"Der Beitrag Jungs zur Psychologie des Kindes"* (Jung's Contribution to the Psychology of the Child). In: *Der Psychologe II. 7/8,* p. 286-294.

Jacobi, Jolande (1971): *Complex/Archetype/Symbol in the Psychology of C.G. Jung.* Princeton: Princeton Press.

Jacobi, Jolande (1973): *The Psychology of C.G. Jung.* New Haven: Yale University Press.

Jones, Ernest (1953): *The Life and Work of Sigmund Freud. Vol. 1. I: The Formative Years and the Great Discoveries 1856–1900.* New York: Basic Books.

Jung, C.G. (1964): *The Collected Works of C.G. Jung, Vol. 7: Two Essays on Analytical Psychology.* Princeton: Princeton University Press. 2nd Edition.

Jung, C.G. (1970): *Collected Works of C.G. Jung, Vol. 8: The Structure and Dynamics of the Psyche.* Princeton: Princeton University Press. 2nd Edition.

Jung, C.G. (1971): *The Collected Works of C.G. Jung, Vol. 6: Psychological Types.* Princeton: Princeton University Press. 3rd Edition.

Jung, C.G. (1971ff.): *Collected Works of C.G. Jung* (CW). 20 Volumes. C.G. Jung, edited by Gerhard Adler, Michael Fordham, Sir Herbert Read. Abingdon-on-Thames: Routledge

Jung, C.G. (1980): *Psychology and Alchemy. CW 12,* § 866. Princeton: Princeton University Press. 2nd Edition.

Jung, C.G. (1972): *The Collected Works of C.G. Jung, Vol. 17: The Development of the Personality.* CW 17, § 866. Princeton: Princeton University Press

Jung, C.G. (1973a): *Briefe II* (Letters II). Bd. 3. 2: 1946–1955. Edited by Aniela Jaffé in cooperation with Gerhard Adler. Olten / Freiburg im Breisgau: Walter (Special Edition. Ostfildern: Edition C.G. Jung in Patmos Verlag, 2012).

Jung, C.G. (1977): *Collected Works of C.G. Jung, Vol. 5: Symbols of Transformation.* Princeton: Princeton University Press. 2nd Edition.

Jung, C.G. (1976): *Collected Works, Vol. 9: The Archetypes and the Collective Unconscious.* Princeton: Princeton University Press. 2nd Edition.

Jung, C.G. (1966): *Collected Works of C.G. Jung, Vol. 16: Practice of Psychotherapy.* Princeton: Princeton University Press. 2nd Edition.

Jung, C.G. (1963): *Memories, Dreams, Reflections.* Edited by Aniela Jaffé. New York: Pantheon Books

Kast, Verena (1997): *Father-Daughter, Mother-Son: Freeing Ourselves from the Complexes That Bind Us.* Rockport: Element Books Ltd.

Kast, Verena (1992): *The Dynamics of Symbols: Fundamentals of Jungian Psychotherapy.* Mt. Prospect: Fromm Intl.

Köhler, T. (1995): *Freuds Psychoanalyse* (Freud's Psychoanalysis). Stuttgart: Kohlhammer.

Mann, Heinrich (2011): *The Small Town Tyrant.* New York: Howard Fertig.

Mentzos, Stavros (1992): *Neurotische Konfliktverarbeitung. Einführung in die psychoanalytische Neurosenlehre unter Berücksichtigung neuer Perspektiven* (Neurotic Conflict Processing: Introduction to the Psychoanalytic Neurosis Theory under Consideration of New Perspectives). Frankfurt am Main: Fischer TB.

Müller, Anette/Müller, Lutz (2003): *Wörterbuch der Analytischen Psychologie* (Dictionary of Analytical Psychology). Düsseldorf: Walter.

Neumann, Erich (1990): *The Child: Structure and Dynamics of the Nascent Personality.* 1st Edition Abingdon-on-Thames: Routledge.

Nickl, Roger (2014): "Nakhutticaihattibiri. Together with a major international project, the psycholinguist Sabine Stoll researches in which ways children come to their native language – such as the Nepalese Chintang with its 1800 verb forms.: In: *Magazine. Die Zeitschrift der Universität Zürich*, Nr. 3, 23. September 2014, p. 19–21.

Novalis (1990): *Henry of Ofterdingen: A Novel.* Long Grove: Waveland Press Inc.

Proust, Marcel (2003): *In Search of Lost Time, Vol. 1.* New York: Modern Library.

Ranke-Graves, Robert (1986): *The Greek Myths: The Complete and Definitive Edition.* New York: Viking Press.

Ring, Thomas (1969): *Astrological Menschenkunde. Bd. 3: Kombinationslehre* (Astrological Anthropology. Vol. 3: Combination Theory). Freiburg im Breisgau: Bauer.

Ring, Thomas (1974): *Die revidierte Astrologie* (Revised Astrology). Seminars in Copenhagen 1974. 10 videos (in German, can be found on YouTube).

Ring, Thomas (1975): *Existenz und Wesen in kosmologischer Sicht* (Existence and Being in the Cosmological Perspective). Freiburg im Breisgau: Aurum.

Ring, Thomas (1979): *Astrologie neu gesehen* (Astrology with New Eyes). 2nd Edition. Freiburg im Breisgau: Aurum.

Ring, Thomas (1980): *Genius und Dämon. Strukturbilder schöpferischer Menschen* (Genius and Demon: Structure Images of Creative People). Freiburg im Breisgau: Aurum.

Ring, Thomas (1985a): *Astrological Menschenkunde. Bd. 1: Kräfte und Kräftebeziehungen* (Astrological Anthropology: Vol. 1. Forces and Relationship Between the Forces). 5th Edition. Freiburg im Breisgau: Bauer.

Ring, Thomas (1985b): *Astrologische Menschenkunde. Bd. 2: Ausdruck und Richtung der Kräfte* (Astrological Anthropology. Vol. 2: Expression and Direction of the Forces). 5th Edition. Freiburg im Breisgau: Bauer.

Ring, Thomas (1985): *Astrologische Menschenkunde. Bd. 4: Das lebende Modell* (Astrological Anthropology. Vol. 4: The Living Model). 3rd Edition. Freiburg im Breisgau: Bauer.

Ring, Thomas (1985d): *Die Olympische Wiederkehr. Ein Gedichtzyklus* (The Olympic Return: A Cycle of Poems). Freiburg im Breisgau: Aurum.

Ring, Thomas (1986): *Das Grundgefüge. Die Stellung des Menschen in Natur und Kosmos* (The Basic Structure: The Human Being's Position in Nature and Cosmos). Freiburg im Breisgau: Aurum.

Ring, Thomas (1995): *Frühe astrologische Schriften* (Early Astrological Writings). Zollikon: Astrodienst-Verlag.

Scharfetter, Christian (1980): *General Psychopathology: An Introduction*. Cambridge: Cambridge University Press.

Stifter, Adalbert (2008): *The Bachelors*. London: Pushkin Press.

Stierlin, Helm (1959): "The Adaption to the 'Stronger' Person's Reality." In: *Psychiatry* 22, p. 143–152.

Stierlin, Helm (1975): *Psychoanalysis and Family Therapy*. New York: Jason Aronson

Stierlin, Helm (1978): *Delegation und Familie* (Delegation and Family). Frankfurt am Main: Suhrkamp.

Stierlin, Helm (1984): Separating *Parents and Children: A Perspective on Running Away, Schizophrenia, and Waywardness*. New York: Jason Aronson Inc.

St. Teresa of Avila (2006): *The Interior Castle*. Washington, DC: ICS Publications.

Winnicott, D. W. (1979): *The Maturational Processes and the Facilitating Environment*. Madison: International Universities Press.

Winnicott, D. W. (1992): *Through Paediatrics to Psycho-Analysis*. New York: Brunner/Mazel.

Winnicott, D. W. (1995): *Playing and Reality*. 2nd Edition. Abingdon-on-Thames: Routledge.

Picture credits

Ill. 1: Karte des Universum Cosmographia. Photo: akg-images.
Ill. 2: Zodiac / G.B.Agnese / 16th century. Photo: akg-images.
Ill. 3: The zodiac with the elements of belonging to the signs. © Marianne Meister.
Ill. 4: The zodiac with the cardinal, fixed, and mutable signs. © Marianne Meister.
Ill. 5: Anatomy of Man / Limburg Brothers / c. 1416. Photo: akg-images.
Ill. 6: The Four Functions of the Self. From: Jolande Jacobi, *Die Psychologie von C.G. Jung*. © Patmos Verlag. Verlagsgruppe Patmos in der Schwabenverlag AG, Ostfildern, 2. Auflage 2012. www.verlagsgruppe-patmos.ce
Ill. 7: The Circle with the Four Quadrants as Life and Value Dimensions. © Marianne Meister.
Ill. 8: The Circle with Left-and-Right and Below-and-Above Subdivision. © Marianne Meister.
Ill. 9: The Circle with the Twelve Houses. © Marianne Meister.

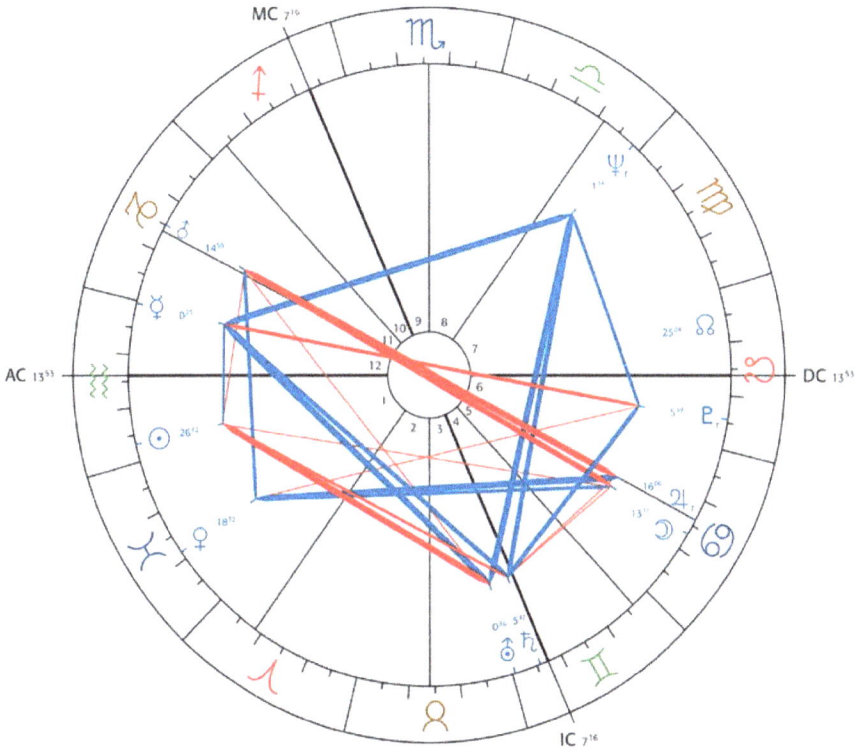

Image 1: Johannes

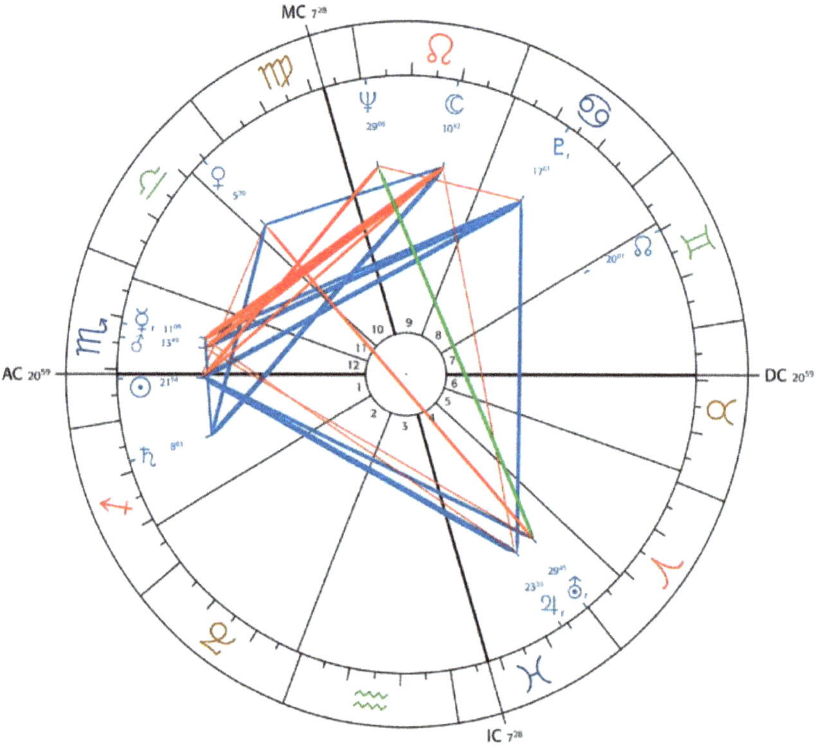

Image 2: Theodor

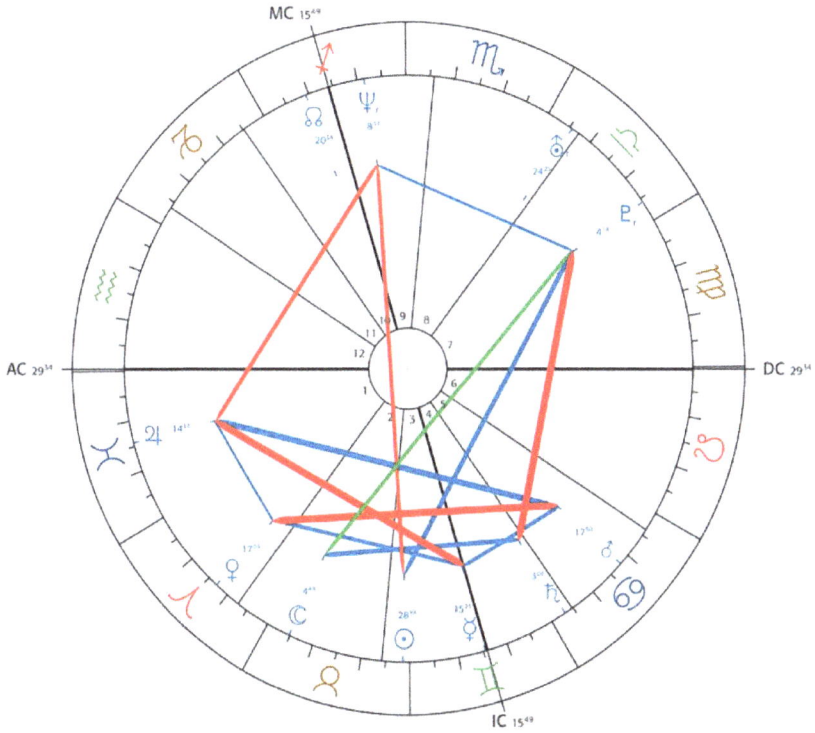

Image 3: Anton

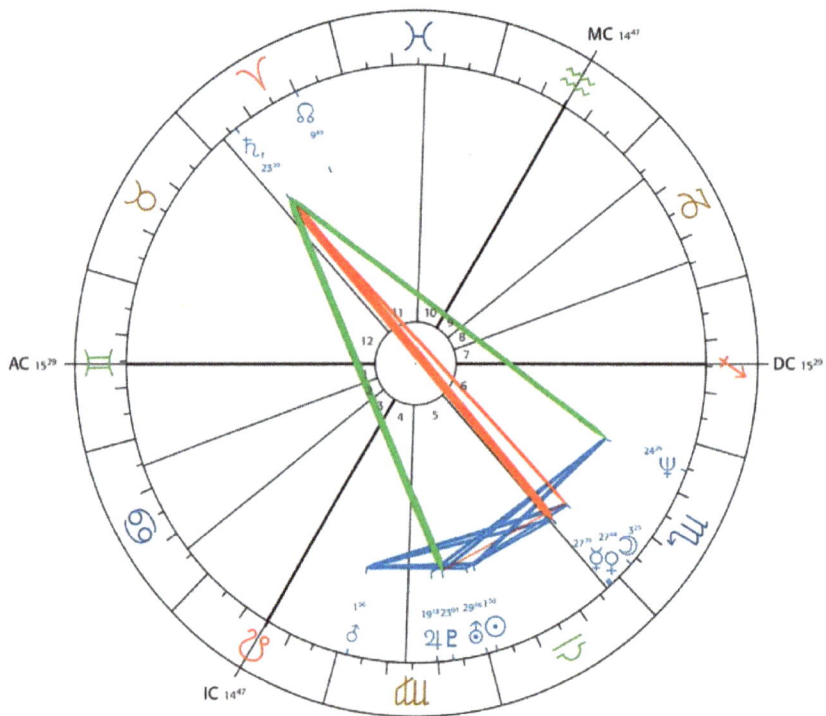

Image 4: Eva

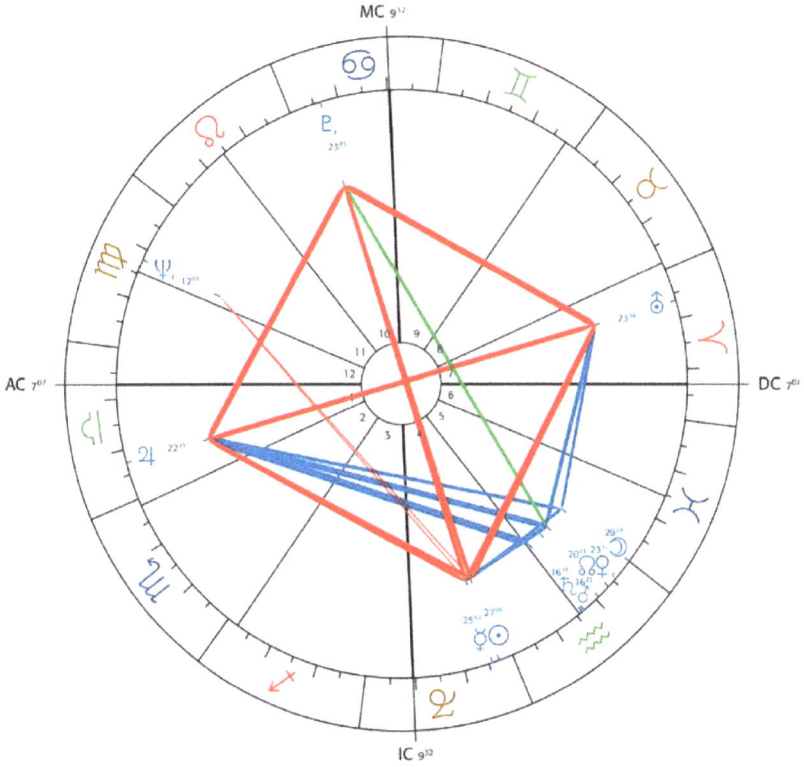

Image 5: Heidi

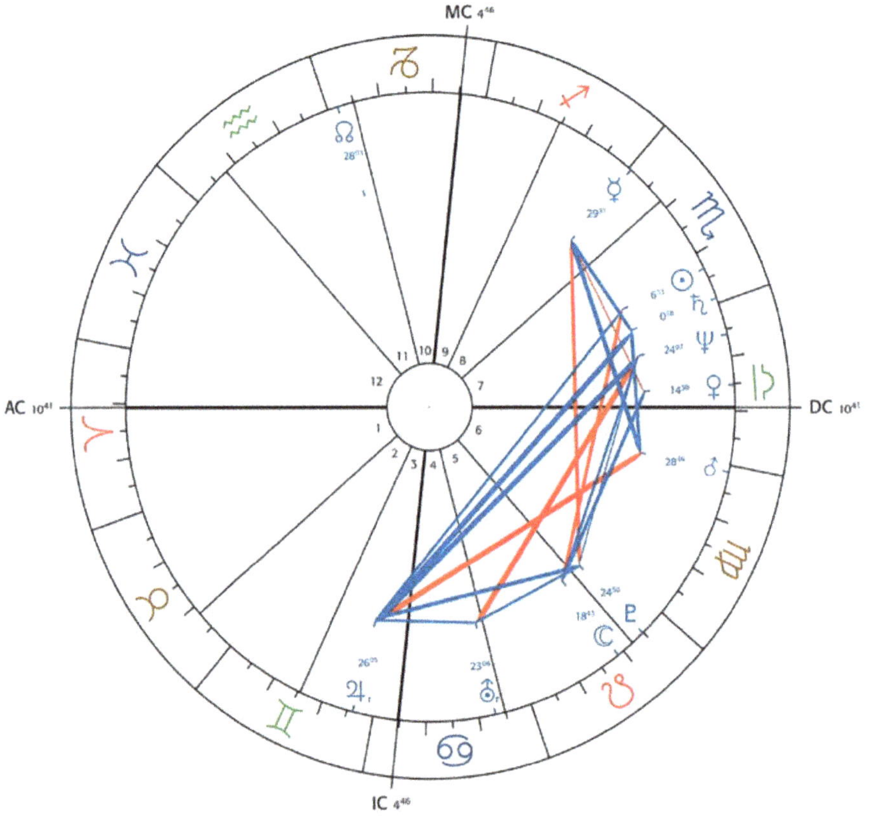

Image 6: Paul

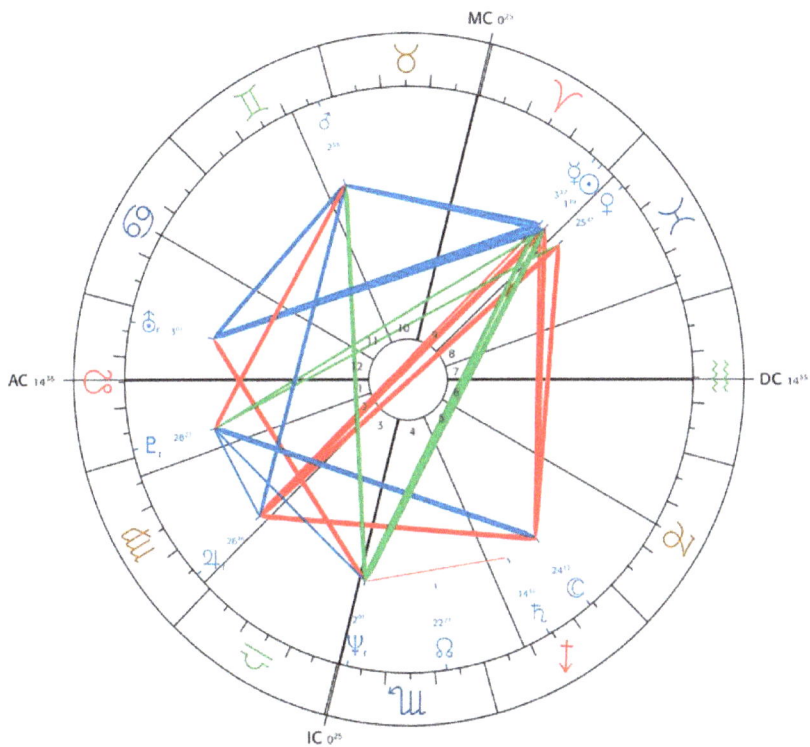

Image 7: Charlotte

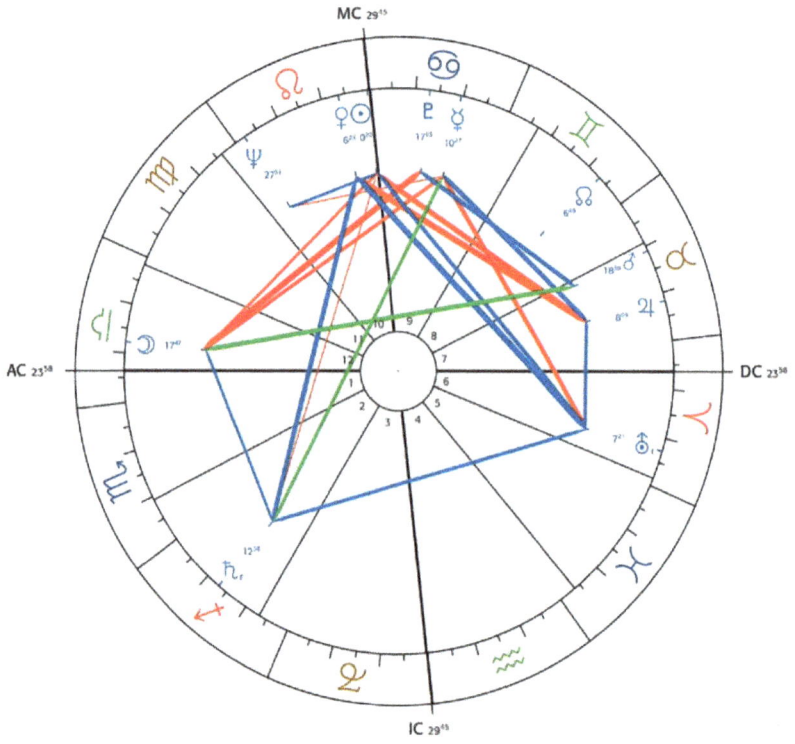

Image 8: Maria